The
Children's
Daily
Devotional
Bible

Robert J. Morgan, General Editor

CONTEMPORARY ENGLISH VERSION

THOMAS NELSON PUBLISHERS
Nashville • Atlanta • London • Vancouver

Quotation Rights for the Contemporary English Version Bible

The American Bible Society is glad to grant authors and publishers the right to use up to one thousand (1,000) verses from the Contemporary English Version text in church, religious and other publications without the need to seek and receive written permission. However, the extent of quotation must not comprise a complete book nor should it amount to more than 50% of the work. The proper copyright notice must appear on the title or copyright page.

When quotations from CEV are used in non-saleable media, such as church bulletins, orders of service, posters, transparencies or similar media, a complete copyright notice is not required, but the initials (CEV) must appear at the end of each quotation.

Requests for quotations in excess of one thousand (1,000) verses in any publication must be directed to, and written approval received from, the American Bible Society, 1865 Broadway, New York, NY 10023.

About the General Editor

Robert John Morgan was born in Elizabethton, Tennessee, in 1952. He was converted to Christ in childhood and called to preach as a teenager. He attended King College in Bristol, Tennessee, and graduated with honors from Columbia Bible College in Columbia, South Carolina, Wheaton Graduate School in Wheaton, Illinois, and Luther Rice Seminary in Atlanta, Georgia.

Mr. Morgan pastored in Greenville, Tennessee from 1976 to 1979. He has pastored The Donelson Fellowship in suburban Nashville since 1980. He has also ministered in seminars in Africa, South America, and Asia. He and his wife, Katrina, have three daughters. He has published articles in several magazines, such as *Focus on the Family* and *Leadership Journal*, and is the author of two books, *Empowered Parenting: Raising Children in the Nurture and Instruction of the Lord* and *Tiny Talks With God*.

Contents

The Devotionals

(Use the boxes to the left of the Devotionals to check off the ones you've read.)

CONTENTS

CONTENTS

Welcome to the
Contemporary English Version

Languages are spoken before they are written. And far more communication is done through the spoken word than through the written word. In fact, more people *hear* the Bible read than read it for themselves. Traditional translations of the Bible count on the *reader's* ability to understand a *written* text. But the *Contemporary English Version* differs from all other English Bibles—past and present—in that it takes into consideration the needs of the *hearer,* as well as those of the reader, who may not be familiar with traditional biblical language.

The *Contemporary English Version* has been described as a "user-friendly" and a "mission-driven" translation that can be *read aloud* without stumbling, *heard* without misunderstanding, and *listened to* with enjoyment and appreciation, because the language is contemporary and the style is lucid and lyrical.

The *Contemporary English Version* invites you to *read*, to *hear*, to *understand* and to *share*

the Word of God now
as never before!

Introduction

Looking for a Best Friend?

We all need one. Someone we can share our secrets with. Someone who likes us. Someone who's fun to be around. We need somebody like that to talk to every day.

The Children's Daily Devotional Bible will help you become best friends with the *best* Best Friend of all—the wonderful God, creator of heaven and earth. He knows all about you, and he likes you very much. He loves you deeply. He's a joy to be with. You can tell him all your secrets. And you can spend time with him every day—for the rest of your life.

God becomes our Best Friend . . .

- when we ask Jesus Christ to forgive our sins and to give us everlasting life, and . . .
- when we begin reading our Bibles and praying every day.

Daily Bible reading and praying is like talking with God himself. He speaks to us when we read his book, the Bible. And we speak to him when we pray. These daily times of Bible study and prayer make us more and more devoted to the Lord . . .

. . . which is why we call them—daily devotions.

Here are seven ways to get the most from *The Children's Daily Devotional Bible:*

1. Use it about the same time each day—maybe in the morning before school or at night just before going to bed.

2. Think of each day's passage as a special message from God just for you.

3. Study the pictures. Each has been drawn to accurately show something about the words you're reading.

4. Use the prayer starters to . . . well, to start your prayers. Then go on to tell the Lord whatever you'd like. Learn to talk to him naturally, just like talking to a friend.

5. Work hard on the memory verses. Collect all 52 in your mind.

6. Use weekends to look over Scriptures you've previously read and to review verses you've already learned.

7. If you *do* occasionally skip a day, make sure you don't miss the next one. Make your daily devotions a habit, and stick to them.

No matter how many—or how few—friends you have, you've got one Best Friend who will never leave you or let you down. And he's waiting for you to get to know him better . . .

. . . just as soon as you turn to page one.

A Word for Parents

My first Bible was given to me in the first grade as an award for memorizing Psalm 23. A year or two later, my parents gave me another Bible, a newer one with larger print. As I advanced through school, they kept updating my Bibles to match my age. I loved to burrow into the bedcovers and read, study, and memorize the Scripture. It's no wonder that at an early age, I gave my life to Christ, and I've been a lover of the Bible ever since.

Now that I'm a parent, my greatest longing is that my children grow up knowing, loving, and serving Jesus Christ. When they were younger, we gathered them around for family devotions. My wife or I would read a Bible story or a few verses then offer a brief prayer. But as they grew, we wanted them to cultivate their own daily devotions. We gave them Bibles appropriate for their ages, and encouraged them to have their "devos" each evening.

Our role shifted a little from instructing to modeling. Notice how Moses puts it in Deuteronomy 6.5-7:

> Love the LORD your God with all your heart, soul, and strength. Memorize his laws and tell them to your children over and over again. Talk about them all the time, whether you're at home or walking along the road or going to bed at night, or getting up in the morning.

The order is important. First, parents should love the Lord with all their hearts. Next we're to memorize his Word, his laws. Then we are to "talk about them all the time . . ." to our children.

The Children's Daily Devotional Bible can help.

- For younger children, use this as a read-to-me picture book of daily devotions.

- For older children, gently monitor their use of this book and help them build the "daily devo" habit into their routine.

- Keep your own copy of the *Children's Daily Devotional Bible* (you can use it for your devotions, too) so you can talk more easily about the Scripture when you're "at home or walking along the road or going to bed at night, or getting up in the morning."

- Provide a full copy of the *Contemporary English Version* so your children can look up surrounding passages for further study.

- Help your child learn the memory verses. John Ruskin, English social critic, said the verses his mother helped him memorize in childhood "set my soul for life." Use charts, stars, incentives, and rewards. Make it a family project.

- Involve your family in a good church with a strong youth ministry.

- Be a spiritual model for your children. The best way to entice your kids into the daily devotional habit is to let them see you enjoying yours.

Our spiritual vitality depends on two aspects of victorious Christian living: conversion and conversation. The first is a matter of heart; the second, of habit.

When we meet Christ at the cross, that's *conversion*. When we meet with him behind the closed door, that's *conversation*.

*The message about **the cross** doesn't make any sense to lost people. But for those of us who are being saved, it is God's power at work (1 Co 1.18).*

*When you pray, go into a room alone and **close the door**. Pray to your Father in private. He knows what is done in private, and he will reward you (Mt 6.6).*

We're converted to Jesus Christ when we trust him as Savior, confessing our sins to him, asking him for eternal life, and committing ourselves to him as Lord and Master. Then the friendship starts. The God of the Universe wants to meet us each day over an old Book at the kitchen table. It's beyond comprehension. It's the *second* most astounding thing I know.

God is both infinite and intimate! He delights in being with his people, hearing us pray and talking to us through his Word. The Master, it seems, occupies two addresses: in the highest heavens and with the humblest hearts.

Our holy God lives forever in the highest heavens,
and this is what he says:
Though I live high above in the holy place,
I am here to help those who are humble
and depend only on me (Is 57.15).

The heavenly Father wants our earthly friendship. Could anything be more astonishing than that?

Only one: many of us can't find time for him. And that's the *most* astounding thing I know. We're too busy for Bible study, and too pooped for prayer.

We rush into each day, bolting from bed like a thoroughbred from the gate. We gulp down our Colombian coffee, throw on designer labels, then veer onto the fast lane. We whirl through our daily tasks like a spinning top, then drive by the restaurant on the way home so they can throw food to us through the window. We drag ourselves to the couch for an hour of celluloid sex and video violence, then stagger to be bed for six hours of sleep.

Whatever happened to green pastures and still waters? We're too frazzled to find them!

It wasn't until my college years that I really understood the joy of spending a quiet half hour in regular conversation with God. Columbia Bible College's daily routine included a mandatory half hour for morning devotions. Now, over 20 years later, I wouldn't trade that habit for anything. It's my daily appointment with God, a personal conversation during which he speaks to me in the Bible and I speak to him in prayer. It enables me to start the day with confidence.

Suppose you go to bed at a reasonable hour and get up a half hour earlier to meet God the next morning—what do you do with those thirty minutes? I'd like to suggest a sequence called *JARS and Rs*.

J=Jot

J stands for "jot." You'll need a notebook for this, but any kind will do. At the top of the page, jot the date. You can then write anything you want about your feelings, your moods, or the circumstances of your life. Or, just use the margin of your Bible to jot down the date and any useful information.

I learned the notebook habit when a college buddy took me to visit Ruth Bell Graham one weekend. She talked with us at length, sharing lessons garnered through a lifetime of unusual ministry. I scribbled down much of what she said, including four words I've never forgotten, for they transformed my devotions: *"Cultivate the notebook habit."*

She explained that for many years she has kept a journal, recording the events of her life and the lessons she has learned from Scripture. When one notebook fills up, she slides it alongside its predecessors on the bookshelf, and starts a new one. Christians throughout history, she told us, have journaled to maintain their emotional equilibrium and to remember lessons they have learned from God.

I immediately went out and purchased a journal. In the two decades since, I've found that the notebook habit focuses my thoughts, especially when I'm troubled, forcing rip-roaring feelings into black ink on white paper so I can deal with them.

After you've jotted a sentence on a page, you're ready for the next step.

A=Ask

Take a moment to ask God to speak to you through his Word. Though some people read the Bible only as a textbook, it's primarily a love letter between the Lord and his people. It's designed to transform and invigorate our lives as the Holy Spirit applies it to our hearts. Repeat David's prayer in Psalm 119.18: *Open my mind and let me discover the wonders of your Law.* Or Samuel's childlike prayer, *I'm listening, LORD. What do you want me to do?* (1 S 3.10).

R=Read

Then read your Bible. Begin each day where you left off the day before. Underline significant phrases. Study cross-references. Diagram sentences. Outline chapters. Check key words in a dictionary. Dig into the text, looking for contrasts and comparisons. Rewrite verses in your own words in your notebook. There are no rules for where or how much to read. The important thing is remembering as you read that God is talking to you as one talks to a friend.

S=Select

As you study the Bible, look for one verse to select as your *Verse-For-The-Day*—a verse that really hammers at your heart. When you find it, copy it in your journal and perhaps on a scrap of paper to carry with you all day. I know one man who writes his *VFTD* on the back of a business card that he props on his desk. Another friend jots hers on a sticky note to post on her dashboard. She memorizes it as she drives to work.

Find your *VFTD* in the morning, carry it in your heart all day, and at night meditate on it as you fall asleep. None sleep as well as those who have a promise for a pillow.

Then having listened to the Lord, it's time to speak to him. The last half of your quiet time centers around the three *Rs* of prayer.

R=Rejoice

Begin by rejoicing, praising, and thanking God for his grace and generosity. A good place to start is with your *VFTD*. Usually when engaged in conversation, I respond and react to the words of the one speaking to me. If he's talking about the Washington Redskins, I don't abruptly begin a discourse on the excavations of Crocodilopolis. I follow the flow of the conversation.

If your VFTD is Matthew 22.37—*Love the Lord your God with all your heart* . . .—tell God how much you love him and thank him for his love for you. Rejoice that you have a love-based relationship with the Almighty.

R=Repent

As you worship the Lord, you may begin to feel inadequate, like Peter in Luke 5.8, who, amazed at Christ's miracle of fish, fell at his knees saying, *"Lord, don't come near me! I am a sinner."*

So we move naturally from rejoicing to repenting. We admit to God faults and failures we've knowingly allowed to mar our lives since we last prayed.

R=Request

Then we're ready to obey Philippians 4.6: *With thankful hearts offer up your prayers and requests to God.* The Lord promises to answer our prayers if we sincerely ask in the name of the Lord Jesus—with one condition inserted for our protection: He only promises to grant us those things that are good for us, that are according to his will (1 John 5.14-15).

So pray with confidence, using your journal to record your requests and to note God's answers. Pray aloud when you can, and talk to God naturally, as though speaking with a friend.

Because you are.

Don't grow discouraged if sometimes you don't feel like praying. Pray anyway.

Don't quit on mornings when you don't enjoy your Bible reading. Read anyway.

Don't despair if you miss a day. Start again the next.

Develop the habit, then the habit will develop you. Cultivate the friendship, and your Friend will stick closer than a brother. For . . .

> *Our holy God lives forever in the highest heavens,*
> *and this is what he says:*
> *Though I live high above in the holy place,*
> *I am here to help those who are humble*
> *and depend only on me (Is 57.15).*

The effect on your children will be for keeps.

People You'll Meet in *The Children's Daily Devotional Bible*

Who in the world is Mephibosheth? Jehoshaphat? Nebuchadnezzar? Ever heard of Ananias and Sapphira?

These hard-to-say names belong to some very interesting people you'll meet in *The Children's Daily Devotional Bible.* The following list can help you get to know them. Beside every name is a helpful guide to pronouncing it correctly, and a description of the person's identity. At the end of each entry you'll find the page number first mentioning that character.

Adam *(ADD um)* **and Eve** *(eev)* - the first man and woman, created by God and placed in the Garden of Eden (p. 2)

Cain *(kane)* **and Abel** *(A buhl)* - Adam and Eve's first two sons (p. 6)

Noah *(NOE uh)* - the man who trusted and obeyed God by building a big boat (p. 8)

Abram/Abraham *(A bruhm/AY bruh ham)* - the man who received God's promise to make his descendants into a great nation (p. 15)

Sarai/Sarah *(SAR eye/SAR uh)* - Abraham's wife; she had her first son when she was 90 years old and Abraham was 100 years old (p. 15)

Lot *(laht)* - Abraham's nephew who traveled with him to the land of Canaan (p. 15)

Isaac *(EYE zik)* - the son of Abraham and Sarah through whom God fulfilled his promise to Abraham (p. 24)

Hagar *(HAY gahr)* - Sarah's Egyptian slave woman (p. 24)

Ishmael *(IHSH may ell)* - the son of Abraham and Hagar (p. 24)

Rebekah *(ruh BEK uh)* - Isaac's wife who was promised and chosen by God (p. 28)

Esau *(EE saw)* - Isaac and Rebekah's son who sold his birthright to his twin brother Jacob (p. 30)

Jacob *(JAY cub)* - Isaac and Rebekah's son who received his father's blessing in place of his twin brother Esau (p. 30)

Laban *(LAY bihn)* - Rebekah's wealthy brother for whom Jacob worked for over 14 years (p. 32)

Leah *(LEE uh)*-Laban's oldest daughter who became Jacob's wife through deceit (p. 32)

Rachel *(RAY chuhl)* - Leah's sister who became Jacob's wife after he had worked 14 years for her father Laban (p. 32)

Joseph *(JOE zeph)* - the second youngest of the twelve sons of Jacob; he became the governor of all Egypt (p. 34)

Moses *(MOE zez)* - the man God used to deliver the children of Israel from Egyptian bondage (p. 42)

Miriam *(MER eh um)* - Moses' older sister who saved his life when he was just a baby (p. 42)

Aaron *(EHR un)* - the older brother of Moses who became his spokesman; he and his sons were the first priests of Israel (p. 48)

Balaam *(BAY lum)* - A magician in Mesopotamia whose donkey was enabled by God to talk (p. 63)

Joshua *(JAHSH oo uh)* - the man who became the leader of Israel following the death of Moses, and who led the nation into the Promised Land (p. 66)

Deborah *(DEB uh rah)* - a prophetess and leader of Israel who was used by God to defeat the enemies of Israel (p. 76)

Barak *(BAR ack)* - the leader of Israel's army who, along with Deborah, defeated the army of Sisera (p. 76)

Gideon *(GIDD ee un)* - the leader God used to rescue Israel from the Midianites with only 300 soldiers (p. 79)

Samson *(SAM suhn)* - a leader of Israel who had great strength when the Holy Spirit came upon him (p. 80)

Delilah (*dih LIE lah*) - the Philistine woman who tricked Samson, causing him to lose his great strength (p. 80)

Naomi (*nay OH mee*) - a woman whose family moved to Moab after a famine in their hometown of Bethlehem (p. 84)

Ruth (*rooth*) - the daughter-in-law of Naomi who returned with Naomi to Bethlehem after the death of both of their husbands (p. 84)

Boaz (*BOE az*) - a wealthy man from Bethlehem, a relative of Naomi's husband, who married Ruth and became an ancestor of David and Jesus (p. 86)

Hannah (*HAN nuh*) - the wife of Elkanah who prayed for a son and dedicated him to God before his birth (p. 89)

Elkanah (*el KAY na*) - a Levite who was the husband of Hannah and the father of Samuel (p. 89)

Eli (*EE lie*) - a priest and judge of Israel (p. 89)

Samuel (*SAM yoo uhl*) - a Hebrew prophet who, as a child, ministered to the Lord by helping Eli the priest (p. 89)

Saul (*sawl*) - the man who was anointed by Samuel as the first king of Israel (p. 93)

David (*DAY vid*) - a musician and warrior for Saul who eventually became king of Israel in Saul's place (p. 98)

Goliath (*goe LIE ahth*) - the gigantic Philistine whom David killed with a slingshot and stone (p. 100)

Jonathan (*JAHN uh thuhn*) - Saul's son and David's best friend (p. 104)

Mephibosheth (*meh FIB oh shehth*) - the son of Jonathan and grandson of Saul; David showed kindness to him for the sake of Jonathan (p. 114)

Solomon (*SAHL uh mun*) - David's son who became king of Israel; he was given special wisdom from God (p. 115)

Ahab (*A hab*) - a wicked king of Israel who built altars to Baal (p. 119)

Elijah (*ee LIE juh*) - a prophet of God during the reign of King Ahab (p. 119)

Elisha (*ee LIE shuh*) - the prophet of God who came after Elijah; he was given twice as much power as the other prophets (p. 124)

Naaman (*NAY a man*) - the commander of the Syrian army who was healed of leprosy (p. 126)

Jezebel (*JEZ uh bel*) - the evil wife of King Ahab and a worshiper of the false god Baal (p. 130)

Hezekiah (*hez uh KIGH uh*) - a king of Judah who trusted in the Lord for defeat of his enemies (p. 132)

Isaiah (*eye ZAY uh*) - a prophet of Judah during the reigns of four kings, including Hezekiah (p. 134)

Josiah (*joe SIGH uh*) - a godly king of Judah who took the throne when he was only eight years old (p. 136)

Jehoshaphat (*juh HAH shuh fat*) - a king of Judah who obeyed and worshiped the Lord; the Lord helped him keep control of his kingdom (p. 139)

Joash (*JOE ash*) - the king of Judah during the time when the temple was repaired (p. 142)

Uzziah (*you ZIE uh*) - the king of Judah who was struck with leprosy as a punishment from the Lord (p. 144)

Ahaz (*A haz*) - a wicked king of Judah who offered sacrifices to Baal (p. 145)

Nehemiah (*knee uh MY ah*) - a Jewish servant of the king of Persia who led in the rebuilding of the walls of Jerusalem (p. 146)

Esther (*ESS ter*) - the Jewish wife of King Xerxes and the queen of Persia who risked her life to save her people (p. 148)

Mordecai (*MAWR deh kie*) - the cousin of Esther and a palace official in Persia (p. 148)

Haman (*HAY mun*) - evil officer in Persia who wanted to destroy all the Jews in the world (p. 148)

Job (*jobe*) - a worshiper of God who trusted the Lord even when tested with the loss of all his possessions (p. 151)

Jeremiah (*jer uh MIGH uh*) - a priest and prophet of God who warned the people of their disobedience to God (p. 188)

Nebuchadnezzar (*neb you kad NEZ ur*) - the king of Babylonia who led his army in an attack on Jerusalem that captured the city (p. 194)

Ezekiel (*ih ZEEK e uhl*) - a priest and

prophet of God before and after the fall of Jerusalem (p. 196)

Daniel *(DAN yuhl)* - a young Jew taken captive by the Babylonians who remained completely faithful to the Lord (p. 199)

Belshazzar *(bel SHAZ zur)* - the last king of Babylon whose evil ways caused the Lord to write a message of doom on the wall of his banquet room (p. 202)

Hosea *(hoe ZAY uh)* - a prophet in Israel for over 40 years (p. 208)

Joel *(JOE uhl)* - a prophet in Israel who used swarms of locusts to describe how God was going to destroy Israel (p. 209)

Amos *(AIM us)* - a man who left his hometown in Judah and went to the northern kingdom of Israel to deliver God's message to the people (p. 212)

Jonah *(JOE nuh)* - a prophet whose disobedience led to his being swallowed by a great fish, but he repented and was sent to preach in Nineveh (p. 213)

Micah *(MIE kuh)* - a prophet who gave messages from the Lord especially to the cities of Samaria and Jerusalem (p. 217)

Nahum *(NAY hum)* - a prophet who told of justice and punishment to come upon Assyria (p. 220)

Habakkuk *(huh BAK uhk)* - a prophet of Judah who praised the Lord's power and glory (p. 221)

Zechariah *(zeck ah RIE a)* - a priest and prophet whose visions were used by God to help the people of Jerusalem with the rebuilding of the temple (p. 222)

Malachi *(MAL ah kie)* - a prophet who reminded the people of Israel to give to God what belonged to him (p. 227)

Jesus *(GEE zus)* - the Son of God, the Savior of the world, who was both God and man (p. 228)

Herod *(HEHR ud)* - the king of Israel when Jesus was born (p. 228)

Mary *(MAIR ee)* - the wife of Joseph and the woman chosen by the Lord as the mother of Jesus (p. 229)

Joseph *(JOE zeph)* - a carpenter from Nazareth; the husband of Mary, mother of Jesus (p. 229)

Simon Peter *(SIGH mun PEE ter)* - a fisherman who was brought to Jesus by his brother Andrew; he became one of Jesus' apostles (p. 235)

James *(jamez)* **and John** *(jahn)* - the sons of Zebedee; fishermen who became apostles of Jesus (p. 238)

Pilate *(PIE lat)* - the Roman governor of Judea during the time of Jesus (p. 243)

Jairus *(jay EYE ruhs)* - a ruler of the Jewish meeting place whose daughter needed healing from Jesus (p. 246)

Pharisees *(FARE uh sees)* - the religious teachers of Jesus' day (p. 249)

Elizabeth *(ee LIZ uh buth)* - the cousin of Mary and the mother of John (p. 256)

John *(jahn)* - the son of Zechariah and Elizabeth; the man God sent to prepare the people to receive Jesus (p. 262)

Judas *(JOO duhs)* - the apostle who betrayed Jesus (p. 278)

Nicodemus *(nick oh DEE mus)* - a Pharisee and Jewish leader who came to Jesus at night (p. 285)

Mary *(MAIR ee)* **and Martha** (MAR thuh) - sisters from the town of Bethany; Jesus was a close friend of their family (p. 291)

Lazarus *(LAZ ah russ)* - the brother of Mary and Martha who was raised from the dead by Jesus (p. 291)

Mary Magdalene *(MAIR ee MAG deh leen)* - a woman from Magdala of Galilee who was one of Jesus' most devoted followers (p. 299)

Ananias *(an uh NYE us)* **and Sapphira** (suh FIGH ruh) - a husband and wife who were struck dead for lying to the Holy Spirit (p. 312)

Stephen *(STEE vun)* - a man of great faith and filled with God's Spirit who was chosen by the twelve apostles to serve God (p. 318)

Simon *(SIGH mun)* - a man of Samaria who practiced witchcraft, but came to believe in Jesus (p. 321)

Philip *(FILL ihp)* - one of seven men chosen by the apostles to serve God by going from place to place telling the good news (p. 321)

Saul *(sawl)* - a man from the city of Tarsus who hated Christians until he came to know Jesus as his Savior; he later became known as Paul, a great preacher of the gospel (p. 323)

Paul *(pawl)* - a faithful follower of Jesus and an apostle to the Gentiles; he took the gospel throughout all the regions north of the Mediterranean Sea; he was originally known as Saul (p. 331)

Barnabas *(BAR nuh bus)* - a devoted follower of the Lord who sold all his goods to give to the work of Christ; he was known as the son of encouragement (p. 333)

Silas *(SIGH lus)* - a loyal companion and friend of Paul who went with him on one of his missionary trips (p. 338)

Timothy *(TIM uh thih)* - a faithful servant of the Lord who was like a son to Paul and served as his assistant (p. 339)

Aquila *(A kwil uh)* **and Priscilla** *(prih SIL uh)* - a Jewish couple who made tents for their living; followers of the Lord and friends of Paul (p. 346)

Philemon *(fie LEE mun)* - a wealthy man who used his large house for church meetings (p. 389)

The Story of Creation

In the beginning God created the heavens and the earth.[a]

2 The earth was barren, with no form of life;[b] it was under a roaring ocean covered with darkness. But the Spirit of God[c] was moving over the water.

3 God said, "I command light to shine!" And light started shining. 4 God looked at the light and saw that it was good. He separated light from darkness 5 and named the light "Day" and the darkness "Night." Evening came and then morning—that was the first day.[d]

6 God said, "I command a dome to separate the water above it from the water below it." 7 And that's what happened. God made the dome 8 and named it "Sky." Evening came and then morning—that was the second day.

9 God said, "I command the water under the sky to come together in one place, so there will be dry ground." And that's what happened. 10 God named the dry ground "Land," and he named the water "Ocean." God looked at what he had done and saw that it was good.

11 God said, "I command the earth to produce all kinds of plants, including fruit trees and grain." And that's what happened. 12 The earth produced all kinds of vegetation. God looked at what he had done, and it was good. 13 Evening came and then morning—that was the third day.

14 God said, "I command lights to appear in the sky and to separate day from night and to show the time for seasons, special days, and years. 15 I command them to shine on the earth." And that's what happened. 16 God made two powerful lights, the brighter one to rule the day and the other[e] to rule the night. He also made the stars.

[a]1.1 *the heavens and the earth:* "The heavens and the earth" stood for the universe. [b]1.1,2 *In . . . life:* Or "When God began to create the heavens and the earth, the earth was barren with no form of life." [c]1.2 *the Spirit of God:* Or "a mighty wind." [d]1.5 *the first day:* A day was measured from evening to evening. [e]1.16 *the brighter . . . the other:* The sun and the moon. But they are not called by their names, because in Old Testament times some people worshiped the sun and the moon as though they were gods.

Prayer Starter: Thank you, Lord, for stars and sky, for trees and grass, and for making the world so beautiful.

Animals and Humans

God said, "I command the earth to give life to all kinds of tame animals, wild animals, and reptiles." And that's what happened. ²⁵God made every one of them. Then he looked at what he had done, and it was good.

²⁶God said, "Now we will make humans, and they will be like us. We will let them rule the fish, the birds, and all other living creatures."

²⁷So God created humans to be like himself: he made men and women. ²⁸God gave them his blessing and said:

Have a lot of children! Fill the earth with people and bring it under your control. Rule over the fish in the ocean, the birds in the sky, and every animal on the earth.

²⁹I have provided all kinds of fruit and grain for you to eat. ³⁰And I have given the green plants as food for everything else that breathes.

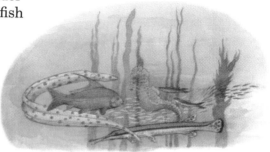

These will be food for animals, both wild and tame, and for birds.

³¹God looked at what he had done. All of it was very good! Evening came and then morning—that was the sixth day.

2 So the heavens and the earth and everything else were created. ²By the seventh day God had finished his work, and so he rested. ³God blessed the seventh day and made it special because on that day he rested from his work.

⁴That's how God created the heavens and the earth.

Prayer Starter: Thank you, Lord, for dogs, cats, fish, and birds. And thank you for men and women and boys and girls—and me.

Memory Verse: God made two powerful lights . . . —*Genesis 1.16*

The First Sin

The snake was sneakier than any of the other wild animals that the Lord God had made. One day it came to the woman and asked, "Did God tell you not to eat fruit from any tree in the garden?"

²The woman answered, "God said we could eat fruit from any tree in the garden, ³except the one in the middle. He told us not to eat fruit from that tree or even to touch it. If we do, we will die."

⁴"No, you won't!" the snake replied. ⁵"God understands what will happen on the day you eat fruit from that tree. You will see what you have done, and you will know the difference between right and wrong, just as God does."

⁶The woman stared at the fruit. It looked beautiful and tasty. She wanted the wisdom that it would give her, and she ate some of the fruit. Her husband was there with her, so she gave some to him, and he ate it too. ⁷Right away they saw what they had done, and they realized they were naked. Then they sewed fig leaves together to make something to cover themselves.

⁸Late in the afternoon a breeze began to blow, and the man and woman heard the Lord God walking in the garden. They were frightened and hid behind some trees.

⁹The Lord called out to the man and asked, "Where are you?"

¹⁰The man answered, "I was naked, and when I heard you walking through the garden, I was frightened and hid!"

¹¹"How did you know you were naked?" God asked. "Did you eat any fruit from that tree in the middle of the garden?"

¹²"It was the woman you put here with me," the man said. "She gave me some of the fruit, and I ate it."

¹³The Lord God then asked the woman, "What have you done?"

"The snake tricked me," she answered. "And I ate some of that fruit."

²⁰The man Adam[a] named his wife Eve[b] because she would become the mother of all who live.

²¹Then the LORD God made clothes out of animal skins for the man and his wife.

²²The LORD said, "These people now know the difference between right and wrong, just as we do. But they must not be allowed to eat fruit from the tree that lets them live forever." ²³So the LORD God sent them out of the Garden of Eden, where they would have to work the ground from which the man had been made. ²⁴Then God put winged creatures at the entrance to the garden and a flaming, flashing sword to guard the way to the life-giving tree.

ᵃ3:20 *The man Adam:* In Hebrew "man" and "Adam" are the same. ᵇ3:20 *Eve:* In Hebrew "Eve" sounds like "living."

Prayer Starter: Father, forgive me for times when I disobey you and do things that make you sad. Help me to please you in all I do and say.

Memory Verse: God made two powerful lights, the brighter one . . .
—*Genesis 1.16*

Cain and Abel

Adam[a] and Eve had a son. Then Eve said, "I'll name him Cain because I got[b] him with the help of the LORD." [2]Later she had another son and named him Abel.

Abel became a sheep farmer, but Cain farmed the land. [3]One day, Cain gave part of his harvest to the LORD, [4]and Abel also gave an offering to the LORD. He killed the first-born lamb from one of his sheep and gave the LORD the best parts of it. The LORD was pleased with Abel and his offering, [5]but not with Cain and his offering. This made Cain so angry that he could not hide his feelings.

[6]The LORD said to Cain:

What's wrong with you? Why do you have such an angry look on your face? [7]If you had done the right thing, you would be smiling.[c] But you did the wrong thing, and now sin is waiting to attack you like a lion. Sin wants to destroy you, but don't let it!

[8]Cain said to his brother Abel, "Let's go for a walk."[d] And when they were out in a field, Cain killed him.

[9]Afterwards the LORD asked Cain, "Where is Abel?"

"How should I know?" he answered. "Am I supposed to look after my brother?"

[10]Then the LORD said:

Why have you done this terrible thing? You killed your own brother, and his blood flowed onto the ground. Now his blood is calling out for

me to punish you. ¹¹And so, I'll put you under a curse. Because you killed Abel and made his blood run out on the ground, you will never be able to farm the land again.

ᵃ4.1 *Adam:* In Hebrew "man" and "Adam" are the same. ᵇ4.1 *Cain . . . got:* In Hebrew "Cain" sounds like "got." ᶜ4.7 *you would be smiling:* Or "I would have accepted your offering." ᵈ4.8 *Cain said to his brother Abel, "Let's . . . walk":* Most ancient translations; Hebrew "Cain spoke to his brother Abel."

Prayer Starter: Lord, help us love each other as you love us. Help me be concerned about others and treat them as I want to be treated.

Memory Verse: God made two powerful lights, the brighter one to rule the day . . . —*Genesis 1.16*

Noah

The LORD saw how bad the people on earth were and that everything they thought and planned was evil. [6]He was very sorry that he had made them, [7]and he said, "I'll destroy every living creature on earth! I'll wipe out people, animals, birds, and reptiles. I'm sorry I ever made them."

[8]But the LORD was pleased with Noah, [9]and this is the story about him. Noah was the only person who lived right and obeyed God. [10]He had three sons: Shem, Ham, and Japheth.

[11-12]God knew that everyone was terribly cruel and violent. [13]So he told Noah:

Cruelty and violence have spread everywhere. Now I'm going to destroy the whole earth and all its people. [14]Get some good lumber and build a boat. Put rooms in it and cover it with tar inside and out. [15]Make it four hundred fifty feet long, seventy-five feet high, and forty-five feet wide. [16]Build a roof[a] on the boat and leave a space of about eighteen inches between the roof and the sides.[b] Make the boat three stories high and put a door on one side.

[17]I'm going to send a flood that will destroy everything that breathes! Nothing will be left alive. [18]But I solemnly promise that you, your wife, your sons, and your daughters-in-law will be kept safe in the boat.[c]

[19-20]Bring into the boat with you a male and a female of every kind of animal and bird, as well as a male and a female of every reptile. I

don't want them to be destroyed. ²¹Store up enough food for yourself and for them.

²²Noah did everything the LORD told him to do.

ᵃ6.16 *roof:* Or "window." ᵇ6.16 *leave . . . sides:* One possible meaning for the difficult Hebrew text. ᶜ6.18 *boat:* One possible meaning for the difficult Hebrew text of verse 18.

Prayer Starter: Dear Lord, give me good friends who will help me to be a better person. Keep me from the wrong kind of friends.

Memory Verse: God made two powerful lights, the brighter one to rule the day and the other to rule the night. — *Genesis 1.16*

The Great Flood

The LORD told Noah:

Take your whole family with you into the boat, because you are the only one on this earth who pleases me. ²Take seven pairs of every kind of animal that can be used for sacrificeᵃ and one pair of all others. ³Also take seven pairs of every kind of bird with you. Do this so there will always be animals and birds on the earth. ⁴Seven days from now I will send rain that will last for forty days and nights, and I will destroy all other living creatures I have made.

⁵⁻⁷Noah was six hundred years old when he went into the boat to escape the flood, and he did everything the LORD had told him to do. His wife, his sons, and his daughters-in-law all went inside with him. ⁸⁻⁹He obeyed God and took a male and a female of each kind of animal and bird into the boat wih him. ¹⁰Seven days later a flood began to cover the earth.

¹¹⁻¹²Noah was six hundred years old when the water under the earth started gushing out everywhere. The sky opened like windows, and rain poured down for forty days and nights.

¹⁷⁻¹⁸And the water became deeper and deeper, until the boat started floating high above the ground. ¹⁹⁻²⁰Finally, the mighty flood was so deep that even the highest mountain peaks were almost twenty-five feet below the surface of the water. ²¹Not a bird, animal, reptile, or human was left alive anywhere on earth. ²²⁻²³The LORD destroyed everything that breathed. Nothing was left alive except Noah and the others on the boat. ²⁴A hundred fifty days later, the water started going down.

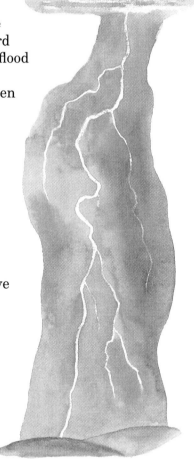

ᵃ7.2 *animal . . . for sacrifice:* Hebrew "clean animals." Animals that could be used for sacrifice were called "clean," and animals that could not be used were called "unclean."

Prayer Starter: I know you are a holy God, dear Father. Make me pure and holy like you are. Keep me from sin.

Memory Verse: Because Noah had faith . . .   *—Hebrews 11.7*

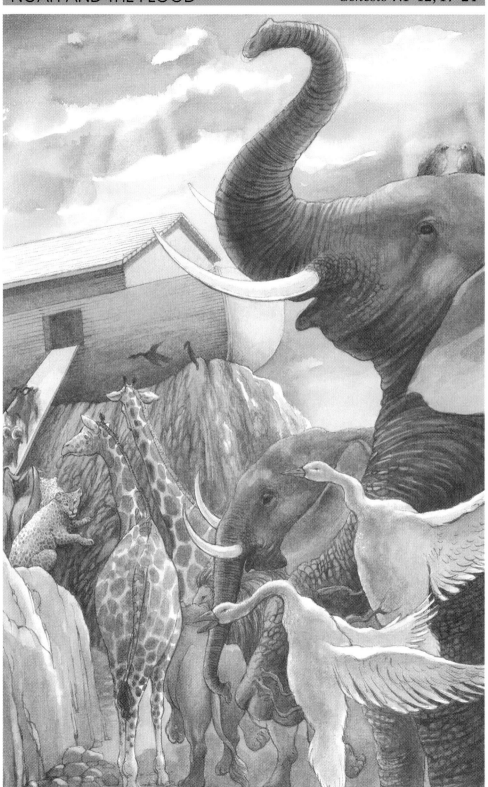

A New Beginning

God did not forget about Noah and the animals with him in the boat. So God made a wind blow, and the water started going down. ²God stopped up the places where the water had been gushing out from under the earth. He also closed up the sky, and the rain stopped. ³For one hundred fifty days the water slowly went down.

⁴Then on the seventeenth day of the seventh month of the year, the boat came to rest somewhere in the Ararat mountains. ⁵The water kept going down, and the mountain tops could be seen on the first day of the tenth month.

⁶⁻⁷Forty days later Noah opened a window to send out a raven, but it kept flying around until the water had dried up. ⁸Noah wanted to find out if the water had gone down, and he sent out a dove. ⁹Deep water was still everywhere, and the dove could not find a place to land. So it flew back to the boat. Noah held out his hand and helped it back in.

¹⁰Seven days later Noah sent the dove out again. ¹¹It returned in the evening, holding in its beak a green leaf from an olive tree. Noah knew that the water was finally going down. ¹²He waited seven more days before sending the dove out again, and this time it did not return.

¹³Noah was now six hundred one years old. And by the first day of that year, almost all the water had gone away. Noah make an opening in the roof of the boatᵃ and saw that the ground was getting dry. ¹⁴By the twenty-seventh day of the second month, the earth was completely dry.

¹⁵God said to Noah, ¹⁶"You, your wife, your sons, and your daughters-in-law may now leave the boat. ¹⁷Let out the birds, animals, and reptiles, so they can mate and live all over the earth."

ᵃ8.13 *made . . . boat:* One possible meaning for the difficult Hebrew text.

Prayer Starter: Thank you for taking care of all the animals and people you have created. You give us food to eat, water to drink, air to breath. We love you, Father.

Memory Verse: Because Noah had faith, he was warned about something . . .   *—Hebrews 11.7*

The Rainbow

God said to Noah and his sons: I am giving you my blessing. Have a lot of children and grandchildren, so people will live everywhere on this earth. ²All animals, birds, reptiles, and fish will be afraid of you. I have placed them under your control.

⁸Again, God said to Noah and his sons:

⁹I am going to make a solemn promise to you and to everyone who will live after you. ¹⁰This includes the birds and the animals that came out of the boat. ¹¹I promise every living creature that the earth and those living on it will never again be destroyed by a flood.

¹²⁻¹³The rainbow that I have put in the sky will be my sign to you and to every living creature on earth. It will remind you that I will keep this promise forever. ¹⁴When I send clouds over the earth, and a rainbow appears in the sky, ¹⁵I will remember my promise to you and to all other living creatures. Never again will I let floodwaters destroy all life. ¹⁶When I see the rainbow in the sky, I will always remember the promise that I have made to every living creature. ¹⁷The rainbow will be the sign of that solemn promise.

¹⁸Noah and his sons, Shem, Ham, and Japheth, came out of the boat. Ham later had a son named Canaan. ¹⁹All people on earth are descendants of Noah's three sons.

Prayer Starter: You made all the colors in the rainbow, dear Lord—green and blue and yellow and red.

Memory Verse: Because Noah had faith, he was warned about something that had not yet happened. . . . *—Hebrews 11.7*

Abram

After Terah [a descendant of Shem] was seventy years old, he had three sons: Abram, Nahor, and Haran, who became the father of Lot. Terah's sons were born in the city of Ur in Chaldea,ᵃ and Haran died there before the death of his father. The following is the story of Terah's descendants.

²⁹⁻³⁰Abram married Sarai, but she was not able to have any children. And Nahor married Milcah, who was the daughter of Haran and the sister of Iscah.

³¹Terah decided to move from Ur to the land of Canaan. He took along Abram and Sarai and his grandson Lot, the son of Haran. But when they came to the city of Haran,ᵇ they decided to settle there instead. ³²Terah lived to be two hundred five years old and died in Haran.

12 The LORD said to Abram:

Leave your country, your family, and your relatives and go to the land that I will show you. ²I will bless you and make your descendants into a great nation. You will become famous and be a blessing to others. ³I will bless anyone who blesses you, but I will put

a curse on anyone who puts a curse on you. Everyone on earth will be blessed because of you.[c]

⁴⁻⁵Abram was seventy-five years old when the LORD told him to leave the city of Haran. He obeyed and left with his wife Sarai, his nephew Lot, and all the possessions and slaves they had gotten while in Haran.

When they came to the land of Canaan, ⁶Abram went as far as the sacred tree of Moreh in a place called Shechem. The Canaanites were still living in the land at that time, ⁷but the LORD appeared to Abram and promised, "I will give this land to your family forever." Abram then built an altar there for the LORD.

⁸Abram traveled to the hill country east of Bethel and camped between Bethel and Ai, where he built another altar and worshiped the LORD. ⁹Later, Abram started out toward the Southern Desert.

[a]11.26-28 *Ur in Chaldea:* Chaldea was a region at the head of the Persian Gulf. Ur was on the main trade routes from Mesopotamia to the Mediterranean Sea. [b]11.31 *Haran:* About 550 miles northwest of Ur. [c]12.3 *Everyone . . . you:* Or "Everyone on earth will ask me to bless them as I have blessed you."

Prayer Starter: Dear Lord, I know that you are wise and wonderful, more than anyone else in the universe. Lead me each day in doing what you wish.

Memory Verse: Because Noah had faith, he was warned about something that had not yet happened. He obeyed and built a boat . . .
—*Hebrews 11.7*

Lot Chooses

Abram and Sarai took everything they owned and went to the Southern Desert. Lot went with them.

²Abram was very rich. He owned many cattle, sheep, and goats, and had a lot of silver and gold. ³Abram moved from place to place in the Southern Desert. And finally, he went north and set up his tents between Bethel and Ai, ⁴where he had earlier camped and built an altar. There he worshiped the LORD.

⁵Lot, who was traveling with him, also had sheep, goats, and cattle, as well as his own family and slaves. ⁶⁻⁷At this time the Canaanites and the Perizzites were living in the same area, and so there wasn't enough pastureland left for Abram and Lot with all of their animals. Besides this, the men who took care of Abram's animals and the ones who took care of Lot's animals started quarreling.

⁸Abram said to Lot, "We are close relatives. We shouldn't argue, and our men shouldn't be fighting one another. ⁹There is plenty of land for you to choose from. Let's separate. If you go north, I'll go south; if you go south, I'll go north."

¹⁰This happened before the LORD had destroyed the cities of Sodom and Gomorrah. And when Lot looked around, he saw there was plenty of water in the Jordan Valley. All the way to Zoar the valley was as green as the garden of the LORD of the land of Egypt. ¹¹So Lot chose the whole Jordan Valley for himself, and as he started toward the east, he and Abram separated. ¹²Abram stayed in the land of Canaan. But Lot settled near the cities of the valley and put up his tents not far from Sodom, ¹³where the people were evil and sinned terribly against the LORD.

¹⁴After Abram and Lot had gone their separate ways, the LORD said to Abram:

Look around to the north, south, east, and west. ¹⁵I will give you and your family all the land you can see. It will be theirs forever! ¹⁶I will give you more descendants than there are specks of dust on the earth, and someday it will be easier to count the specks of dust than

to count your descendants. ¹⁷Now walk back and forth across the land, because I am giving it to you.

¹⁸Abram took down his tents and went to live near the sacred trees of Mamre at Hebron, where he built an altar in honor of the LORD.

Prayer Starter: Father, I want to be unselfish. Keep me from complaining and bickering and being jealous. May I love others like you do.

Memory Verse: Because Noah had faith, he was warned about something that had not yet happened. He obeyed and built a boat that saved him and his family.
　　　　　　　　　　　　　　　　　　　　—*Hebrews 11.7*

Abraham Believed the Lord

Later the LORD spoke to Abram in a vision, "Abram, don't be afraid! I will protect you and reward you greatly."

²But Abram answered, "LORD All-Powerful, you have given me everything I could ask for, except children. And when I die, Eliezer of Damascus will get all I own.ᵃ ³You have not given me any children, and this servant of mine will inherit everything."

⁴The LORD replied, "No, he won't! You will have a son of your own, and everything you have will be his." ⁵Then the LORD took Abram outside and said, "Look at the sky and see if you can count the stars. That's how many descendants you will have." ⁶Abram believed the LORD, and the LORD was pleased with him.

17 Abram was ninety-nine years old when the LORD appeared to him again and said, "I am God All-Powerful. If you obey me and always do right, ²I will keep my solemn promise to you and give you more descendants than can be counted." ³Abram bowed with his face to the ground, and God said:

⁴⁻⁵I promise that you will be the father of many nations. That's why I now change your name from Abram to Abraham.ᵇ ⁶I will give you a lot of descendants, and in the future they will become great nations. Some of them will even be kings.

⁷I will always keep the promise I have made to you and your descendants, because I am your God and their God. ⁸I will give you and them the land in which you are now a foreigner. I will give the whole land of Canaan to your family forever, and I will be their God.

¹⁵Abraham, your wife's name will now be Sarah instead of Sarai. ¹⁶I will bless her, and you will have a son by her. She will become the mother of nations, and some of her descendants will even be kings.

ᵃ15.2 *And . . . own:* One possible meaning for the difficult Hebrew text.
ᵇ17.4,5 *Abraham:* In Hebrew "Abraham" sounds like "father of many nations."

Prayer Starter: Father, thank you for Jesus Christ, and for your promise of eternal life. Give me faith in Christ, and may I serve him each day.

Memory Verse: But Abraham never doubted . . . —*Romans 4.20*

Abraham's Guests

One hot summer afternoon Abraham was sitting by the entrance to his tent near the sacred trees of Mamre, when the Lord appeared to him. [2]Abraham looked up and saw three men standing nearby. He quickly ran to meet them, bowed with his face to the ground, [3]and said, "Please come to my home where I can serve you. [4]I'll have some water brought, so you can wash your feet, then you can rest under the tree. [5]Let me get you some food to give you strength before you leave. I would be honored to serve you."

"Thank you very much," they answered. "We accept your offer."

[6]Abraham quickly went to his tent and said to Sarah, "Hurry! Get a large sack of flour and make some bread." [7]After saying this, he rushed off to his herd of cattle and picked out one of the best calves, which his servant quickly prepared. [8]He then served his guests some yogurt and milk together with the meat.

While they were eating, he stood near them under the trees, [9]and they asked, "Where is your wife Sarah?"

"She is right there in the tent," Abraham answered.

[10]One of the guests was the Lord, and he said, "I'll come back about this time next year, and when I do, Sarah will already have a son."

Sarah was behind Abraham, listening at the entrance to the tent. [11]Abraham and Sarah were very old, and Sarah was well past the age for having children. [12]So she laughed and said to herself, "Now that I am worn out and my husband is old, will I really know such happiness?"[a]

[13]The Lord asked Abraham, "Why did Sarah laugh? Does she doubt that she can have a child in her old age? [14]I am the Lord! There is nothing too difficult for me. I'll come back next year at the time I promised, and Sarah will already have a son."

[a]18.12 *know such happiness:* Either the joy of making love or the joy of having children.

Prayer Starter: Heavenly father, you are very great. You know the past, the present, and the future. Thank you for having a plan for my life.

Memory Verse: But Abraham never doubted or questioned . . .
—*Romans 4.20*

Sodom and Gomorrah

That evening the two angels[a] arrived in Sodom, while Lot was sitting near the city gate.[b] When Lot saw them, he got up, bowed down low, ²and said, "Gentlemen, I am your servant. Please come to my home. You can wash your feet, spend the night, and be on your way in the morning."

¹²⁻¹³The two angels said to Lot, "The LORD has heard many terrible things about the people of Sodom, and he has sent us here to destroy the city. Take your family and leave. Take every relative you have in the city, as well as the men your daughters are going to marry."

¹⁴Lot went to the men who were engaged to his daughters and said, "Hurry and get out of here! The LORD is going to destroy this city." But they thought he was joking, and they laughed at him.

¹⁵Early the next morning the two angels tried to make Lot hurry and leave. They said, "Take your wife and your two daughters and get out of here as fast as you can! If you don't, every one of you will be killed when the LORD destroys the city." ¹⁶At first, Lot just stood there. But the LORD wanted to save him. So the angels took Lot, his wife, and his two daughters by the hand and led them out of the city.

²³The sun was coming up as Lot reached the town of Zoar, ²⁴and the LORD sent burning sulphur down like rain on Sodom and Gomorrah. ²⁵He destroyed those cities and everyone who lived in them, as well as their land and the trees and grass that grew there. ²⁶On the way, Lot's wife looked back and was turned into a block of salt.

[a]19.1 *two angels:* The two men of 18.2. [b]19.1 *near the city gate:* In a large area where the people would gather for community business and for meeting with friends.

Prayer Starter: Father, help me to never doubt or question your promises. I know you are faithful. May I trust you more and more.

Memory Verse: But Abraham never doubted or questioned God's promise. . . .
—*Romans 4.20*

22

Hagar's Son

The LORD was good to Sarah and kept his promise. ²Although Abraham was very old, Sarah had a son exactly at the time God had said. ³Abraham named his son Isaac.

⁹⁻¹⁰One day, Sarah noticed Hagar's son Ishmaelᵃ playing,ᵇ and she said to Abraham, "Get rid of that Egyptian slave woman and her son! I don't want him to inherit anything. It should all go to my son."ᶜ

¹¹Abraham was worried about Ishmael. ¹²But God said, "Abraham, don't worry about your slave woman and the boy. Just do what Sarah tells you. Isaac will inherit your family name, ¹³but the son of the slave woman is also your son, and I will make his descendants into a great nation."

¹⁴Early the next morning Abraham gave Hagar an animal skin full of water and some bread. Then he put the boy on her shoulder and sent them away.

They wandered around in the desert near Beersheba, ¹⁵and after they had run out of water, Hagar put her son under a bush. ¹⁶Then she sat down a long way off, because she could not bear to watch him die. And she cried bitterly.

¹⁷When God heard the boy crying, the angel of God called out to Hagar from heaven and said, "Hagar, why are you worried? Don't be afraid. I have heard your son crying. ¹⁸Help him up and hold his hand, because I will make him the father of a great nation." ¹⁹Then God let her see a well. So she went to the well and filled the skin with water, then gave some to her son.

²⁰⁻²¹God blessed Ishmael, and as the boy grew older, he became an expert with his bow and arrows. He lived in the Paran Desert, and his mother chose an Egyptian woman for him to marry.

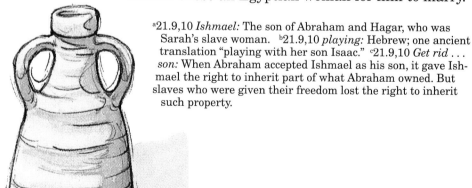

ᵃ21.9,10 *Ishmael:* The son of Abraham and Hagar, who was Sarah's slave woman. ᵇ21.9,10 *playing:* Hebrew; one ancient translation "playing with her son Isaac." ᶜ21.9,10 *Get rid . . . son:* When Abraham accepted Ishmael as his son, it gave Ishmael the right to inherit part of what Abraham owned. But slaves who were given their freedom lost the right to inherit such property.

Prayer Starter: Lord, many people around the world are hungry and thirsty. Please provide for their needs, and give me what I need each day, too.

Memory Verse: But Abraham never doubted or questioned God's promise. His faith made him strong . . .
—Romans 4.20

The Test

The LORD said, "Go get Isaac, your only son, the one you dearly love! Take him to the land of Moriah, and I will show you a mountain where you must sacrifice him to me on the fires of an altar." ³So Abraham got up early the next morning and chopped wood for the fire. He put a saddle on his donkey and left with Isaac and two servants for the place where God had told him to go.

⁶Abraham put the wood on Isaac's shoulder, but he carried the hot coals and the knife. As the two of them walked along, ⁷⁻⁸Isaac said, "Father, we have the coals and the wood, but where is the lamb for the sacrifice?"

"My son," Abraham answered, "God will provide the lamb."

The two of them walked on, and ⁹when they reached the place that God had told him about, Abraham built an altar and placed the wood on it. Next, he tied up his son and put him on the wood. ¹⁰He then took the knife and got ready to kill his son. ¹¹But the LORD's angel shouted from heaven, "Abraham! Abraham!"

"Here I am!" he answered.

¹²"Don't hurt the boy or harm him in any way!" the angel said. "Now I know that you truly obey God, because you were willing to offer him your only son."

¹³Abraham looked up and saw a ram caught by its horns in the bushes. So he took the ram and sacrificed it in place of his son.

¹⁴Abraham named that place "The LORD Will Provide." And even now people say, "On the mountain of the LORD it will be provided."[a]

---

[a]22.14 *The LORD Will Provide . . . it will be provided:* Or "The LORD Will Be Seen . . . the LORD will be seen" or "It (a ram) Will Be Seen . . . it (a ram) will be seen."

Prayer Starter: Thank you, Lord, for helping me to love you more than anything else in the world. I love you because you first loved me.

Memory Verse: But Abraham never doubted or questioned God's promise. His faith made him strong, and he gave all the credit to God.
—*Romans 4.20*

A Wife for Isaac

So the servant gave Abraham his word that he would do everything he had been told to do.

[10]Soon after that, the servant loaded ten of Abraham's camels with valuable gifts. Then he set out for the city in northern Syria,[a] where Abraham's brother Nahor lived.

[11]When he got there, he let the camels rest near the well outside the city. It was late afternoon, the time when the women came out for water. [12]The servant prayed:

You, LORD, are the God my master Abraham worships. Please keep your promise to him and let me find a wife for Isaac today. [13]The young women of the city will soon come to this well for water, [14]and I'll ask one of them for a drink. If she gives me a drink and then offers to get some water for my camels, I'll know she is the one you have chosen and that you have kept your promise to my master.

[15-16]While he was still praying, a beautiful unmarried young woman came by with a water jar on her shoulder. She was Rebekah, the daughter of Bethuel, the son of Abraham's brother Nahor and his wife Milcah. Rebekah walked past Abraham's servant, then went over to the well, and filled her water jar. When she started back, [17]Abraham's servant ran to her and said, "Please let me have a drink of water."

[18]"I'll be glad to," she answered. Then she quickly took the jar from her shoulder and held it while he drank. [19-20]After he had finished, she said, "Now I'll give your camels all the water they want." She quickly poured out water for them, and she kept going back for more, until his camels had drunk all they wanted.

[a]24.10 *northern Syria:* The Hebrew text has "Aram-Naharaim," probably referring to the land around the city of Haran.

Prayer Starter: You lead those who trust you, Lord. Please be my guide and show me what to do and how to live all my life.

Memory Verse: We know that God . . .   —*Romans 8.28*

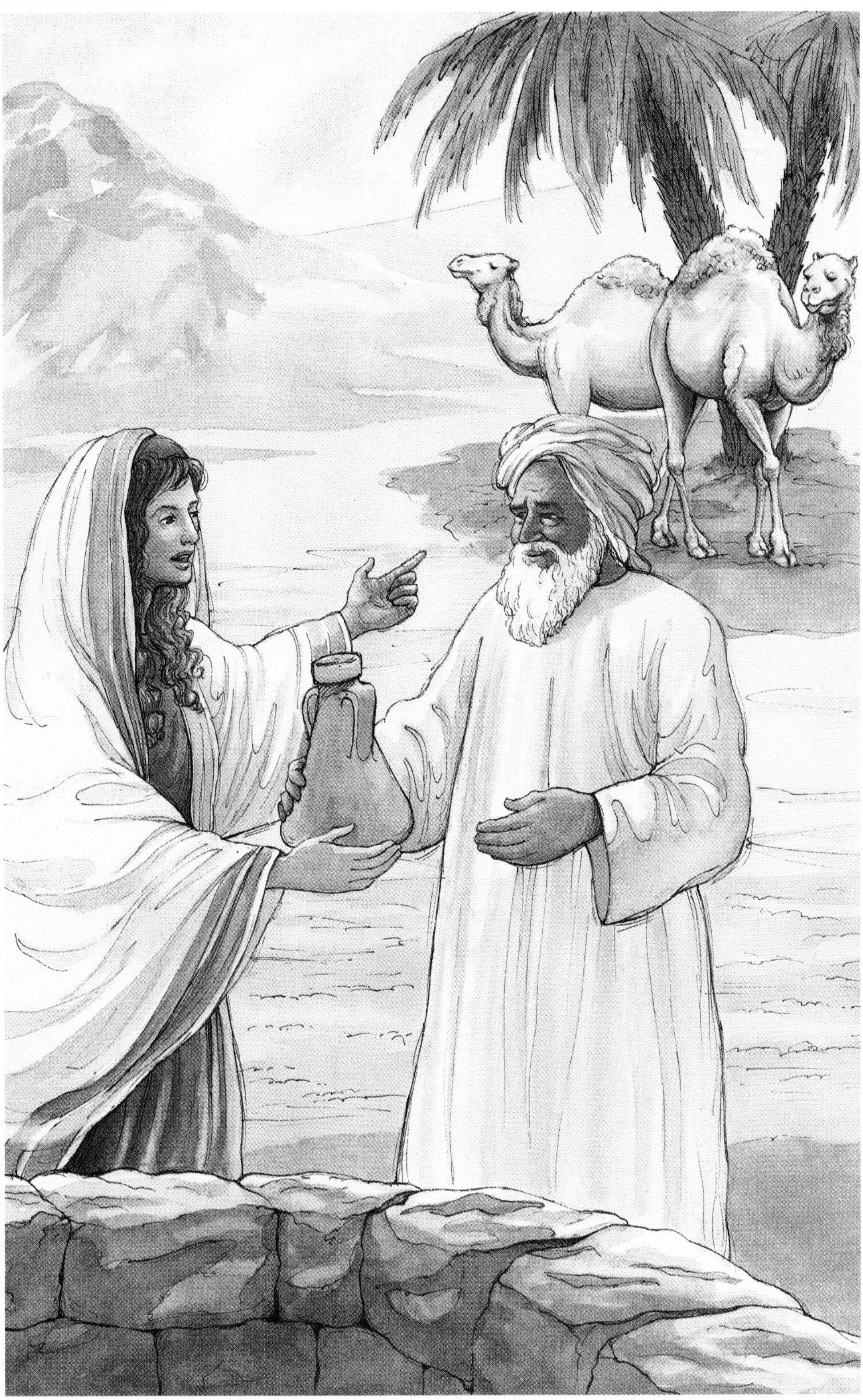

<table>
<tr><td>

Jacob and Esau

</td></tr>
</table>

Isaac was the son of Abraham, [20]and he was forty years old when he married Rebekah, the daughter of Bethuel. She was also the sister of Laban, the Aramean from northern Syria.[a]

Almost twenty years later, [21]Rebekah still had no children. So Isaac asked the LORD to let her have a child, and the LORD answered his prayer.

[22]Before Rebekah gave birth, she knew she was going to have twins.

[24]When Rebekah gave birth, [25]the first baby was covered with red hair, so he was named Esau.[b] [26]The second baby grabbed on to his brother's heel, so they named him Jacob.[c] Isaac was sixty years old when they were born.

[27]As Jacob and Esau grew older, Esau liked the outdoors and became a good hunter, while Jacob settled down and became a shepherd. [28]Esau would take the meat of wild animals to his father Isaac, and so Isaac loved him more, but Jacob was his mother's favorite son.

[29]One day, Jacob was cooking some stew, when Esau came home hungry [30]and said, "I'm starving to death! Give me some of that red stew right now!" That's how Esau got the name "Edom."[d]

[31]Jacob replied, "Sell me your rights as the first-born son."[e]

[32]"I'm about to die," Esau answered. "What good will those rights do me?"

³³But Jacob said, "Promise me your birthrights, here and now!" And that's what Esau did. ³⁴Jacob then gave Esau some bread and some of the bean stew, and when Esau had finished eating and drinking, he just got up and left, showing how little he thought of his rights as the first-born.

ª25.20 *northern Syria:* The Hebrew text has "Aram-Naharaim," probably referring to the land around the city of Haran. ᵇ25.25 *Esau:* In Hebrew "Esau" sounds like "hairy." ᶜ25.26 *Jacob:* In Hebrew "Jacob" sounds like "heel." ᵈ25.30 *Edom:* In Hebrew "Edom" sounds like "red." ᵉ25.31 *rights . . . son:* The first-born son inherited the largest amount of property, as well as the leadership of the family.

Prayer Starter: If I have friends who tempt me to do what is wrong, Lord, help me to say "No." May I always do what pleases you.

Memory Verse: We know that God is always at work . . .
—Romans 8.28

Jacob and Rachel

As Jacob continued on his way to the east, ²he looked out in a field and saw a well where shepherds took their sheep for water. Three flocks of sheep were lying around the well, which was covered with a large rock. ³Shepherds would roll the rock away when all their sheep had gathered there. Then after the sheep had been watered, the shepherds would roll the rock back over the mouth of the well.

⁴Jacob asked the shepherds, "Where are you from?"

"We're from Haran," they answered.

⁵Then he asked, "Do you know Nahor's grandson Laban?"

"Yes we do," they replied.

⁶"How is he?" Jacob asked.

"He's fine," they answered. "And here comes his daughter Rachel with the sheep."

⁷Jacob told them, "Look, the sun is still high up in the sky, and it's too early to bring in the rest of the flocks. Water your sheep and take them back to the pasture."

[8]But they replied, "We can't do that until they all get here, and the rock has been rolled away from the well."

[9]While Jacob was still talking with the men, his cousin Rachel came up with her father's sheep. [10]When Jacob saw her and his uncle's sheep, he rolled the rock away and watered the sheep. [11]He then kissed Rachel and started crying, because he was so happy. [12]He told her that he was the son of her aunt Rebekah, and she ran and told her father about him.

[13]As soon as Laban heard the news, he ran out to meet Jacob. He hugged and kissed him and brought him to his home, where Jacob told him everything that had happened. [14]Laban said, "You are my nephew, and you are like one of my own family."

After Jacob had been there for a month, [15]Laban said to him, "You shouldn't have to work without pay, just because you are a relative of mine. What do you want me to give you?"

[16-17]Laban had two daughters. Leah was older than Rachel, but her eyes didn't sparkle,[a] while Rachel was beautiful and had a good figure. [18]Since Jacob was in love with Rachel, he answered, "If you will let me marry Rachel, I'll work seven years for you."

[19]Laban replied, "It's better for me to let you marry Rachel than for someone else to have her. So stay and work for me." [20]Jacob worked seven years for Laban, but the time seemed like only a few days, because he loved Rachel so much.

[22]So Laban gave a big feast and invited all their neighbors. [23]But that evening he brought Leah to Jacob, who married her and spent the night with her. [24]Laban also gave Zilpah to Leah as her servant woman.

[a]29.16,17 *but her eyes didn't sparkle:* Or "and her eyes sparkled."

Prayer Starter: Thank you for my family. Help us to always take care of each other.

Memory Verse: We know that God is always at work for the good of everyone . . .   *—Romans 8.28*

Jacob's Name Is Changed

As Jacob was on his way back home, some of God's angels came and met him. ²When Jacob saw them, he said, "This is God's camp." So he named the place Mahanaim.ª

³Jacob sent messengers on ahead to Esau, who lived in the land of Seir, also known as Edom. ⁴Jacob told them to say to Esau, "Master, I am your servant! I have lived with Laban all this time, ⁵and now I own cattle, donkeys, and sheep, as well as many slaves. Master, I am sending these messengers in the hope that you will be kind to me."

⁶When the messengers returned, they told Jacob, "We went to your brother Esau, and now he is heading this way with four hundred men."

⁷Jacob was so frightened that he divided his people, sheep, cattle, and camels into two groups. ⁸He thought, "If Esau attacks one group, perhaps the other can escape."

¹⁶Jacob put servants in charge of each herd and told them, "Go ahead of me and keep a space between each herd." ¹⁷Then he said to the servant in charge of the first herd, "When Esau meets you, he will ask whose servant you are. He will want to know where you are going and who owns those animals in front of you. ¹⁸So tell him, 'They belong to your servant Jacob, who is coming this way. He is sending them as a gift to his master Esau.'"

¹⁹Jacob also told the men in charge of the second and third herds and those who followed to say the same thing when they met Esau. ²⁰And Jacob told them to be sure to say that he was right behind them. Jacob hoped the gifts would make Esau friendly, so Esau would be glad to see him when they met. ²¹Jacob's men took the gifts on ahead of him, but he spent the night in camp.

²²⁻²³Jacob got up in the middle of the night and took his wives, his eleven children, and everything he owned across to the other side of the Jabbok River for safety. ²⁴Afterwards, Jacob went back and spent the rest of the night alone.

A man came and fought with Jacob until just before daybreak. ²⁵When the man saw that he could not win, he struck Jacob on the hip and threw it out of joint. ²⁶They kept on wrestling until the man said, "Let go of me! It's almost daylight."

"You can't go until you bless me," Jacob replied.

²⁷Then the man asked, "What is your name?"

"Jacob," he answered.

²⁸The man said, "Your name will no longer be Jacob. You have wrestled with God and with men, and you have won. That's why your name will be Israel."ᵇ

²⁹Jacob said, "Now tell me your name."

"Don't you know who I am?" he asked. And he blessed Jacob.

³⁰Jacob said, "I have seen God face to face, and I am still alive." So he

named the place Peniel.[c] [31]The sun was coming up as Jacob was leaving Peniel. He was limping because he had been struck on the hip, [32]and the muscle on his hip joint had been injured. That's why even today the people of Israel don't eat the hip muscle of any animal.

[a]*32.2 Mahanaim:* In Hebrew "Manahaim" means "two camps." [b]*32.28 Israel:* In Hebrew one meaning of "Israel" is "a man who wrestles with God." [c]*32.30 Peniel:* In Hebrew "Peniel" means "face of God."

Prayer Starter: May I be strong and cheerful, for I know you give me victory.

Memory Verse: We know that God is always at work for the good of everyone who loves him. . . .   *—Romans 8.28*

Twenty Pieces of Silver

Oone day when Joseph's brothers had taken the sheep to a pasture near Shechem, ¹³his father Jacob said to him, "I want you to go to your brothers. They are with the sheep near Shechem."

"Yes, sir," Joseph answered.

¹⁷Joseph left and found his brothers in Dothan. ¹⁸But before he got there, they saw him coming and made plans to kill him. ¹⁹They said to one another, "Look, here comes the hero of those dreams! ²⁰Let's kill him and throw him into a pit and say that some wild animal ate him. Then we'll see what happens to those dreams."

²³When Joseph came to his brothers, they pulled off his fancy coatᵃ ²⁴and threw him into a dry well.

²⁵As Joseph's brothers sat down to eat, they looked up and saw a caravan of Ishmaelites coming from Gilead. Their camels were loaded with all kinds of spices that they were taking to Egypt. ²⁶So Judah said, "What will we gain if we kill our brother and hide his body? ²⁷Let's sell him to the Ishmaelites and not harm him. After all, he is our brother." And the others agreed.

²⁸When the Midianite merchants came by, Joseph's brothers took him out of the well, and for twenty pieces of silver they sold him to the Ishmaelitesᵇ who took him to Egypt.

39The Ishmaelites took Joseph to Egypt and sold him to Potiphar, the king'sᶜ official in charge of the palace guard.

ᵃ37.23 *fancy coat:* Or "a coat of many colors" or "a coat with long sleeves." ᵇ37.28 *Midianite . . . Ishmaelites:* It is possible that in this passage "Ishmaelite" has the meaning "nomadic traders," while "Midianite" refers to their ethnic origin. ᶜ39.1 *the king's:* The Hebrew text has "Pharaoh's," a Hebrew word sometimes used for the king of Egypt.

Prayer Starter: Protect me from bad people, Lord. Keep me safe from those who could harm me. And keep me from ever harming another person.

Memory Verse: We know that God is always at work for the good of everyone who loves him. They are the ones God has chosen. —*Romans 8.28*

The King's Dream

Two years later the king[a] of Egypt dreamed he was standing beside the Nile River. [2]Suddenly, seven fat, healthy cows came up from the river and started eating grass along the bank. [3]Then seven ugly, skinny cows came up out of the river and [4]ate the fat, healthy cows. When this happened, the king woke up.

[8]The next morning the king was upset. So he called in his magicians and wise men and told them what he had dreamed. None of them could tell him what the dreams meant.

[14]The king sent for Joseph, who was quickly brought out of jail. He shaved, changed his clothes, and went to the king.

[15]The king said to him, "I had a dream, yet no one can explain what it means. I am told that you can interpret dreams."

[16]"Your Majesty," Joseph answered, "I can't do it myself, but God can give a good meaning to your dreams."

[29]For seven years Egypt will have more than enough grain, [30]but that will be followed by seven years when there won't be enough. The good years of plenty will be forgotten, and everywhere in Egypt people will be starving. [31]The famine will be so bad that no one will remember that once there had been plenty.

[33]Your Majesty, you should find someone who is wise and will know what to do, so that you can put him in charge of all Egypt. [34]Then appoint some other officials to collect one-fifth of every crop harvested in Egypt during the seven years when there is plenty. [35]Give them the power to collect the grain during those good years and to store it in your cities. [36]It can be stored until it is needed during the seven years when there won't be enough grain in Egypt. This will keep the country from being destroyed because of the lack of food.

[37]The king[b] and his officials liked this plan. [38]So the king said to them, "No one could possibly handle this better than Joseph, since the Spirit of God is with him."

[a]41.1 *the king:* The Hebrew text has "Pharaoh," a Hebrew word sometimes used for the king of Egypt. [b]41.37 *The king:* The Hebrew text has "Pharaoh," a Hebrew word sometimes used for the king of Egypt.

Prayer Starter: Thank you for always being at work for Joseph's good—and for mine. May I love you and be chosen for your purpose.

Memory Verse: Don't mistreat someone . . . —*Romans 12.17–18*

Joseph Becomes Governor

The king told Joseph, "God is the one who has shown you these things. No one else is as wise as you are or knows as much as you do. [40]I'm putting you in charge of my palace, and everybody will have to obey you. No one will be over you except me. [41]You are now governor of all Egypt!"

[42]Then the king took off his royal ring and put it on Joseph's finger. He gave him fine clothes to wear and placed a gold chain around his neck. [43]He also let him ride in the chariot next to his own, and people shouted, "Make way for Joseph!" So Joseph was governor of Egypt.

[44]The king told Joseph, "Although I'm king, no one in Egypt is to do anything without your permission." [45]He gave Joseph the Egyptian name Zaphenath Paneah. And he let him marry Asenath, the daughter of Potiphera, a priest in the city of Heliopolis.[a] Joseph traveled all over Egypt.

[46]Joseph was thirty when the king made him governor, and he went everywhere for the king. [47]For seven years there were big harvests of grain. [48]Joseph collected and stored up the extra grain in the cities of Egypt near the fields where it was harvested. [49]In fact, there was so much grain that they stopped keeping record, because it was like counting the grains of sand along the beach.

[a]41.45 *Heliopolis:* The Hebrew text has "On," which is better known by its Greek name "Heliopolis."

Prayer Starter: Make me wise, O Lord, that I might help other people like Joseph did.

Memory Verse: Don't mistreat someone who has mistreated you. . . .
    —Romans 12.17–18

God Sent Me Here

When Jacob found out there was grain in Egypt, he said to his sons, "Why are you just sitting here, staring at one another? ²I have heard there is grain in Egypt. Now go down and buy some, so we won't starve to death."

⁶Since Joseph was governor of Egypt and in charge of selling grain, his brothers came to him and bowed with their faces to the ground. ⁷⁻⁸They did not recognize Joseph, but right away he knew who they were, though he pretended not to know. Instead, he spoke harshly and asked, "Where do you come from?"

"From the land of Canaan," they answered. "We've come here to buy grain.". . .

45 Joseph asked his brothers if his father was still alive, but they were too frightened to answer. ⁴Joseph told them to come closer to him, and when they did, he said:

Yes, I am your brother Joseph, the one you sold into Egypt. ⁵Don't worry or blame yourselves for what you did. God is the one who sent me ahead of you to save lives.

Prayer Starter: Don't let me mistreat those who mistreat me. Help me do my best to live at peace with others.

Memory Verse: Don't mistreat someone who has mistreated you. But try to earn the respect of others . . .   —*Romans 12.17–18*

My Son Is Alive!

So the king said to Joseph:
Tell your brothers to load their donkeys and return to Canaan. [18]Have them bring their father and their families here. I will give them the best land in Egypt, and they can eat and enjoy everything that grows on it.

[21]Jacob's sons agreed to do what the king had said. And Joseph gave them wagons and food for their trip home, just as the king had ordered. [22]Joseph gave some new clothes to each of his brothers, but to Benjamin he gave five new outfits and three hundred pieces of silver. [23]To his father he sent ten donkeys loaded with the best things in Egypt, and ten other donkeys loaded with grain and bread and other food for the return trip. [24]Then he sent his brothers off and told them, "Don't argue on the way home!"

[25]Joseph's brothers left Egypt, and when they arrived in Canaan, [26]they told their father that Joseph was still alive and was the ruler of Egypt. But their father was so surprised that he could not believe them. [27]Then they told him everything Joseph had said. When he saw the wagons Joseph had sent, he felt much better [28]and said, "Now I can believe you! My son Joseph must really be alive and I will get to see him before I die."

46 Jacob packed up everything he owned and left for Egypt. On the way he stopped near the town of Beersheba and offered sacrifices to the God his father Isaac had worshiped. [2]That night, God spoke to him and said, "Jacob! Jacob!"

"Here I am," Jacob answered.

[3]God said, "I am God, the same God your father worshiped. Don't be afraid to go to Egypt. I will give you so many descendants that one day they will become a nation. [4]I will go with you to Egypt, and later I will bring your descendants back here. Your son Joseph will be at your side when you die."

[5-7]Jacob and his family set out from Beersheba and headed for Egypt. His sons put him in the wagon that the king[a] had sent for him, and they put their small children and their wives in the other wagons. Jacob's whole family went to Egypt.

[a]46.5-7 *the king:* The Hebrew text has "Pharaoh," a Hebrew word sometimes used for the king of Egypt.

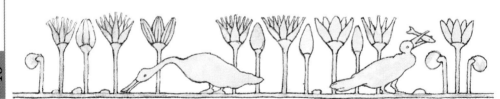

Prayer Starter: Bless my family, Lord, those I love. May we praise you together.

Memory Verse: Don't mistreat someone who has mistreated you. But try to earn the respect of others, and do your best . . . —*Romans 12.17–18*

Baby on the Nile

Many years later a new king came to power. He did not know what Joseph had done for Egypt, [9]and he told the Egyptians:

There are too many of those Israelites in our country, and they are becoming more powerful than we are. [10]If we don't outsmart them, their families will keep growing larger. And if our country goes to war, they could easily fight on the side of our enemies and escape from Egypt.

[11]The Egyptians put slave bosses in charge of the people of Israel and tried to wear them down with hard work.

[15]Finally, the king called in Shiphrah and Puah, the two women who helped the Hebrew[a] mothers when they gave birth. [16]He told them, "If a Hebrew woman gives birth to a girl, let the child live. If the baby is a boy, kill him!"

[17]But the two women were faithful to God and did not kill the boys, even though the king had told them to.

2 A man from the Levi tribe married a woman from the same tribe, [2]and she later had a baby boy. He was a beautiful child, and she kept him inside for three months. [3]But when she could no longer keep him hidden, she made a basket out of reeds and covered it with tar. She put him in the basket and placed it in the tall grass along the edge of the Nile River. [4]The baby's older sister[b] stood off at a distance to see what would happen to him.

[5]About that time one of the king's[c] daughters came down to take a bath in the river, while her servant women walked along the river bank. She saw the basket in the tall grass and sent one of the young women to pull it out of the water. [6]When the king's daughter opened the basket, she saw the baby and felt sorry for him because he was crying. She said, "This must be one of the Hebrew babies."

[7]At once the baby's older sister came up and asked, "Do you want me to get a Hebrew woman to take care of the baby for you?"

[8]"Yes," the king's daughter answered.

So the girl brought the baby's mother, [9]and the king's daughter told her, "Take care of this child, and I will pay you."

Prayer Starter: Lord, watch over me each night as I'm asleep and keep me from all harm. May your angels keep me safe.

Memory Verse: Don't mistreat someone who has mistreated you. But try to earn the respect of others, and do your best to live at peace with everyone.   *—Romans 12.17–18*

The baby's mother carried him home and took care of him. [10]And when he was old enough, she took him to the king's daughter, who adopted him. She named him Moses.[d]

[a]1.15 *Hebrew:* An earlier term for "Israelite." [b]2.4 *older sister:* Miriam, the sister of Moses and Aaron. [c]2.5 *the king's:* The Hebrew text has "Pharaoh's," a Hebrew word sometimes used for the title of the king of Egypt. [d]2.10 *Moses:* In Hebrew "Moses" sounds like "pull out."

The Burning Bush

One day, Moses was taking care of the sheep and goats of his father-in-law Jethro, the priest of Midian, and Moses decided to lead them across the desert to Sinai,[a] the holy mountain. [2]There an angel of the LORD appeared to him from a burning bush.

Moses saw that the bush was on fire, but it was not burning up. [3]"This is strange!" he said to himself. "I'll go over and see why the bush isn't burning up."

[4]When the LORD saw Moses coming near the bush, he called him by name, and Moses answered, "Here I am."

[5]God replied, "Don't come any closer. Take off your sandals—the ground where you are standing is holy. [6]I am the God who was worshiped by your ancestors Abraham, Isaac, and Jacob."

Moses was afraid to look at God, and so he hid his face.

[7]The LORD said:

I have seen how my people are suffering as slaves in Egypt, and I have heard them beg for my help because of the way they are being mistreated. I feel sorry for them, [8]and I have come down to rescue them from the Egyptians.

I will bring my people out of Egypt into a country where there is good land, rich with milk and honey. I will give them the land where the Canaanites, Hittites, Amorites, Perizzites, Hivites, and Jebusites now live. [9]My people have begged for my help, and I have seen how cruel the Egyptians are to them. [10]Now go to the king! I am sending you to lead my people out of his country.

[a]3.1 *Sinai:* The Hebrew text has "Horeb," another name for Sinai.

Prayer Starter: Dear Lord, you are the God worshiped by Abraham, Joseph, and Moses. Help us to honor and worship and praise you, too.

Memory Verse: Our LORD, no other gods . . .   —*Exodus 15.11*

What's That in Your Hand?

Moses asked the LORD, "Suppose everyone refuses to listen to my message, and no one believes that you really appeared to me?"

²The LORD answered, "What's that in your hand?"

"A walking stick," Moses replied.

³"Throw it down!" the LORD commanded. So Moses

threw the stick on the ground. It immediately turned into a snake, and Moses jumped back.

⁴"Pick it up by the tail!" the LORD told him. And when Moses did this, the snake turned back into a walking stick.

⁵"Do this," the LORD said, "and the Israelites will believe that you have seen me, the God who was worshiped by their ancestors Abraham, Isaac, and Jacob."

⁶Next, the LORD commanded Moses, "Put your hand inside your shirt." Moses obeyed, and when he took it out, his hand had turned white as snow—like someone with leprosy.[a]

⁷"Put your hand back inside your shirt," the LORD told him. Moses did so, and when he took it out again, it was as healthy as the rest of his body.

⁸⁻⁹Then the LORD said, "If no one believes either of these miracles, take some water from the Nile River and pour it on the ground. The water will immediately turn into blood."

¹⁰Moses replied, "I have never been a good speaker. I wasn't one before you spoke to me, and I'm not one now. I am slow at speaking, and I can never think of what to say."

¹¹But the LORD answered, "Who makes people able to speak or makes them deaf or unable to speak? Who gives them sight or makes them blind? Don't you know that I am the one who does these things? ¹²Now go! When you speak, I will be with you and give you the words to say."

¹³Moses begged, "LORD, please send someone else to do it."

¹⁴The LORD became irritated with Moses and said:

What about your brother Aaron, the Levite? I know he is a good

Prayer Starter: Lord, help me to speak up for you whenever I need to. Give me great courage and wise words. May I be your witness.

Memory Verse: Our LORD, no other gods compare with you . . .
—*Exodus 15.11*

speaker. He is already on his way here to visit you, and he will be happy to see you again. ¹⁵⁻¹⁶Aaron will speak to the people for you, and you will be like me, telling Aaron what to say. I will be with both of you as you speak, and I will tell each of you what to do. ¹⁷Now take this walking stick and use it to perform miracles.

ᵃ4.6 *leprosy:* The word translated "leprosy" was used for many different kinds of skin diseases.

**River
of Blood**

The LORD said to Moses:
The Egyptian king[a] stubbornly refuses to change his mind and let the people go. [15]Tomorrow morning take the stick that turned into a snake, then wait beside the Nile River for the king. [16]Tell him, "The LORD God of the Hebrews sent me to order you to release his people, so they can worship him in the desert. But until now, you have paid no attention.

[17]"The LORD is going to do something to show you that he really is the LORD. I will strike the Nile with this stick, and the water will turn to blood. [18]The fish will die, the river will stink, and none of you Egyptians will be able to drink the water.

[19]Moses, then command Aaron to hold his stick over the water. And when he does, every drop of water in Egypt will turn into blood, including rivers, canals, ponds, and even the water in buckets and jars.

[20]Moses and Aaron obeyed the LORD. Aaron held out his stick, then struck the Nile, as the king and his officials watched. The river turned into blood, [21]the fish died, and the water smelled so bad that none of the Egyptians could drink it. Blood was everywhere in Egypt.

[a]7.14 *The Egyptian king:* The Hebrew text has "Pharaoh," a Hebrew word sometimes used for the title of the king of Egypt.

Prayer Starter: Thank you for being more powerful than anything or anyone else in all the universe, Lord. And thank you for your powerful love to me.

Memory Verse: Our LORD, no other gods compare with you—
Majestic and holy! . . .   —*Exodus 15.11*

48

Leave Us Alone!

Moses called the leaders of Israel together and said:

Each family is to pick out a sheep and kill it for Passover. ²²Make a brush from a few small branches of a hyssop plant and dip the brush in the bowl that has the blood of the animal in it. Then brush some of the blood above the door and on the posts at each side of the door of your house. After this, everyone is to stay inside.

²³During that night the LORD will go through the country of Egypt and kill the first-born son in every Egyptian family. He will see where you have put the blood, and he will not come into your house. His angel that brings death will pass over and not kill your first-born sons.

²⁴⁻²⁵After you have entered the country promised to you by the LORD, you and your children must continue to celebrate Passover each year. ²⁶Your children will ask you, "What are we celebrating?" ²⁷And you will answer, "The Passover animal is killed to honor the LORD. We do these things because on that night long ago the LORD passed over the homes of our people in Egypt. He killed the first-born sons of the Egyptians, but he saved our children from death."

After Moses finished speaking, the people of Israel knelt down and worshiped the LORD. ²⁸Then they left and did what Moses and Aaron had told them to do.

²⁹At midnight the LORD killed the first-born son of every Egyptian family, from the son of the king[a] to the son of every prisoner in jail. He also killed the first-born male of every animal that belonged to the Egyptians.

³⁰That night the king, his officials, and everyone else in Egypt got up and started crying bitterly. In every Egyptian home, someone was dead.

³¹During the night the king[b] sent for Moses and Aaron and told them, "Get your people out of my country and leave us alone! Go and worship the LORD, as you have asked. ³²Take your sheep, goats, and cattle, and get out. But ask your God to be kind to me."

[a]12.29 *the king:* The Hebrew text has "Pharaoh," a Hebrew word sometimes used for the title of the king of Egypt. [b]12.31 *the king:* The Hebrew text has "Pharaoh," a Hebrew word sometimes used for the title of the king of Egypt.

Prayer Starter: O Lord, no other gods compare with you. You are majestic and holy. I love you.

Memory Verse: Our LORD, no other gods compare with you— Majestic and holy! Fearsome and glorious! . . .   —*Exodus 15.11*

Walls of Water

When the king of Egypt heard that the Israelites had finally left, he and his officials changed their minds and said, "Look what we have done! We let them get away, and they will no longer be our slaves."

⁶The king got his war chariot and army ready. ⁷He commanded his officers in charge of his six hundred best chariots and all his other chariots to start after the Israelites. ⁸The LORD made the king so stubborn that he went after them, even though the Israelites proudly° went on their way. ⁹But the king's horses and chariots and soldiers caught up with them while they were camping by the Red Sea near Pi-Hahiroth and Baal-Zephon.

¹⁰When the Israelites saw the king coming with his army, they were frightened and begged the LORD for help.

¹³But Moses answered, "Don't be afraid! Be brave, and you will see the LORD save you today. These Egyptians will never bother you again. ¹⁴The LORD will fight for you, and you won't have to do a thing."

¹⁵The LORD said to Moses, "Why do you keep calling out to me for help? Tell the Israelites to move forward. ¹⁶Then hold your walking stick over the sea. The water will open up and make a road where they can walk through on dry ground. ¹⁷I will make the Egyptians so stubborn that they will go after you. Then I will be praised because of what happens to the king and his chariots and cavalry. ¹⁸The Egyptians will know for sure that I am the LORD."

²¹Moses stretched his arm over the sea, and the LORD sent a strong east wind that blew all night until there was dry land where the water had been. The sea opened up, ²²and the Israelites walked through on dry land with a wall of water on each side.

°14.8 *proudly:* Or "victoriously."

Prayer Starter: Thank you, Lord, for the story of Moses and the children of Israel. Help me to trust you just as Moses did.

Memory Verse: Our LORD, no other gods compare with you— Majestic and holy! Fearsome and glorious! Miracle worker!　　*—Exodus 15.11*

What Is It?

On the fifteenth day of the second month after the Israelites had escaped from Egypt, they left Elim and started through the western edge of the Sinai Desert[a] in the direction of Mount Sinai. [2]There in the desert they started complaining to Moses and Aaron, [3]"We wish the LORD had killed us in Egypt. When we lived there, we could at least sit down and eat all the bread and meat we wanted. But you have brought us out here into this desert, where we are going to starve."

[4]The LORD said to Moses, "I will send bread[b] down from heaven like rain. Each day the people can go out and gather only enough for that day. That's how I will see if they obey me. [5]But on the sixth day of each week they must gather and cook twice as much."

[6]Moses and Aaron told the people, "This evening you will know that the LORD was the one who rescued you from Egypt. [7]And in the morning you will see his glorious power, because he has heard your complaints against him. Why should you grumble to us? Who are we?"

[13]That evening a lot of quails came and landed everywhere in the camp, and the next morning dew covered the ground. [14]After the dew had gone, the desert was covered with thin flakes that looked like frost. [15]The people had never seen anything like this, and they started asking each other, "What is it?"[c]

Moses answered, "This is the bread that the LORD has given you to eat. [16]And he orders you to gather about two quarts for each person in your family—that should be more than enough."

[17]They did as they were told. Some gathered more and some gathered less.

[a]16.1 *the western edge of the Sinai Desert:* Hebrew "the Sin Desert." [b]16.4 *bread:* This was something like a thin wafer, and it was called "Manna," which in Hebrew means, "What is it?" [c]16.15 *What is it:* This was something like a thin wafer, and it was called "Manna," which in Hebrew means, "What is it?"

Prayer Starter: Give us each day the food we need, Lord. Give me clothes and shelter and friends and family. Please provide for all my needs.

Memory Verse: Respect your father and your mother . . .

—Exodus 20.12

Water from a Rock

The Israelites left the desert and moved from one place to another each time the LORD ordered them to. Once they camped at Rephidim,[a] but there was no water for them to drink.

[2]The people started complaining to Moses, "Give us some water!"

Moses replied, "Why are you complaining to me and trying to put the LORD to the test?"

[3]But the people were thirsty and kept on complaining, "Moses, did you bring us out of Egypt just to let us and our families and our animals die of thirst?"

[4]Then Moses prayed to the LORD, "What am I going to do with these people? They are about to stone me to death!"

[5]The LORD answered, "Take some of the leaders with you and go ahead of the rest of the people. Also take along the walking stick you used to strike the Nile River, [6]and when you get to the rock at Mount Sinai,[b] I will be there with you. Strike the rock with the stick, and water will pour out for the people to drink." Moses did this while the leaders watched.

[a]17.1 *Rephidim:* The last stopping place for the Israelites between the Red Sea and Mount Sinai; the exact location is not known. [b]17.6 *Sinai:* The Hebrew text has "Horeb," another name for Sinai.

Prayer Starter: Thank you, Lord, for making water. Thanks for giving us water for drinking, bathing, and swimming.

Memory Verse: Respect your father and your mother, and you will live . . .
— *Exodus 20.12*

God's Commands

On the morning of the third day there was thunder and lightning. A thick cloud covered the mountain, a loud trumpet blast was heard, and everyone in camp trembled with fear. ¹⁷Moses led them out of the camp to meet God, and they stood at the foot of the mountain.

¹⁸Mount Sinai was covered with smoke because the LORD had come down in a flaming fire. Smoke poured out of the mountain just like a furnace, and the whole mountain shook. ¹⁹The trumpet blew louder and louder. Moses spoke, and God answered him with thunder.

20 God said to the people of Israel:
²I am the LORD your God, the one who brought you out of Egypt where you were slaves.

³Do not worship any god except me.

⁴Do not make idols that look like anything in the sky or on earth or in the ocean under the earth.

⁷Do not misuse my name.ᵃ I am the LORD your God, and I will punish anyone who misuses my name.

⁸Remember that the Sabbath Day belongs to me. . . .

¹²Respect your father and your mother, and you will live a long time in the land I am giving you.

¹³Do not murder.

¹⁴Be faithful in marriage.

¹⁵Do not steal.

¹⁶Do not tell lies about others.

¹⁷Do not want anything that belongs to someone else. Don't want anyone's house, wife or husband, slaves, oxen, donkeys or anything else.

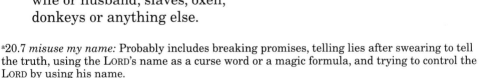

ᵃ20.7 *misuse my name:* Probably includes breaking promises, telling lies after swearing to tell the truth, using the LORD's name as a curse word or a magic formula, and trying to control the LORD by using his name.

Prayer Starter: O Lord, you are the Lord my God. May I never worship anyone except you.

Memory Verse: Respect your father and your mother, and you will live a long time . . .
—*Exodus 20.12*

The Broken Law

After the people saw that Moses had been on the mountain for a long time, they went to Aaron and said, "Make us an image of a god who will lead and protect us. Moses brought us out of Egypt, but nobody knows what has happened to him."

²Aaron told them, "Bring me the gold earrings that your wives and sons and daughters are wearing."

³Everybody took off their earrings and brought them to Aaron, ⁴then he melted them and made an idol in the shape of a young bull.

All the people said to one another, "This is the god who brought us out of Egypt!"

⁵When Aaron saw what was happening, he built an altar in front of the idol and said, "Tomorrow we will celebrate in honor of the LORD." ⁶The people got up early the next morning and killed some animals to be used for sacrifices and others to be eaten. Then everyone ate and drank so much that they began to carry on like wild people.

⁷The LORD said to Moses:

Hurry back down! Those people you led out of Egypt are acting like fools.

¹⁵⁻¹⁶Moses went back down the mountain with the two flat stones on which God had written all of his laws with his own hand, and he had used both sides of the stones.

¹⁹As Moses got closer to the camp, he saw the idol, and he also saw the people dancing around. This made him so angry that he threw down the stones and broke them to pieces at the foot of the mountain.

Prayer Starter: Dear Lord, I know that many people act badly in this world. Keep me from following their example.

Memory Verse: Respect your father and your mother, and you will live a long time in the land . . .
—*Exodus 20.12*

His Face Was Shining

Ohne day the LORD said to Moses, "Cut two flat stones like the first ones I made, and I will write on them the same commandments that were on the two you broke. ²Be ready tomorrow morning to come up Mount Sinai and meet me at the top.

⁵The LORD God came down in a cloud and stood beside Moses there on the mountain. God spoke his holy name, "the LORD."ª

²⁸Moses stayed on the mountain with the LORD for forty days and nights, without eating or drinking. And he wrote down the Ten Commandments, the most important part of God's agreement with his people.

²⁹Moses came down from Mount Sinai, carrying the Ten Commandments. His face was shining brightly because the LORD had been speaking to him. But Moses did not know at first that his face was shining. ³⁰When Aaron and the others looked at Moses, they saw that his face was shining, and they were afraid to go near him. ³¹Moses called out for Aaron and the leaders to come to him, and he spoke with them. ³²Then the rest of the people of Israel gathered around Moses, and he gave them the laws that the LORD had given him on Mount Sinai.

³³The face of Moses kept shining, and after he had spoken with the people, he covered his face with a veil. ³⁴Moses would always remove the veil when he went into the sacred tent to speak with the LORD. And when he came out, he would tell the people everything the LORD had told him to say. ³⁵They could see that his face was still shining. So after he had spoken with them, he would put the veil back on and leave it on until the next time he went to speak with the LORD.

ª34.5 *the LORD:* The Hebrew text has "Yahweh," which is usually translated "LORD" in the CEV. Since it seems related to the word translated "I am," it may mean "I am the one who is" or "I will be what I will be" or "I am the one who brings into being."

Prayer Starter: Give me a cheerful face, dear Lord. Help me to smile easily. Give me eyes that express your love.

Memory Verse: Respect your father and your mother, and you will live a long time in the land I am giving you.   —*Exodus 20.12*

Two Goats

T wo of Aaron's sons had already lost their lives for disobeying the LORD, so the LORD told Moses to say to Aaron:

I, the LORD, appear in a cloud over the place of mercy on the sacred chest, which is behind the inside curtain[a] of the sacred tent. And I warn you not to go there except at the proper time. Otherwise, you will die!

³Before entering this most holy place, you must offer a bull as a sacrifice for your sins and a ram as a sacrifice to please me.[b] ⁴You will take a bath and put on the sacred linen clothes, including the underwear, the robe, the sash, and the turban. ⁵Then the community of Israel will bring you a ram and two goats, both of them males. The goats are to be used as sacrifices for sin, and the ram is to be used as a sacrifice to please me.

⁶Aaron, you must offer the bull as a sacrifice of forgiveness for your own sins and for the sins of your family. ⁷Then you will lead the two goats into my presence at the front of the sacred tent, ⁸where I will show you[c] which goat will be sacrificed to me and which one will be sent into the desert to the demon Azazel.[d] ⁹After you offer the first goat as a sacrifice for sin, ¹⁰the other one must be presented to me alive, before you send it into the desert to take away the sins of the people.

[a]16.1,2 *inside curtain:* That separated the holy place from the most holy place. [b]16.3 *sacrifice to please me:* These sacrifices have traditionally been called "whole burnt offerings" because the whole animal was burned on the altar. A main purpose of such sacrifices was to please the LORD with the smell of the sacrifice, and so in the CEV they are often called "sacrifices to please the LORD." [c]16.8 *I will show you:* The Hebrew text has "you must cast lots to find out." Pieces of wood or stone (called "lots") were used to find out what God wanted his people to do. [d]16.8 *Azazel:* It was believed that a demon named Azazel lived in the desert.

Prayer Starter: O Lord, help me to understand more and more about what Christ has done for me.

Memory Verse: And the Son of Man . . .   *—John 3.14*

Twelve Spies

Moses sent twelve tribal leaders from Israel's camp in the Paran Desert.

¹⁷Before Moses sent them into Canaan, he said:

After you go through the Southern Desert of Canaan, continue north into the hill country ¹⁸and find out what those regions are like. Be sure to remember how many people live there, how strong they are, ¹⁹⁻²⁰and if they live in open towns or walled cities. See if the land is good for growing crops and find out what kinds of trees grow there. It's time for grapes to ripen, so try to bring back some of the fruit that grows there.

²¹The twelve men left to explore Canaan from the Zin Desert in the south all the way to the town of Rehob near Lebo-Hamath in the north. ²²As they went through the Southern Desert, they came to the town of Hebron, which was seven years older than the Egyptian town of Zoan. In Hebron, they saw the three Anakimᵃ clans of Ahiman, Sheshai, and Talmai. ²³⁻²⁴When

they got to Bunch Valley,ᵇ they cut off a branch with such a huge bunch of grapes, that it took two men to carry it on a pole. That's why the place was called Bunch Valley. Along with the grapes, they also took back pomegranatesᶜ and figs.

²⁵After exploring the land of Canaan forty days, ²⁶the twelve men returned to Kadesh in the Paran Desert and told Moses, Aaron, and the people what they had seen. They showed them the fruit ²⁷and said:

Look at this fruit! The land we explored is rich with milk and honey. ²⁸But the people who live there are strong, and their cities are large and walled.

³⁰Caleb calmed down the crowd and said, "Let's go and take the land. I know we can do it!"

ᵃ13.22 *Anakim:* Perhaps a group of very large people. ᵇ13.23,24 *Bunch Valley:* Or "Eshcol Valley." ᶜ13.23,24 *pomegranates:* A bright red fruit that looks like an apple.

Prayer Starter: Give me more and more faith in you, O Lord. Help me to trust your word.

Memory Verse: And the Son of Man must be lifted up . . .
—John 3.14

The Bronze Snake

The Israelites had to go around the territory of Edom, so when they left Mount Hor, they headed south toward the Red Sea.ᵃ But along the way, the people became so impatient ⁵that they complained against God and said to Moses, "Did you bring us out of Egypt, just to let us die in the desert? There's no water out here, and we can't stand this awful food!"

⁶Then the LORD sent poisonous snakes that bit and killed many of them.

⁷Some of the people went to Moses and admitted, "It was wrong of us to insult you and the LORD. Now please ask him to make these snakes go away."

Moses prayed, ⁸and the LORD answered, "Make a snake out of bronze and place it on top of a pole. Anyone who gets bitten can look at the snake and won't die."

⁹Moses obeyed the LORD. And all of those who looked at the bronze snake lived, even though they had been bitten by the poisonous snakes.

¹⁰As the Israelites continued their journey to Canaan, they camped at Oboth, ¹¹then at Iye-Abarim in the desert east of Moab, ¹²and then in the Zered Gorge. ¹³After that, they crossed the Arnon River gorge and camped in the Moabite desert bordering Amorite territory. The Arnon

was the border between the Moabites and the Amorites. ¹⁴A song in *The Book of the LORD's Battles*ᵇ mentions the town of Waheb with its creeks in the territory of Suphah. It also mentions the Arnon River, ¹⁵with its valleys that lie alongside the Moabite border and extend to the town of Ar.

¹⁶From the Arnon, the Israelites went to the well near the town of Beer, where the LORD had said to Moses, "Call the people together, and I will give them water to drink."

¹⁷That's also the same well the Israelites sang about in this song:

> Let's celebrate! The well has given us water.
> ¹⁸ With their royal scepters, our leaders pointed out
>   where to dig the well.

The Israelites left the desert and camped near the town of Mattanah, ¹⁹then at Nahaliel, and then at Bamoth. ²⁰Finally, they reached Moabite territory, where they camped near Mount Pisgahᶜ in a valley overlooking the desert north of the Dead Sea.

ᵃ21.4 *Red Sea:* Hebrew *yam suph,* here referring to the Gulf of Aqaba, since the term is extended to include the northeastern arm of the Red Sea. ᵇ21.14 *The Book of the LORD's Battles:* This may have been a collection of ancient war songs. ᶜ21.20 *Mount Pisgah:* This probably refers to the highest peak in the Abarim Mountains in Moab.

Prayer Starter: Forgive me, Lord, when I complain and grumble and make others unhappy. Give me a happy spirit.

Memory Verse: And the Son of Man must be lifted up, just as that metal snake . . .
                                                              —John 3.14

Balaam's Donkey

Balaam was riding his donkey to Moab, and two of his servants were with him. But God was angry that Balaam had gone, so one of the LORD's angels stood in the road to stop him. ²³When Balaam's donkey saw the angel standing there with a sword, it walked off the road and into an open field. Balaam had to beat the donkey to get it back on the road.

²⁴Then the angel stood between two vineyards, in a narrow path with a stone wall on each side. ²⁵When the donkey saw the angel, it walked so close to one of the walls that Balaam's foot scraped against the wall. Balaam beat the donkey again.

²⁶The angel moved once more and stood in a spot so narrow that there was no room for the donkey to go around. ²⁷So it just lay down. Balaam lost his temper, then picked up a stick and smacked the donkey.

²⁸When that happened, the LORD told the donkey to speak, and it asked Balaam, "What have I done to you that made you beat me three times?"

²⁹"You made me look stupid!" Balaam answered. "If I had a sword, I'd kill you here and now!"

³⁰"But you're my owner," replied the donkey, "and you've ridden me many times. Have I ever done anything like this before?"

"No," Balaam admitted.

³¹Just then, the LORD let Balaam see the angel standing in the road, holding a sword, and Balaam bowed down.

³²The angel said, "You had no right to treat your donkey like that! I was the one who blocked your way, because I don't think you should go to Moab.ᵃ ³³If your donkey had not seen me and stopped those three times, I would have killed you and let the donkey live."

³⁴Balaam replied, "I was wrong."

ᵃ22.32 *I don't think you should go to Moab:* One possible meaning for the difficult Hebrew text.

Prayer Starter: How wonderful you are, dear Lord. How wise and powerful!

Memory Verse: And the Son of Man must be lifted up, just as that metal snake was lifted up by Moses . . .   *—John 3.14*

The Death of Moses

Sometime later, Moses left the lowlands of Moab. He went up Mount Pisgah to the peak of Mount Nebo,[a] which is across the Jordan River from Jericho. The LORD showed him all the land as far north as Gilead and the town of Dan. ²He let Moses see the territories that would soon belong to the tribes of Naphtali, Ephraim, Manasseh, and Judah, as far west as the Mediterranean Sea. ³The LORD also showed him the land in the south, from the valley near the town of Jericho, known as The City of Palm Trees, down to the town of Zoar.

⁴The LORD said, "Moses, this is the land I was talking about when I solemnly promised Abraham, Isaac, and Jacob that I would give land to their descendants. I have let you see it, but you will not cross the Jordan and go in."

⁵And so, Moses the LORD's servant died there in Moab, just as the LORD had said. ⁶The LORD buried him in a valley near the town of Beth-Peor, but even today no one knows exactly where. ⁷Moses was a hundred twenty years old when he died, yet his eyesight was still good, and his body was strong.

⁸The people of Israel stayed in the lowlands of Moab, where they mourned and grieved thirty days for Moses, as was their custom.

⁹Before Moses died, he had placed his hands on Joshua, and the LORD had given Joshua wisdom. The Israelites paid attention to what Joshua said and obeyed the commands that the LORD had given Moses.

[a]34.1 *Mount Pisgah . . . Mount Nebo:* Mount Nebo was probably one peak of the ridge known as Mount Pisgah.

Prayer Starter: I love your promises in the Bible, dear Lord. Thank you for each one.

Memory Verse: And the Son of Man must be lifted up, just as that metal snake was lifted up by Moses in the desert.   —*John 3.14*

> Rahab

Joshua chose two men as spies and sent them from their camp at Acacia with these instructions: "Go across the river and find out as much as you can about the whole region, especially about the town of Jericho."

The two spies left the Israelite camp at Acacia and went to Jericho, where they decided to spend the night at the house of a prostitute[a] named Rahab.

²But someone found out about them and told the king of Jericho, "Some Israelite men came here tonight, and they are spies." ³⁻⁷So the king sent soldiers to Rahab's house to arrest the spies.

Meanwhile, Rahab had taken the men up to the flat roof of her house and had hidden them under some piles of flax plants[b] that she had put there to dry.

The soldiers came to her door and demanded, "Let us have the men who are staying at your house. They are spies."

She answered, "Some men did come to my house, but I didn't know where they had come from. They left about sunset, just before it was time to close the town gate.[c] I don't know where they were going, but if you hurry, maybe you can catch them."

⁸Rahab went back up to her roof. The spies were still awake, so she told them:

⁹I know that the LORD has given Israel this land. Everyone shakes with fear because of you.

¹²Please promise me in the LORD's name that you will be as kind to my family as I have been to you. Do something to show ¹³that you won't let your people kill my father and mother and my brothers and sisters and their families.

¹⁴"Rahab," the spies answered, "if you keep quiet about what we're doing, we promise to be kind to you when the LORD gives us this land."

[a]2.1 *prostitute:* Rahab was possibly an innkeeper. [b]2.3-7 *flax plants:* The stalks of flax plants were harvested, soaked in water, and dried, then their fibers were separated and spun into thread, which was woven into linen cloth. [c]2.3-7 *gate:* Many towns and cities had walls with heavy gates that were closed at night for protection.

Prayer Starter: Keep me safe each day, O Lord, and protect me throughout every night.

Memory Verse: I've commanded you to be strong . . . —*Joshua 1.9*

Amazing Things

Joshua told the people, "Make yourselves accept-able[a] to worship the LORD, because he is going to do some amazing things for us."

[6]Then Joshua turned to the priests and said, "Take the chest and cross the Jordan River ahead of us." So the priests picked up the chest by its carrying poles and went on ahead.

[7]The LORD told Joshua, "Beginning today I will show the people that you are their leader, and they will know that I am helping you as I helped Moses. [8]Now, tell the priests who are carrying the chest to go a little way into the river and stand there."

[14]The Israelites packed up and left camp. The priests carry-ing the chest walked in front, [15]until they came to the Jordan River. The water in the river had risen over its banks, as it often does in springtime.[b] But as soon as the feet of the priests touched the water, [16-17]the river stopped flowing, and the water started piling up at the town of Adam near Zarethan. No water flowed toward the Dead Sea, and the priests stood in the middle of the dry riverbed near Jericho while every-one else crossed over.

[a]3.5 *Make yourselves acceptable:* People had to do certain things to make them-selves acceptable to worship the LORD. [b]3.15 *springtime:* Or "har-vest time"; the grain harvest was in late spring.

Prayer Starter: Lord, help me to worship you as I should, because you are going to do amazing things for me.

Memory Verse: I've commanded you to be strong and brave. . . .

—*Joshua 1.9*

The Walls of Jericho

Joshua called the priests together and said, "Take the chest and have seven priests carry trumpets and march ahead of it."

7-10Next, he gave the army their orders: "March slowly around Jericho. A few of you will go ahead of the chest to guard it, but most of you will follow it. Don't shout the battle cry or yell or even talk until the day I tell you to. Then let out a shout!"

As soon as Joshua finished giving the orders, the army started marching. One group of soldiers led the way, with seven priests marching behind them and blowing trumpets. Then came the priests carrying the chest, followed by the rest of the soldiers. ¹¹They obeyed Joshua's orders and carried the chest once around the town before returning to camp for the night.

¹²⁻¹⁴Early the next morning, Joshua and everyone else started marching around Jericho in the same order as the day before. One group of soldiers was in front, followed by the seven priests with trumpets and the priests who carried the chest. The rest of the army came next. The seven priests blew their trumpets while everyone marched slowly around Jericho and back to camp. They did this once a day for six days.

¹⁵On the seventh day, the army got up at daybreak. They marched slowly around Jericho the same as they had done for the past six days, except on this day they went around seven times. ¹⁶Then the priests blew the trumpets, and Joshua yelled:

Get ready to shout! The LORD will let you capture this town.

²⁰The priests blew their trumpets again, and the soldiers shouted as loud as they could. The walls of Jericho fell flat. Then the soldiers rushed up the hill, went straight into the town, and captured it.

Prayer Starter: You are a God who does miracles, Lord. I praise and worship you.

Memory Verse: I've commanded you to be strong and brave. Don't ever be afraid or discouraged! . . .   *—Joshua 1.9*

The Longest Day

Joshua marched all night from Gilgal to Gibeon and made a surprise attack on the Amorite camp. ¹⁰The LORD made the enemy panic, and the Israelites started killing them right and left. They[a] chased the Amorite troops up the road to Beth-Horon and kept on killing them, until they reached the towns of Azekah and Makkedah.[b] ¹¹And while these troops were going down through Beth-Horon Pass,[c] the LORD made huge hailstones fall on them all the way to Azekah. More of the enemy soldiers died from the hail than from the Israelite weapons.

¹²⁻¹³The LORD was helping the Israelites defeat the Amorites that day. So about noon, Joshua prayed to the LORD loud enough for the Israelites to hear:

"Our LORD, make the sun stop in the sky over Gibeon,
and the moon stand still over Aijalon Valley."[d]
So the sun and the moon stopped and stood still
until Israel defeated its enemies.

This poem can be found in *The Book of Jashar.*[e] The sun stood still and didn't go down for about a whole day. ¹⁴Never before and never since has the LORD done anything like that for someone who prayed. The LORD was really fighting for Israel.

[a]10.10 *They:* Or "The LORD." [b]10.10 *Makkedah:* A total distance of about twenty-five miles. [c]10.11 *Beth-Horon Pass:* A two-mile long, steeply-sloping valley between the towns of Upper Beth-Horon and Lower Beth-Horon. [d]10.12,13 *Aijalon Valley:* A valley southwest of Beth-Horon Pass. [e]10.12,13 *Book of Jashar:* This book may have been a collection of ancient war songs.

Prayer Starter: Thank you, Father, for the sun and moon. And thank you for the day they stood still.

Memory Verse: I've commanded you to be strong and brave. Don't ever be afraid or discouraged! I am the LORD your God . . .   *—Joshua 1.9*

Choose Right Now!

Joshua called the tribes of Israel together for a meeting at Shechem. He had the leaders, including the old men, the judges, and the officials, come up and stand near the sacred tent.ᵃ ²Then Joshua told everyone to listen to this message from the LORD, the God of Israel:

Long ago your ancestors lived on the other side of the Euphrates River, and they worshiped other gods. This continued until the time of your ancestor Terah and his two sons, Abraham and Nahor. ³But I brought Abraham across the Euphrates River and led him through the land of Canaan. I blessed him by giving him Isaac, the first in a line of many descendants. ⁴Then I gave Isaac two sons, Jacob and Esau. I had Esau live in the hill country of Mount Seir, but your ancestor Jacob and his children went to live in Egypt.

⁵⁻⁶Later I sent Moses and his brother Aaron to help your people, and I made all those horrible things happen to the Egyptians. I brought your ancestors out of Egypt, but the Egyptians got in their chariots and on their horses and chased your ancestors, catching up with them at the Red Sea.ᵇ ⁷Your people cried to me for help, so I put a dark cloud between them and the Egyptians. Then I opened up the sea and let your people walk across on dry ground. But when the Egyptians tried to follow, I commanded the sea to swallow them, and they drowned while you watched.

You lived in the desert for a long time, ⁸then I brought you into the land east of the Jordan River. The Amorites were living there, and they fought you. But with my help, you defeated them, wiped them out, and took their land. ⁹King Balak decided that his nation Moab would go to war against you, so he asked Balaam° to come and put a curse on you. ¹⁰But I wouldn't listen to Balaam, and I rescued you by making him bless you instead of curse you.

¹¹You crossed the Jordan River and came to Jericho. The rulers of Jericho fought you, and so did the Amorites, the Perizzites, the Canaanites, the Hittites, the Girgashites, the Hivites, and the Jebusites. I helped you defeat them all. ¹²Your enemies ran from you, but not because you had swords and bows and arrows. I made your enemies panic and run away, as I had done with the two Amorite kings east of the Jordan River.

¹³You didn't have to work for this land—I gave it to you. Now you live in towns you didn't build, and you eat grapes and olives from vineyards and trees you didn't plant.

¹⁴Then Joshua told the people:

Worship the LORD, obey him, and always be faithful. Get rid of the idols your ancestors worshiped when they lived on the other side of the Euphrates River and in Egypt. ¹⁵But if you don't want to worship the LORD, then choose right now! Will you worship the same idols your ancestors did? Or since you're living on land that once belonged to the Amorites, maybe you'll worship their gods. I won't. My family and I are going to worship and obey the LORD!

ª24.1 *near . . . tent:* Or "in front of the sacred chest"; Hebrew "in the presence of God." ᵇ24.5,6 *Red Sea:* Hebrew *yam suph* "Sea of Reeds," one of the marshes or fresh water lakes near the eastern part of the Nile Delta. ᶜ24.9 *King Balak . . . Balaam:* The Hebrew text has "King Balak the son of Zippor . . . Balaam the son of Beor."

Prayer Starter: Father, may my family and I worship and obey the Lord!

Memory Verse: I've commanded you to be strong and brave. Don't ever be afraid or discouraged! I am the LORD your God, and I will be there to help you wherever you go.   *—Joshua 1.9*

<table>
<tr><td>**Deborah and Barak**</td></tr>
</table>

Deborah the wife of Lappidoth was a prophet and a leader[a] of Israel during those days. [5]She would sit under Deborah's Palm Tree between Ramah and Bethel in the hill country of Ephraim, where Israelites would come and ask her to settle their legal cases.

[6]One day, Barak the son of Abinoam was in Kedesh in Naphtali, and Deborah sent word for him to come and talk with her. When he arrived, she said:

I have a message for you from the LORD God of Israel! You are to get together an army of ten thousand men from the Naphtali and Zebulun tribes and lead them to Mount Tabor. [7]The LORD will trick Sisera into coming out to fight you at the Kishon River. Sisera will be leading King Jabin's army as usual, and they will have their chariots, but the LORD has promised to help you defeat them.

[8]"I'm not going unless you go!" Barak told her.

[9]"All right, I'll go!" she replied. "But I'm warning you that the LORD is going to let a woman defeat Sisera, and no one will honor you for winning the battle."

Deborah and Barak left for Kedesh, [10]where Barak called together the troops from Zebulun and Naphtali. Ten thousand soldiers gathered there, and Barak led them out from Kedesh. Deborah went too.

[a]4.4 *leader:* The Hebrew text has "judges." In addition to leading Israelites in battle, these special leaders also decided legal cases and sometimes performed religious duties.

Prayer Starter: Father, help my friends to live for you as they should. May they love and serve Jesus.

Memory Verse: Dear friends, God is good. . . .   —*Romans 12.1*

We Praise You, Lord!

After the battle was over that day, Deborah and Barak sang this song:

² We praise you, Lord! Our soldiers volunteered,
    ready to follow you.
³ Listen, kings and rulers, while I sing for the Lord,
    the God of Israel.

⁴ Our Lord, God of Israel, when you came from Seir,
    where the Edomites live,
⁵ rain poured from the sky, the earth trembled,
    and mountains shook.

⁶ In the time of Shamgar son of Anath,
  and now again in Jael's time,
        roads were too dangerous
        for caravans.
  Travelers had to take
  the back roads,
⁷   and villagers couldn't work
        in their fields.ᵃ
  Then Deborahᵇ took command,
  protecting Israel
        as a mother protects her children.

⁸ The Israelites worshiped other gods,
  and the gates of their towns were then attacked.ᶜ
        But they had no shields or spears to fight with.
⁹ I praise you, Lord, and I am grateful
        for those leaders and soldiers who volunteered.
¹⁰ Listen, everyone!
  Whether you ride a donkey with a padded saddle
        or have to walk.
¹¹ Even those who carry waterᵈ to the animals
  will tell you, "The Lord has won victories,
        and so has Israel."

ᵃ5.7 *villagers . . . fields:* One possible meaning for the difficult Hebrew text. ᵇ5.7 *Deborah:* Or "I, Deborah." ᶜ5.8 *The Israelites . . . attacked:* One possible meaning for the difficult Hebrew text. ᵈ5.11 *Even . . . water:* One possible meaning for the difficult Hebrew text.

Prayer Starter: We praise you, O Lord, for giving us each day what we need. Thank you for loving me so much.

Memory Verse: Dear friends, God is good. So I beg you . . .
                                                              —*Romans 12.1*

Gideon

One day an angel from the LORD went to the town of Ophrah and sat down under the big tree that belonged to Joash, a member of the Abiezer clan. Joash's son Gideon was nearby, threshing grain in a shallow pit, where he could not be seen by the Midianites.

¹²The angel appeared and spoke to Gideon, "The LORD is helping you, and you are a strong warrior."

¹³Gideon answered, "Please don't take this wrong, but if the LORD is helping us, then why have all of these awful things happened? We've heard how the LORD performed miracles and rescued our ancestors from Egypt. But those things happened long ago. Now the LORD has abandoned us to the Midianites."

¹⁴Then the LORD himself said, "Gideon, you will be strong, because I am giving you the power to rescue Israel from the Midianites."

¹⁵Gideon replied, "But how can I rescue Israel? My clan is the weakest one in Manasseh, and everyone else in my family is more important than I am."

¹⁶"Gideon," the LORD answered, "you can rescue Israel because I am going to help you!"

Prayer Starter: When I'm tempted to doubt your promises, Lord, strengthen my faith. Help me trust you as I should.

Memory Verse: Dear friends, God is good. So I beg you to offer your bodies . . .
—*Romans 12.1*

Samson and Delilah

Some time later, Samson fell in love with a woman named Delilah, who lived in the Sorek Valley. [5]The Philistine rulers[a] went to Delilah and said, "Trick Samson into telling you what makes him so strong and what can make him weak. Then we can tie him up so he can't get away. If you find out his secret, we will each give you eleven hundred pieces of silver."[b]

[15]"Samson," Delilah said, "you claim to love me, but you don't mean it! You've made me look like a fool three times now, and you still haven't told me why you are so strong." [16]Delilah started nagging and pestering him day after day, until he couldn't stand it any longer.

[17]Finally, Samson told her the truth. "I have belonged to God[c] ever since I was born, so my hair has never been cut. If it were ever cut off, my strength would leave me, and I would be as weak as anyone else."

[18]Delilah realized that he was telling the truth. So she sent someone to tell the Philistine rulers, "Come to my house one more time. Samson has finally told me the truth."

The Philistine rulers went to Delilah's house, and they brought along the silver they had promised her. [19]Delilah had lulled Samson to sleep with his head resting in her lap. She signalled to one of the Philistine men as she began cutting off Samson's seven braids. And by the time she was finished, Samson's strength was gone. Delilah tied him up [20]and shouted, "Samson, the Philistines are attacking!"

Samson woke up and thought, "I'll break loose and escape, just as I always do." He did not realize that the LORD had stopped helping him.

[21]The Philistines grabbed Samson and poked out his eyes. They took him to the prison in Gaza and chained him up. Then they put him to work, turning a millstone to grind grain. [22]But they didn't cut his hair any more, so it started growing back.

[a]16.5 *Philistine rulers:* There were five rulers, each one controlling part of Philistia. [b]16.5 *silver:* About 140 pounds of silver altogether. [c]16.17 *belonged to God:* The Hebrew text has "be a Nazirite of God." Nazirites were dedicated to God and had to follow special rules to stay that way.

Prayer Starter: Keep me from sin, Lord, and keep me from making foolish mistakes.

Memory Verse: Dear friends, God is good. So I beg you to offer your bodies to him as a living sacrifice . . .   —*Romans 12.1*

One Last Time

The Philistine rulers threw a big party and sacrificed a lot of animals to their god Dagon. The rulers said:

> Samson was our enemy, but our god Dagon
> helped us capture him!

²⁴⁻²⁵Everyone there was having a good time, and they shouted, "Bring out Samson—he's still good for a few more laughs!"

The rulers had Samson brought from the prison, and when the people saw him, this is how they praised their god:

> Samson ruined our crops and killed our people.
> He was our enemy, but our god
> helped us capture him.

They made fun of Samson for a while, then they told him to stand near the columns that supported the roof.

²⁸Samson prayed, "Please remember me, LORD God. The Philistines poked out my eyes, but make me strong one last time, so I can take revenge for at least one of my eyes!"[a]

²⁹Samson was standing between the two middle columns that held up the roof. He felt around and found one column with his right hand, and the other with his left hand. ³⁰Then he shouted, "Let me die with the Philistines!" He pushed against the columns as hard as he could, and the temple collapsed with the Philistine rulers and everyone else still inside. Samson killed more Philistines when he died than he had killed during his entire life.

[a]16.28 *one of my eyes:* Or "my eyes."

Prayer Starter: Help those in prison, dear Lord. May they learn to love and serve you.

Memory Verse: Dear friends, God is good. So I beg you to offer your bodies to him as a living sacrifice, pure and pleasing. *—Romans 12.1*

Ruth and Naomi

Before Israel was ruled by kings, Elimelech from the tribe of Ephrath lived in the town of Bethlehem. His wife was named Naomi, and their two sons were Mahlon and Chilion. But when their crops failed they moved to the country of Moab.ᵃ And while they were there, ³Elimelech died, leaving Naomi with only her two sons.

⁴Later, Naomi's sons married Moab women. One was named Orpah and the other Ruth. About ten years later, ⁵Mahlon and Chilion also died. Now Naomi had no husband or sons.

⁶⁻⁷When Naomi heard that the Lord had given his people a good harvest, she and her two daughters-in-law got ready to leave Moab and go to Judah. As they were on their way there, ⁸Naomi said to them, "Don't you want to go back home to your own mothers? You were kind to my husband and sons, and you have always been kind to me. I pray that the LORD will be just as kind to you. ⁹May he give each of you another husband and a home of your own."

Naomi kissed them. They cried ¹⁰and said, "We want to go with you and live among your people."

¹¹But she replied, "My daughters, why don't you return home? What good will it do you to go with me? Do you think I could have more sons for you to marry?ᵇ ¹²You must go back home, because I am too old to marry again. Even if I got married tonight and later had more sons, ¹³would you wait for them to become old enough to marry? No, my daughters! Life is harder for me than it is for you, because the LORD has turned against me."ᶜ

[14]They cried again. Orpah kissed her mother-in-law good-by, but Ruth held on to her. [15]Naomi then said to Ruth, "Look, your sister-in-law is going back to her people and to her gods! Why don't you go with her?"

[16]Ruth answered,

"Please don't tell me to leave you
  and return home!
I will go where you go,
I will live where you live;
    your people will be my people,
    your God will be my God.
[17] I will die where you die
    and be buried beside you.
May the LORD punish me if we are ever separated,
    even by death!"[d]

[18]When Naomi saw that Ruth had made up her mind to go with her, she stopped urging her to go back.

[19]They reached Bethlehem, and the whole town was excited to see them.

---

[a]1.1,2 *Moab:* The people of Moab worshiped idols and were usually enemies of the people of Israel. [b]1.11 *for you to marry:* When a married man died and left no children, it was the custom for one of his brothers to marry his widow. Any children they had would then be thought of as those of the dead man, so that his family name would live on. [c]1.13 *Life . . . me:* Or "I'm sorry that the LORD has turned against me and made life so hard for you." [d]1.17 *even by death:* Or "by anything but death."

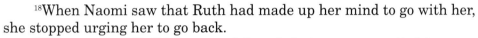

Prayer Starter: Thanks for giving us families, Lord. Bless my family today.

Memory Verse: When you pray . . .   *—Matthew 6.6*

Boaz

One day, Ruth said to Naomi, "Let me see if I can find someone who will let me pick up the grain left in the fields by the harvest workers."[a]

Naomi answered, "Go ahead, my daughter." So right away, Ruth went out to pick up grain in a field owned by Boaz. He was a relative of Naomi's husband Elimelech, as well as a rich and important man.

[4]When Boaz left Bethlehem and went out to his field, he said to the harvest workers, "The LORD bless you!"

They replied, "And may the LORD bless you!"

[5]Then Boaz asked the man in charge of the harvest workers, "Who is that young woman?"

[6]The man answered, "She is the one who came back from Moab with Naomi. [7]She asked if she could pick up grain left by the harvest workers, and she has been working all morning without a moment's rest."[b]

[8]Boaz went over to Ruth and said, "I think it would be best for you not to pick up grain in anyone else's field. Stay here with the women [9]and follow along behind them, as they gather up what the men have cut. I have warned the men not to bother you, and whenever you are thirsty, you can drink from the water jars they have filled."

[10]Ruth bowed down to the ground and said, "You know I come from another country. Why are you so good to me?"

[11]Boaz answered, "I've heard how you've helped your mother-in-law ever since your husband died. You even left your own father and mother to come and live in a foreign land among people you don't know. [12]I pray that the LORD God of Israel will reward you for what you have done. And now that you have come to him for protection, I pray that he will bless you."

[a]2.1-3 *grain left . . . workers:* It was the custom at harvest time to leave some grain in the field for the poor to pick up. [b]2.7 *she has . . . rest:* One possible meaning for the difficult Hebrew text.

Prayer Starter: Lead me each day, dear Father. Guide me to the people you want me to meet, and to the work you want me to do.

Memory Verse: When you pray, go into a room alone and close the door. . . .
                                       —*Matthew 6.6*

**More than
Seven Sons**

Boaz told the town leaders and everyone else:

All of you are witnesses that today I have bought from Naomi the property that belonged to Elimelech and his two sons, Chilion and Mahlon. ⁹You are also witnesses that I have agreed to marry Mahlon's widow Ruth, the Moabite woman. This will keep the property in his family's name, and he will be remembered in this town. ¹¹The town leaders and the others standing there said:

We are witnesses to this. And we pray that the LORD will give your wife many children, just as he did Leah and Rachel, the wives of Jacob. May you be a rich man in the tribe of Ephrathah and an important man in Bethlehem. ¹²May the children you have by this young woman make your family as famous as the family of Perez,ᵃ the son of Tamar and Judah.

¹³Boaz married Ruth, and the LORD blessed her with a son. ¹⁴After his birth, the women said to Naomi:

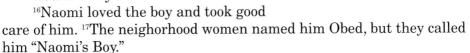

Praise the LORD! Today he has given you a grandson to take care of you. We pray that the boy will grow up to be famous everywhere in Israel. ¹⁵He willᵇ make you happy and take care of you in your old age, because he is the son of your daughter-in-law. And she loves you more than seven sons of your own would love you.

¹⁶Naomi loved the boy and took good care of him. ¹⁷The neighorhood women named him Obed, but they called him "Naomi's Boy."

When Obed grew up he had a son named Jesse, who later became the father of King David.

ᵃ4.12 *Perez:* One of the sons of Judah; he was an ancestor of Boaz and of many others who lived in Bethlehem. ᵇ4.14,15 *We pray that . . . famous . . . ¹⁵He will:* Or "We pray that the LORD will be praised everywhere in Israel. ¹⁵Your grandson will."

Prayer Starter: Thank you for my parents, Lord. And for my grandparents, too.

Memory Verse: When you pray, go into a room alone and close the door. Pray to your Father in private. . . .   —*Matthew 6.6*

Hannah Prayed Silently

When the sacrifice had been offered, and they had eaten the meal, Hannah got up and went to pray. Eli was sitting in his chair near the door to the place of worship. ¹⁰Hannah was brokenhearted and was crying as she prayed, ¹¹"LORD All-Powerful, I am your servant, but I am so miserable! Please let me have a son. I will give him to you for as long as he lives, and his hair will never be cut."ᵃ

¹²⁻¹³Hannah prayed silently to the LORD for a long time. But her lips were moving, and Eli thought she was drunk. ¹⁴"How long are you going to stay drunk?" he asked. "Sober up!"

¹⁵⁻¹⁶"Sir, please don't think I'm no good!" Hannah answered. "I'm not drunk, and I haven't been drinking. But I do feel miserable and terribly upset. I've been praying all this time, telling the LORD about my problems."

¹⁷Eli replied, "You may go home now and stop worrying. I'm sure the God of Israel will answer your prayer."

ᵃ1.11 *his hair . . . cut:* Never cutting the child's hair would be a sign that he would belong to the LORD.

Prayer Starter: Lord, I am sure you answer prayer. Please help me pray to you each day.

Memory Verse: When you pray, go into a room alone and close the door. Pray to your Father in private. He knows what is done in private . . .
—*Matthew 6.6*

The Little Boy

Elkanah and his family got up early the next morning and worshiped the LORD. Then they went back home to Ramah. Later the LORD blessed Elkanah and Hannah [20]with a son. She named him Samuel because she had asked the LORD for him.[a]

[21]The next time Elkanah and his family went to offer their yearly sacrifice, he took along a gift that he had promised to give to the LORD. [22]But Hannah stayed home, because she had told Elkanah, "Samuel and I won't go until he's old enough for me to stop nursing him. Then I'll give him to the LORD, and he can stay there at Shiloh for the rest of his life."

[23]"You know what's best," Elkanah said. "Stay here until it's time to stop nursing him. I'm sure the LORD will help you do what you have promised."[b] Hannah did not go to Shiloh until she stopped nursing Samuel.

[24-25]When it was the time of year to go to Shiloh again, Hannah and Elkanah[c] took Samuel to the LORD's house. They brought along a three-year-old bull,[d] a twenty-pound sack of flour, and a clay jar full of wine. Hannah and Elkanah offered the bull as a sacrifice, then brought the little boy to Eli.

[26]"Sir," Hannah said, "a few years ago I stood here beside you and asked the LORD [27]to give me a child. Here he is! The LORD gave me just what I asked for. [28]Now I am giving him to the LORD, and he will be the LORD's servant for as long as he lives."

[a]1.20 *him:* In Hebrew "Samuel" sounds something like "Someone from God" or "The name of God" or "His name is God." [b]1.23 *the LORD . . . promised:* The Dead Sea Scrolls and two ancient translations; the Standard Hebrew Text "the LORD will do what he said." [c]1.24,25 *When it was the time of year to go to Shiloh again, Hannah and Elkanah:* The Dead Sea Scrolls and one ancient translation; the Standard Hebrew Text "she." [d]1.24,25 *a three-year-old bull:* The Dead Sea Scrolls and two ancient translations; the Standard Hebrew Text "three bulls."

Prayer Starter: I want to be your servant as long as I live, dear Lord.

Memory Verse: When you pray, go into a room alone and close the door. Pray to your Father in private. He knows what is done in private, and he will reward you.

—*Matthew 6.6*

I'm Listening, Lord

Samuel served the LORD by helping Eli the priest, who was by that time almost blind. In those days, the LORD hardly ever spoke directly to people, and he did not appear to them in dreams very often. But one night, Eli was asleep in his room, ³and Samuel was sleeping on a mat near the sacred chest in the LORD's house. They had not been asleep very longᵃ ⁴when the LORD called out Samuel's name.

"Here I am!" Samuel answered. ⁵Then he ran to Eli and said, "Here I am. What do you want?"

"I didn't call you," Eli answered. "Go back to bed."

Samuel went back.

⁶Again the LORD called out Samuel's name. Samuel got up and went to Eli. "Here I am," he said. "What do you want?"

Eli told him, "Son, I didn't call you. Go back to sleep."

⁷The LORD had not spoken to Samuel before, and Samuel did not recognize the voice. ⁸When the LORD called out his name for the third time, Samuel went to Eli again and said, "Here I am. What do you want?"

Eli finally realized that it was the LORD who was speaking to Samuel. ⁹So he said, "Go back and lie down! If someone speaks to you again, answer, 'I'm listening, LORD. What do you want me to do?'"

Once again Samuel went back and lay down.

¹⁰The LORD then stood beside Samuel and called out as he had done before, "Samuel! Samuel!"

"I'm listening," Samuel answered. "What do you want me to do?"

¹¹The LORD said:

Samuel, I am going to do something in Israel that will shock everyone who hears about it! ¹²I will punish Eli and his family, just as I promised. ¹³He knew that his sons refused to respect me,ᵇ and he let them get away with it, even though I said I would punish his family forever. ¹⁴I warned Eli that sacrifices or offerings could never make things right! His family has done too many disgusting things.

ᵃ3.3 *They . . . long:* The Hebrew text has "The lamp was still burning." An olive oil lamp would go out after a few hours if the wick was not adjusted. ᵇ3.13 *refused . . . me:* Or "were insulting everyone."

Prayer Starter: I'm listening to your word each day, dear Lord. Help me to do what you want me to do.

Memory Verse: "Tell me," Samuel said. . . .   —*1 Samuel 15.22*

Saul Anointed King

S amuel took a small jar of olive oil and poured it on Saul's head. Then he kissed[a] Saul and told him:

The LORD has chosen you to be the leader and ruler of his people.[b] 2When you leave me today, you'll meet two men near Rachel's tomb at Zelzah in the territory of Benjamin. They'll tell you, "The donkeys you've been looking for have been found. Your father has forgotten about them, and now he's worrying about you! He's wondering how he can find you."

3Go on from there until you reach the big oak tree at Tabor, where you'll meet three men on their way to worship God at Bethel. One of them will be leading three young goats, another will be carrying three round loaves of bread, and the last one will be carrying a clay jar of wine. 4After they greet you, they'll give you two loaves of bread.

5Next, go to Gibeah,[c] where the Philistines have an army camp. As you're going into the town, you'll meet a group of prophets coming down from the place of worship. They'll be going along prophesying while others are walking in front of them, playing small harps, small drums, and flutes.

6The Spirit of the LORD will suddenly take control of you.[d] You'll become a different person and start prophesying right along with them. 7After these things happen, do whatever you think is right! God will help you.

[a]10.1 *kissed:* Relatives or close friends often greeted one another with a kiss. But this may have been a ceremonial kiss after Samuel poured oil on Saul's head to show that he was to be king. [b]10.1 *people:* One ancient translation adds "You will rule the LORD's people and save them from their enemies who are all around them. These things will prove that what I say is true." [c]10.5 *Gibeah:* The Hebrew text has "Gibeah of God," which may or may not have been the same Gibeah as Saul's hometown. [d]10.6 *take . . . you:* Or "will take control of you in a powerful way."

Prayer Starter: Father, I know you have a plan for my life. Thanks for loving me so much.

Memory Verse: "Tell me," Samuel said. "Does the LORD really want sacrifices and offerings? . . ."
—*1 Samuel 15.22*

That Was Stupid!

Saul was a young man[a] when he became king, and he ruled Israel for two years. [2]Then[b] he chose three thousand men from Israel to be full-time soldiers and sent everyone else[c] home. Two thousand of these troops stayed with him in the hills around Michmash and Bethel. The other thousand were stationed with Jonathan[d] at Gibeah[e] in the territory of Benjamin.

[5]The Philistines called their army together to fight Israel. They had three thousand[f] chariots, six thousand cavalry, and as many foot soldiers as there are grains of sand on the beach. They went to Michmash and set up camp there east of Beth-Aven.[g]

[6]The Israelite army realized that they were outnumbered and were going to lose the battle. Some of the Israelite men hid in caves or in clumps of bushes,[h] and some ran to places where they could hide among large rocks. Others hid in tombs[i] or in deep dry pits. [7]Still others[j] went to Gad and Gilead on the other side of the Jordan River.

Saul stayed at Gilgal. His soldiers were shaking with fear, [8]and they were starting to run off and leave him. Saul waited there seven days, just as Samuel had ordered him to do, but Samuel did not come. [9]Finally, Saul commanded, "Bring me some animals, so we can offer sacrifices to please the LORD and ask for his help."

Saul killed one of the animals, [10]and just as he was placing it on the altar, Samuel arrived. Saul went out to welcome him.

[11]"What have you done?" Samuel asked.

Saul answered, "My soldiers were leaving in all directions, and you didn't come when you were supposed to. The Philistines were gathering at Michmash, [12]and I was worried that they would attack me here at Gilgal. I hadn't offered a sacrifice to ask for the LORD's help, so I forced myself to offer a sacrifice on the altar fire."

[13]"That was stupid!" Samuel said. "You didn't obey the LORD your God. If you had obeyed him, someone from your family would always have been king of Israel. [14]But no, you disobeyed, and so the LORD won't choose anyone else from your family to be king. In fact, he has already chosen the one he wants to be the next leader of his people." [15]Then Samuel left Gilgal.

Part of Saul's army had not deserted him, and he led them to Gibeah in Benjamin to join his other troops. Then he counted them[k] and found that he still had six hundred men. [16]Saul, Jonathan, and their army set up camp at Geba in Benjamin.

[a]13.1 *a young man:* One possible meaning for the difficult Hebrew text; several manuscripts of one ancient translation have "thirty years old." [b]13.1,2 *for . . . Then:* One possible meaning for the difficult Hebrew text. [c]13.2 *everyone else:* People who were not full-time soldiers, but fought together with the army when the nation was in danger. [d]13.2 *Jonathan:* Saul's son. [e]13.2 *Michmash . . . Bethel . . . Gibeah:* These three towns form a triangle, with Bethel to the north. [f]13.5 *three thousand:* Some ancient translations; Hebrew "thirty thousand." [g]13.5 *Beth-Aven:* This Beth-Aven was probably located about a mile southwest of Michmash, between Michmash and Geba. [h]13.6 *in . . . bushes:* Or "in cracks in the rocks." [i]13.6 *tombs:* The Hebrew word may mean a room cut into solid rock and used as a burial place, or it may mean a cellar. [j]13.7 *Still others:* This translates a Hebrew word which may be used of wandering groups of people who sometimes became outlaws or hired soldiers. [k]13.15 *Then Samuel . . . counted them:* Two ancient translations; Hebrew "Then Samuel left Gilgal and went to Gibeah in Benjamin. Saul counted his army."

Prayer Starter: Forgive us, Lord, when we aren't as patient as you want us to be.

Memory Verse: "Tell me," Samuel said. "Does the LORD really want sacrifices and offerings? No! . . ."   *—1 Samuel 15.22*

He Wants You to Obey

The LORD told Samuel, [11]"Saul has stopped obeying me, and I'm sorry that I made him king."

Samuel was angry, and he cried out in prayer to the LORD all night. [12]Early the next morning he went to talk with Saul. Someone told him, "Saul went to Carmel, where he had a monument built so everyone would remember his victory. Then he left for Gilgal."

[13]Samuel finally caught up with Saul,[a] and Saul told him, "I hope the LORD will bless you! I have done what the LORD told me."

[14]"Then why," Samuel asked, "do I hear sheep and cattle?"

[15]"The army took them from the Amalekites," Saul explained. "They kept the best sheep and cattle, so they could sacrifice them to the LORD your God. But we destroyed everything else."

[16]"Stop!" Samuel said. "Let me tell you what the LORD told me last night."

"All right," Saul answered.

[17]Samuel continued, "You may not think you're very important, but the LORD chose you to be king, and you are in charge of the tribes of Israel. [18]When the LORD sent you on this mission, he told you to wipe out those worthless Amalekites. [19]Why didn't you listen to the LORD? Why did you keep the animals and make him angry?"

[a]15.13 *Saul:* One ancient translation adds "Saul had sacrificed to the LORD the best animals they had taken from Amalek, when Samuel came up to him . . ."

Prayer Starter: I know you want me to obey you, Lord. Give me an obedient heart.

Memory Verse: "Tell me," Samuel said. "Does the LORD really want sacrifices and offerings? No! He doesn't want your sacrifices . . . ."

—1 Samuel 15.22

David's Harp

The Spirit of the LORD had left Saul, and an evil spirit from the LORD was terrifying him. ¹⁵"It's an evil spirit from God that's frightening you," Saul's officials told him. ¹⁶"Your Majesty, let us go and look for someone who is good at playing the harp. He can play for you whenever the evil spirit from God bothers you, and you'll feel better."

¹⁷"All right," Saul answered. "Find me someone who is good at playing the harp and bring him here."

¹⁸"A man named Jesse who lives in Bethlehem has a son who can play the harp," one official said. "He's a brave warrior, he's good-looking, he can speak well, and the LORD is with him."

¹⁹Saul sent a message to Jesse: "Tell your son David to leave your sheep and come here to me."

²⁰Jesse loaded a donkey with bread and a goatskin full of wine,^a then he told David to take the donkey and a young goat to Saul. ²¹David went to Saul and started working for him. Saul liked him so much that he put David in charge of carrying his weapons. ²²Not long after this, Saul sent another message to Jesse: "I really like David. Please let him stay with me."

²³Whenever the evil spirit from God bothered Saul, David would play his harp. Saul would relax and feel better, and the evil spirit would go away.

^a16.20 *wine:* Wine was sometimes kept in bottles made of goatskin sewn up with the fur on the outside.

Prayer Starter: So many people are sad, dear Lord. Give me a message to cheer them up.

Memory Verse: "Tell me," Samuel said. "Does the LORD really want sacrifices and offerings? No! He doesn't want your sacrifices. He wants you to obey him."   *—1 Samuel 15.22*

David's Sling

The Philistines got ready for war and brought their troops together to attack the town of Socoh in Judah. They set up camp at Ephes-Dammin, between Socoh and Azekah.[a]

⁴The Philistine army had a hero named Goliath who was from the town of Gath and was over nine feet[b] tall.

¹³⁻¹⁴David was Jesse's youngest son. ¹⁵He took care of his father's sheep, and he went back and forth between Bethlehem and Saul's camp.

¹⁷One day, Jesse told David, "Hurry and take this sack of roasted grain and these ten loaves of bread to your brothers at the army camp."

²⁴When the Israelite soldiers saw Goliath, they were scared and ran off.

³¹Some soldiers overheard David talking, so they told Saul what David had said. Saul sent for David, and David came. ³²"Your Majesty," he said, "this Philistine shouldn't turn us into cowards. I'll go out and fight him myself!"

⁴²When Goliath saw that David was just a healthy, good-looking boy, he made fun of him. ⁴³"Do you think I'm a dog?" Goliath asked. "Is that why you've come after me with a stick?" He cursed David in the name of the Philistine gods ⁴⁴and shouted, "Come on! When I'm finished with you, I'll feed you to the birds and wild animals!"

⁴⁵David answered:

You've come out to fight me with a sword and a spear and a dagger. But I've come out to fight you in the name of the LORD All-Powerful. He is the God of Israel's army, and you have insulted him too!

⁴⁶Today the LORD will help me defeat you. I'll knock you down and cut off your head, and I'll feed the bodies of the other Philistine soldiers to the birds and wild animals. Then the whole world will know that Israel has a real God. ⁴⁷Everybody here will see that the LORD doesn't need swords or spears to save his people. The LORD always wins his battles, and he will help us defeat you.

⁴⁸When Goliath started forward, David ran toward him. ⁴⁹He put a rock in his sling and swung the sling around by its straps. When he let go of one strap, the rock flew out and hit Goliath on the forehead. It cracked his skull, and he fell facedown on the ground.

[a]17.1 *Socoh and Azekah:* Socoh was controlled by the Israelites, while Azekah was in Philistine hands. [b]17.4 *over nine feet:* The Standard Hebrew Text; the Dead Sea Scrolls and some manuscripts of one ancient translation have "almost seven feet."

Prayer Starter: Keep me strong and safe against bullies, dear Lord, and against everyone who might harm me.

Memory Verse: I can lie down . . .   *—Psalm 4.8*

Saul Grows Angry

David was a success in everything that Saul sent him to do, and Saul made him a high officer in his army. That pleased everyone, including Saul's other officers.

⁶David had killed Goliath, the battle was over, and the Israelite army set out for home. As the army went along, women came out of each Israelite town to welcome King Saul. They were singing happy songs and dancing to the music of tambourines and harps. ⁷They sang:

> Saul has killed a thousand enemies;
>   David has killed ten thousand enemies!

⁸This song made Saul very angry, and he thought, "They are saying that David has killed ten times more enemies than I ever did. Next they will want to make him king." ⁹Saul never again trusted David.

¹⁰The next day the LORD let an evil spirit take control of Saul, and he began acting like a crazy man inside his house. David came to play the

harp for Saul as usual, but this time Saul had a spear in his hand. ¹¹Saul thought, "I'll pin David to the wall." He threw the spear at David twice, but David dodged and got away both times.

¹²Saul was afraid of David, because the LORD was helping David and was no longer helping him. ¹³Saul put David in charge of a thousand soldiers and sent him out to fight. ¹⁴The LORD helped David, and he and his soldiers always won their battles. ¹⁵This made Saul even more afraid of David. ¹⁶But everyone else in Judah and Israel was loyal to[a] David, because he led the army in battle.

³⁰The Philistine rulers kept coming to fight Israel, but whenever David fought them, he won. He was famous because he won more battles against the Philistines than any of Saul's other officers.

[a]18.16 *was loyal to:* Or "loved."

Prayer Starter: Father, don't let me become jealous toward others. May I be happy when others are successful.

Memory Verse: I can lie down and sleep soundly . . .   *—Psalm 4.8*

Good Friends Part

"Why do you want to kill David?" Jonathan asked. "What has he done?"

³³Saul threw his spear at Jonathan and tried to kill him. Then Jonathan was sure that his father really did want to kill David. ³⁴Jonathan was angry that his father had insulted David[a] so terribly. He got up, left the table, and didn't eat anything all that day.

³⁵In the morning, Jonathan went out to the field to meet David. He took a servant boy along ³⁶and told him, "When I shoot the arrows, you run and find them for me."

The boy started running, and Jonathan shot an arrow so that it would go beyond him. ³⁷When the boy got near the place where the arrow had landed, Jonathan shouted, "Isn't the arrow on past you?" ³⁸Jonathan shouted to him again, "Hurry up! Don't stop!"

The boy picked up the arrows and brought them back to Jonathan. ⁴⁰Jonathan gave his weapons to the boy and told him, "Take these back into town."

⁴¹After the boy had gone, David got up from beside the mound[b] and bowed very low three times. Then he and Jonathan kissed[c] each other and cried, but David cried louder. ⁴²Jonathan said, "Take care of yourself. And remember, we each have asked the LORD to watch and make sure that we and our descendants keep our promise forever."

David left and Jonathan went back to town.

[a]20.34 *insulted David:* Or "insulted him" (that is, Jonathan). [b]20.41 *the mound:* One ancient translation; Hebrew "from the south side." [c]20.41 *kissed:* A common way of greeting or saying good-by in biblical times.

Prayer Starter: Thank you for good friends. Please take care of them.

Memory Verse: I can lie down and sleep soundly because you, LORD . . .
—Psalm 4.8

Is That
You?

Saul led three thousand of Israel's best soldiers out to look for David and his men near Wild Goat Rocks at En-Gedi. ³There were some sheep pens along the side of the road, and one of them was built around the entrance to a cave. Saul went into the cave to relieve himself.

David and his men were hiding at the back of the cave. ⁴They whispered to David, "The LORD told you he was going to let you defeat your enemies and do whatever you want with them. This must be the day the LORD was talking about."

David sneaked over and cut off a small pieceᵃ of Saul's robe, but Saul didn't notice a thing. ⁵Afterward, David was sorry that he had even done that, ⁶⁻⁷and he told his men, "Stop talking foolishly. We're not going to attack Saul. He's my king, and I pray that the LORD will keep me from doing anything to harm his chosen king."

Saul left the cave and started down the road. ⁸Soon, David also got up and left the cave. "Your Majesty!" he shouted from a distance.

Saul turned around to look. David bowed down very low ⁹and said:

Your Majesty, why do you listen to people who say that I'm trying to harm you? ¹⁰You can see for yourself that the LORD gave me the chance to catch you in the cave today. Some of my men wanted to

kill you, but I wouldn't let them do it. I told them, "I will not harm the LORD's chosen king!" ¹¹Your Majesty, look at what I'm holding. You can see that it's a piece of your robe. If I could cut off a piece of your robe, I could have killed you. But I let you live, and that should prove I'm not trying to harm you or to rebel. I haven't done anything to you, and yet you keep trying to ambush and kill me.

¹²I'll let the LORD decide which one of us has done right. I pray that the LORD will punish you for what you're doing to me, but I won't do anything to you. ¹³An old proverb says, "Only evil people do evil things," and so I won't harm you.

¹⁶"David, my son—is that you?" Saul asked. Then he started crying ¹⁷and said:

David, you're a better person than I am. You treated me with kindness, even though I've been cruel to you. ¹⁸You've told me how you were kind enough not to kill me when the LORD gave you the chance. ¹⁹If you really were my enemy, you wouldn't have let me leave here alive. I pray that the LORD will give you a big reward for what you did today.

²⁰I realize now that you will be the next king, and a powerful king at that. ²¹Promise me with the LORD as your witness, that you won't wipe out my descendants. Let them live to keep my family name alive.

²²So David promised, and Saul went home. David and his men returned to their hideout.

ᵃ24.4 *small piece:* Hebrew "corner" or "lower hem."

Prayer Starter: Bless the leaders of my country today, Lord. Give them wisdom.

Memory Verse: I can lie down and sleep soundly because you, LORD, will keep me . . .
—*Psalm 4.8*

The Spear and Water Jar

Once again, some people from Ziph went to Gibeah to talk with Saul. "David has a hideout on Mount Hachilah near Jeshimon out in the desert," they told him.

²Saul took three thousand of Israel's best soldiers and went to look for David there in the Ziph Desert. ³Saul set up camp on Mount Hachilah, which is across the road from Jeshimon. But David was hiding out in the desert.

When David heard that Saul was following him, ⁴he sent some spies to find out if it was true. ⁵Then he sneaked up to Saul's camp. He noticed that Saul and his army commander Abner the son of Ner were sleeping in the middle of the camp, with soldiers sleeping all around them. ⁶David asked Ahimelech the Hittite and Joab's brother Abishai,ᵃ "Which one of you will go with me into Saul's camp?"

"I will!" Abishai answered.

⁷That same night, David and Abishai crept into the camp. Saul was sleeping, and his spear was stuck in the ground not far from his head. Abner and the soldiers were sound asleep all around him.

⁸Abishai whispered, "This time God has let you get your hands on your enemy! I'll pin him to the ground with one thrust of his own spear."

⁹"Don't kill him!" David whispered back. "The LORD will punish anyone who kills his chosen king. ¹⁰As surely as the LORD lives, the LORD will kill Saul, or Saul will die a natural death or be killed in battle. ¹¹But I pray that the LORD will keep me from harming his chosen king. Let's grab his spear and his water jar and get out of here!"

¹²David took the spear and the water jar, then left the camp. None of Saul's soldiers knew what had happened or even woke up—the LORD had made all of them fall sound asleep.

ᵃ26.6 *Abishai:* Hebrew "Abishai the son of Zeruiah." Zeruiah was David's older sister, so Abishai and Joab were David's nephews.

Prayer Starter: Lord, you make the day and night, the light and the darkness. Bless me by day and keep me safe by night.

Memory Verse: I can lie down and sleep soundly because you, LORD, will keep me safe.
—*Psalm 4.8*

The Ghost of Samuel

Samuel had died some time earlier, and people from all over Israel had attended his funeral in his hometown of Ramah.

Meanwhile, Saul had been trying to get rid of everyone who spoke with the spirits of the dead.[a] But one day the Philistines brought their soldiers together to attack Israel.

⁵Saul took one look at the Philistine army and started shaking with fear. ⁶So he asked the LORD what to do. But the LORD would not answer, either in a dream or by a priest or a prophet. ⁷Then Saul told his officers, "Find me a woman who can talk to the spirits of the dead. I'll go to her and find out what's going to happen."

His servants told him, "There's a woman at Endor who can talk to spirits of the dead."

⁸That night, Saul put on different clothing so nobody would recognize him. Then he and two of his men went to the woman, and asked, "Will you bring up the ghost of someone for us?"

⁹The woman said, "Why are you trying to trick me and get me killed? You know King Saul has gotten rid of everyone who talks to the spirits of the dead!"

¹⁰Saul replied, "I swear by the living LORD that nothing will happen to you because of this."

¹¹"Who do you want me to bring up?" she asked.

"Bring up the ghost of Samuel," he answered.

¹²When the woman saw Samuel, she screamed. Then she turned to Saul and said, "You've tricked me! You're the king!"

¹³"Don't be afraid," Saul replied. "Just tell me what you see."

¹⁴"What does it look like?"

"It looks like an old man wearing a robe."

¹⁵"Why are you bothering me by bringing me up like this?" Samuel asked.

"I'm terribly worried," Saul answered. "The Philistines are about to attack me. God has turned his back on me and won't answer any more by prophets or by dreams. What should I do?"

¹⁶Samuel said:

If the LORD has turned away from you and is now your enemy, don't ask me what to do. ¹⁷I've already told you: The LORD has sworn to take the kingdom from you and give it to David. And that's just what he's doing!

---

[a]28.1-3 *dead:* Many people believed that it was possible to talk to spirits of the dead, and that these spirits could tell the future.

Prayer Starter: Keep us safe from the devil, Father. Protect us from the evil one.

Memory Verse: Do what the LORD . . .   *—1 Kings 2.3a*

Saul and His Sons Die

Meanwhile, the Philistines were fighting Israel at Mount Gilboa. Israel's soldiers ran from the Philistines, and many of them were killed. ²The Philistines closed in on Saul and his sons, and they killed his sons Jonathan, Abinadab, and Malchishua. ³The fighting was fierce around Saul, and he was badly wounded by enemy arrows.

⁴Saul told the soldier who carried his weapons, "Kill me with your sword! I don't want those worthless Philistines to torture me and make fun." But the soldier was afraid to kill him.

Saul then took out his own sword; he stuck the blade into his stomach, and fell on it. ⁵When the soldier knew that Saul was dead, he killed himself in the same way.

⁶Saul was dead, his three sons were dead, and the soldier who carried his weapons was dead. They and all his soldiers died on that same day. ⁷The Israelites on the other side of Jezreel Valley[a] and the other side of the Jordan learned that Saul and his sons were dead. They saw that the Israelite army had run away. So they ran away too, and the Philistines moved into the towns the Israelites had left behind.

[a]31.7 *Jezreel Valley:* Hebrew "valley." Shunem and Gilboa were across the Jezreel Valley from each other.

Prayer Starter: Dear Father, so many people are sad and afraid. Help me point them to Jesus.

Memory Verse: Do what the LORD your God commands . . .
—1 Kings 2.3a

David and the Sacred Chest

David brought together thirty thousand of Israel's best soldiers and ²led them to Baalah in Judah, which was also called Kiriath-Jearim. They were going there^a to get the sacred chest and bring it back to Jerusalem. The throne of the LORD All-Powerful is above the winged creatures^b on top of this chest, and he is worshiped there.^c

³They put the sacred chest on a new ox cart and started bringing it down the hill from Abinadab's house. Abinadab's sons Uzzah and Ahio were guiding the ox cart, ⁴with Ahio^d walking in front of it. ⁵Some of the

people of Israel were playing music on small harps and other stringed instruments, and on tambourines, castanets, and cymbals. David and the others were happy, and they danced for the LORD with all their might.

⁶But when they came to Nacon's threshing-floor, the oxen stumbled, so Uzzah reached out and took hold of the sacred chest. ⁷The LORD God was very angry at Uzzah for doing this, and he killed Uzzah right there beside the chest.

⁸David got angry at God for killing Uzzah. He named that place "Bursting Out Against Uzzah,"^e and that's what it's still called.

⁹David was afraid of the LORD and thought, "Should I really take the sacred chest to my city?" ¹⁰He decided not to take it there. Instead, he turned off the road and took it to the home of Obed Edom, who was from Gath.ᶠ

¹¹⁻¹²The chest stayed there for three months, and the LORD greatly blessed Obed Edom, his family, and everything he owned. Then someone told King David, "The LORD has done this because the sacred chest is in Obed Edom's house."

Right away, David went to Obed Edom's house to get the chest and bring it to David's City. Everyone was celebrating. ¹³The people carrying the chest walked six steps, then David sacrificed an ox and a choice cow. ¹⁴He was dancing for the LORD with all his might, but he wore only a linen cloth.ᵍ ¹⁵He and everyone else were celebrating by shouting and blowing horns while the chest was being carried along.

¹⁶Saul's daughter Michal looked out her window and watched the chest being brought into David's City. But when she saw David jumping and dancing for the LORD, she was disgusted.

¹⁷They put the chest inside a tent that David had set up for it. David worshiped the LORD by sacrificing animals and burning them on an altar,ʰ ¹⁸then he blessed the people in the name of the LORD All-Powerful. ¹⁹He gave all the men and women in the crowd a small loaf of bread, some meat, and a handful of raisins, and everyone went home.

ᵃ6.2 *to Baalah . . . there:* The Dead Sea Scrolls; the Standard Hebrew Text "from Baalah in Judah. They had gone there." ᵇ6.2 *winged creatures:* Two golden statues of winged creatures were on top of the sacred chest and were symbols of the LORD's throne on earth. ᶜ6.2 *he is worshiped there:* Or "the chest belongs to him." ᵈ6.3,4 *Ahio . . . Ahio:* Or "his brother . . . his brother." ᵉ6.8 *Bursting . . . Uzzah:* Or "Perez-Uzzah." ᶠ6.10 *Gath:* Or perhaps, "Gittaim." ᵍ6.14 *only a linen cloth:* The Hebrew word is "ephod," which can mean either a piece of clothing like a skirt that went from the waist to the knee or a garment like a vest or a jacket that only the priests wore. ʰ6.17 *sacrificing . . . altar:* The Hebrew mentions two kinds of sacrifices. In one kind of sacrifice, the whole animal was burned on the altar. In the other kind, only part was burned, and the worshipers ate the rest, as in verse 19.

Prayer Starter: Sometimes I don't do the right thing, Lord, but please continue to show me how to follow you.

Memory Verse: Do what the LORD your God commands and follow his teachings. . . .   —*1 Kings 2.3a*

Mephibosheth

One day, David thought, "I wonder if any of Saul's family are still alive. If they are, I will be kind to them, because I made a promise to Jonathan." ²David called in Ziba, one of the servants of Saul's family. David said, "So you are Ziba."

"Yes, Your Majesty, I am."

³David asked, "Are any of Saul's family still alive? If there are, I want to be kind to them."

Ziba answered, "One of Jonathan's sons is still alive, but he can't walk."

⁴"Where is he?" David asked.

Ziba replied, "He lives in Lo-Debar with Machir the son of Ammiel."

⁵⁻⁶David sent some servants to bring Jonathan's son from Lo-Debar. His name was Mephibosheth,ᵃ and he was the grandson of Saul. He came to David and knelt down.

David asked, "Are you Mephibosheth?"

"Yes, I am, Your Majesty."

⁷David said, "Don't be afraid. I'll be kind to you because Jonathan was your father. I'm going to give you back the land that belonged to your grandfather Saul. Besides that, you will always eat with me at my table."

⁸Mephibosheth knelt down again and said, "Why should you care about me? I'm worth no more than a dead dog."

⁹David called in Ziba, Saul's chief servant, and told him, "Since Mephibosheth is Saul's grandson, I've given him back everything that belonged to your master Saul and his family.

¹¹⁻¹³Mephibosheth was lame, but he lived in Jerusalem and ate at David'sᵇ table, just like one of David's own sons. And he had a young son of his own, named Mica.

ᵃ9.5,6 *Mephibosheth:* Or "Mephibaal." ᵇ9.11-13 *David's:* Hebrew "my."

Prayer Starter: Give us kind hearts toward one another, Lord, for you are kind toward us.

Memory Verse: Do what the LORD your God commands and follow his teachings. Obey everything . . .   *—1 Kings 2.3a*

David Speaks to His Son

Not long before David died, he told Solomon: [2]My son, I will soon die, as everyone must. But I want you to be strong and brave. [3]Do what the LORD your God commands and follow his teachings. Obey everything written in the Law of Moses. Then you will be a success, no matter what you do or where you go. [4]You and your descendants must always faithfully obey the LORD. If you do, he will keep the solemn promise he made to me that someone from our family will always be king of Israel.

[10-11]David was king of Israel forty years. He ruled seven years from Hebron and thirty-three years from Jerusalem. Then he died and was buried in Jerusalem.[a]

3 One night while Solomon was in Gibeon, the LORD God appeared to him in a dream and said, "Solomon, ask for anything you want, and I will give it to you."

[6]Solomon answered:

My father David, your servant, was honest and did what you commanded. You were always loyal to him, and you gave him a son who is now king. [7]LORD God, I'm your servant, and you've made me king in my father's place. But I'm very young and know so little about being a leader. [8]And now I must rule your chosen people, even though there are too many of them to count.

[9]Please make me wise and teach me the difference between right and wrong. Then I will know how to rule your people. If you don't, there is no way I could rule this great nation of yours.

[10-11]God said:

Solomon, I'm pleased that you asked for this. [12]I'll make you wiser than anyone who has ever lived or ever will live.

[a]2.10,11 *Jerusalem:* Hebrew "the city of David."

Prayer Starter: Give me wisdom, dear Lord, and help me to think clearly.

Memory Verse: Do what the LORD your God commands and follow his teachings. Obey everything written in the Law of Moses. —*1 Kings 2.3a*

Oone day two women[a] came to King Solomon, [17]and one of them said:

The Two Mothers

Your Majesty, this woman and I live in the same house. Not long ago my baby was born at home, [18]and three days later her baby was born. Nobody else was there with us.

[19]One night while we were all asleep, she rolled over on her baby, and he died. [20]Then while I was still asleep, she got up and took my son out of my bed. She put him in her bed, then she put her dead baby next to me.

[21]In the morning when I got up to feed my son, I saw that he was dead. But when I looked at him in the light, I knew he wasn't my son.

[22]"No!" the other woman shouted. "He was your son. My baby is alive!"

"The dead baby is yours," the woman yelled. "Mine is alive!"

They argued back and forth in front of Solomon, [23]until finally he said, "Both of you say this live baby is yours. [24]Someone bring me a sword."

A sword was brought, and Solomon ordered, [25]"Cut the baby in half! That way each of you can have part of him."

[26]"Please don't kill my son," the baby's mother screamed. "Your Majesty, I love him very much, but give him to her. Just don't kill him."

The other woman shouted, "Go ahead and cut him in half. Then neither of us will have the baby."

[27]Solomon said, "Don't kill the baby." Then he pointed to the first woman, "She is his real mother. Give the baby to her."

[28]Everyone in Israel was amazed when they heard how Solomon had made his decision. They realized that God had given him the wisdom to judge fairly.

[a]3.16 *women:* Hebrew "prostitutes."

Prayer Starter: Use me, dear Lord, to help others solve their problems. Make me wise.

Memory Verse: The prayer of an innocent person . . .

　　　　　　　　　　　　　　　　—James 5.16b–17a

The Queen of Sheba

The Queen of Sheba heard how famous Solomon was, so she went to Jerusalem to test him with difficult questions. ²She took along several of her officials, and she loaded her camels with gifts of spices, jewels, and gold. When she arrived, she and Solomon talked about everything she could think of. ³He answered every question, no matter how difficult it was.

⁴⁻⁵The Queen was amazed at Solomon's wisdom. She was breathless when she saw his palace, the food on his table, his officials, his servants in their uniforms, the people who served his food, and the sacrifices he offered at the LORD's temple. ⁶She said:

Solomon, in my own country I had heard about your wisdom and all you've done. ⁷But I didn't believe it until I saw it with my own eyes! And there's so much I didn't hear about. You are wiser and richer than I was told. ⁸Your wivesª and officials are lucky to be here where they can listen to the wise things you say.

⁹I praise the LORD your God. He is pleased with you and has made you king of Israel. The LORD loves Israel, so he has given them a king who will rule fairly and honestly.

¹⁰The Queen of Sheba gave Solomon almost five tons of gold, many jewels, and more spices than anyone had ever brought into Israel.

¹¹⁻¹³In return, Solomon gave her the gifts he would have given any other ruler, but he also gave her everything else she wanted. Then she and her officials went back to their own country.

King Hiram's ships brought gold, juniper wood, and jewels from the country of Ophir. Solomon used the wood to make stepsᵇ for the temple and palace, and harps and other stringed instruments for the musicians. It was the best juniper wood anyone in Israel had ever seen.

ª10.8 *wives:* Two ancient translations; Hebrew "men." ᵇ10.11-13 *steps:* Or "stools" or "railings."

Prayer Starter: Thank you for all you give us, dear Lord. Thanks for my home, my bed, my clothes, my food.

Memory Verse: The prayer of an innocent person is powerful . . .
—*James 5.16b–17a*

Fed by Ravens

Ahab son of Omri became king of Israel in the thirty-eighth year of Asa's rule in Judah, and he ruled twenty-two years from Samaria. ³⁰Ahab did more things to disobey the LORD than any king before him. ³¹He acted just like Jeroboam. Even worse, he married Jezebel the daughter of King Ethbaal of Sidon[a] and started worshiping Baal. ³²Ahab built an altar and temple for Baal in Samaria ³³and set up a sacred pole[b] for worshiping the goddess Asherah. Ahab did more to make the LORD God of Israel angry than any king of Israel before him.

³⁴While Ahab was king, a man from Bethel named Hiel rebuilt the town of Jericho. But while Hiel was laying the foundation for the town wall, his oldest son Abiram died. And while he was finishing the gates, his youngest son Segub died. This happened just as the LORD had told Joshua to say many years ago.

17 Elijah was a prophet from Tishbe in Gilead.[c] One day he went to King Ahab and said, "I'm a servant of the living LORD, the God of Israel. And I swear in his name that it won't rain until I say so. There won't even be any dew on the ground."

²Later, the LORD said to Elijah, ³"Leave and go across the Jordan River so you can hide near Cherith Creek. ⁴You can drink water from the creek, and eat the food I've told the ravens to bring you."

⁵Elijah obeyed the LORD and went to live near Cherith Creek.

[a]16.31 *Sidon:* One of the most important cities in Phoenicia. It was located on the coast of the Mediterranean Sea, north of Israel, in what is today southern Lebanon. [b]16.33 *sacred pole:* Or "trees," used as symbols of Asherah, the goddess of fertility. [c]17.1 *from Tishbe in Gilead:* Or "From the settlers in Gilead."

Prayer Starter: Thank you for the stories in the Bible, Father. Help me to pray like Elijah.

Memory Verse: The prayer of an innocent person is powerful, and it can help a lot. . . .   *—James 5.16b–17a*

A Handful of Flour

The LORD told Elijah, ⁹"Go to the town of Zarephath in Sidon and live there. I've told a widow in that town to give you food."

¹⁰When Elijah came near the town gate of Zarephath, he saw a widow gathering sticks for a fire. "Would you please bring me a cup of water?" he asked.

¹¹As she left to get it, he asked, "Would you also please bring me a piece of bread?"

¹²The widow answered, "In the name of the living LORD your God, I swear that I don't have any bread. All I have is a handful of flour and a little olive oil. I'm on my way home now with these few sticks to cook what I have for my son and me. After that, we will starve to death."

¹³Elijah said, "Everything will be fine. Do what you said. Go home and fix something for you and your son. But first, please make a small piece of bread and bring it to me. ¹⁴The LORD God of Israel has promised that your jar of flour won't run out and your bottle of oil won't dry up before he sends rain for the crops."

¹⁵The widow went home and did exactly what Elijah had told her. She and Elijah and her family had enough food for a long time. ¹⁶The LORD kept the promise that his prophet Elijah had made, and she did not run out of flour or oil.

¹⁷Several days later, the son of the woman who owned the houseᵃ got sick, and he kept getting worse, until finally he died.

¹⁸The woman shouted at Elijah, "What have I done to you? I thought you were God's prophet. Did you come here to cause the death of my son as a reminder that I've sinned against God?"ᵇ

¹⁹"Bring me your son," Elijah said. Then he took the boy from her arms and carried him upstairs to the room where he was staying. Elijah laid the boy on his bed ²⁰and prayed, "LORD God, why did you do such a terrible thing to this woman? She's letting me stay here and now you've let her son die." ²¹Elijah stretched himself out over the boy three times, while praying, "LORD God, bring this boy back to life!"

²²The LORD answered Elijah's prayer, and the boy started breathing again. ²³Elijah picked him up and carried him downstairs. He gave the boy to his mother and said, "Look, your son is alive."

²⁴"You are God's prophet!" the woman replied. "Now I know that you really do speak for the LORD."

ᵃ17.17 *the woman who owned the house:* This may or may not be the same woman as the widow in verses 8-16. ᵇ17.18 *Did you . . . God:* In ancient times people sometimes thought that if they sinned, something terrible would happen to them.

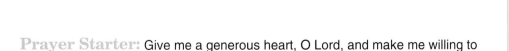

Prayer Starter: Give me a generous heart, O Lord, and make me willing to share.

Memory Verse: The prayer of an innocent person is powerful, and it can help a lot. Elijah was just . . .   *—James 5.16b–17a*

The Lord Is God!

Elijah said to Baal's prophets, "There are more of you, so you go first. Pick out a bull and get it ready, but don't light the fire. Then pray to your god." ²⁶They chose their bull, then they got it ready and prayed to Baal all morning, asking him to start the fire. They danced around the altar and shouted, "Answer us, Baal!" But there was no answer.

²⁷At noon, Elijah began making fun of them. "Pray louder!" he said. "Baal must be a god. Maybe he's daydreaming or using the toilet or traveling somewhere. Or maybe he's asleep, and you have to wake him up."

²⁸The prophets kept shouting louder and louder, and they cut themselves with swords and knives until they were bleeding. This was the way they worshiped, ²⁹and they kept it up all afternoon. But there was no answer of any kind.

³⁰Elijah told everyone to gather around him while he repaired the LORD's altar. ³¹⁻³²Then he used twelve stones to build an altar in honor of the LORD. Each stone stood for one of the tribes of Israel, which was the name the LORD had given to their ancestor Jacob. Elijah dug a ditch around the altar, large enough to hold about thirteen quarts. ³³He placed the wood on the altar, then they cut the bull into pieces and laid the meat on the wood.

He told the people, "Fill four large jars with water and pour it over the meat and the wood." After they did this, ³⁴he told them to do it two more times. They did exactly as he said ³⁵until finally, the water ran down the altar and filled the ditch.

³⁶When it was time for the evening sacrifice, Elijah prayed:

Our LORD, you are the God of Abraham, Isaac, and Israel. Now, prove that you are the God of this nation,ᵃ and that I, your servant, have done this at your command. ³⁷Please answer me, so these people will know that you are the LORD God, and that you will turn their hearts back to you.ᵇ

³⁸The LORD immediately sent fire, and it burned up the sacrifice, the wood, and the stones. It scorched the ground everywhere around the altar and dried up every drop of water in the ditch. ³⁹When the crowd saw what had happened, they all bowed down and shouted, "The LORD is God! The LORD is God!"

ᵃ18.36 *this nation:* Hebrew "Israel." ᵇ18.37 *will turn . . . to you:* One possible meaning for the difficult Hebrew text.

Prayer Starter: I want to be true to you, Lord, even if I'm the only Christian in my group. Keep me faithful.

Memory Verse: The prayer of an innocent person is powerful, and it can help a lot. Elijah was just as human as we are. —*James 5.16b–17a*

Chariot of Fire

Elijah then said, "Elisha, now the LORD wants me to go to Jericho, but you must stay here."

Elisha replied, "I swear by the living LORD and by your own life, that I will stay with you no matter what!" And he went with Elijah to Jericho.

⁵A group of prophets who lived there asked Elisha, "Do you know that today the LORD is going to take away your master?"

"Yes, I do," Elisha answered. "But don't remind me of it."

⁶Elijah then said to Elisha, "Now the LORD wants me to go to the Jordan River, but you must stay here."

Elisha replied, "I swear by the living LORD and by your own life that I will never leave you!" So the two of them walked on together.

⁷Fifty prophets followed Elijah and Elisha from Jericho, then stood at a distance and watched as the two men walked toward the river. ⁸When they got there, Elijah took off his coat, then he rolled it up and struck the water with it. At once a path opened up through the river, and the two of them walked across on dry ground.

⁹After they had reached the other side, Elijah said, "Elisha, the LORD will soon take me away. What can I do for you before that happens?"

Elisha answered, "Please give me twice as much of your power as you give the other prophets, so I can be the one who takes your place as their leader."

¹⁰"It won't be easy," Elijah answered. "It can happen only if you see me as I am being taken away."

¹¹Elijah and Elisha were walking along and talking, when suddenly there appeared between them a flaming chariot pulled by fiery horses. Right away, a strong wind took Elijah up into heaven. ¹²Elisha saw this and shouted, "Israel's cavalry and chariots have taken my master away!"ᵃ After Elijah had gone, Elisha tore his clothes in sorrow.

ᵃ2.12 *Israel's . . . away:* Or "Master, you were like cavalry and chariots for the people of Israel!"

Prayer Starter: I praise you, Lord, for eternal life. Thank you for all the Bible says about heaven.

Memory Verse: Our God says, "Calm down . . ."   —*Psalm 46.10*

Naaman's Leprosy

Naaman was the commander of the Syrian army. The LORD had helped him and his troops defeat their enemies, so the king of Syria respected Naaman very much. Naaman was a brave soldier, but he had leprosy.[a]

²One day while the Syrian troops were raiding Israel, they captured a girl, and she became a servant of Naaman's wife. ³Some time later the girl said, "If your husband Naaman would go to the prophet in Samaria, he would be cured of his leprosy."

⁴When Naaman told the king what the girl had said, ⁵the king replied, "Go ahead! I will give you a letter to take to the king of Israel."

Naaman left and took along seven hundred fifty pounds of silver, one hundred fifty pounds of gold, and ten new outfits. ⁶He also carried the letter to the king of Israel. It said, "I am sending my servant Naaman to you. Would you cure him of his leprosy?"

⁷When the king of Israel read the letter, he tore his clothes in fear and shouted, "That Syrian king believes I can cure this man of leprosy!

Does he think I'm God with power over life and death? He must be trying to pick a fight with me."

⁸As soon as Elisha the prophet[b] heard what had happened, he sent the Israelite king this message: "Why are you so afraid? Send the man to me, so that he will know there is a prophet in Israel."

⁹Naaman left with his horses and chariots and stopped at the door of Elisha's house. ¹⁰Elisha sent someone outside to say to him, "Go wash seven times in the Jordan River. Then you'll be completely cured."

¹¹But Naaman stormed off, grumbling, "Why couldn't he come out and talk to me? I thought for sure he would stand in front of me and pray to the LORD his God, then wave his hand over my skin and cure me. ¹²What about the Abana River[c] or the Pharpar River? Those rivers in Damascus are just as good as any river in Israel. I could have washed in them and been cured."

¹³His servants went over to him and said, "Sir, if the prophet had told you to do something difficult, you would have done it. So why don't you do what he said? Go wash and be cured."

¹⁴Naaman walked down to the Jordan; he waded out into the water and stooped down in it seven times, just as Elisha had told him. Right away, he was cured, and his skin became as smooth as a child's.

¹⁵Naaman and his officials went back to Elisha. Naaman stood in front of him and announced, "Now I know that the God of Israel is the only God in the whole world."

ᵃ5.1 *leprosy:* The word translated "leprosy" was used for many different kinds of skin diseases. ᵇ5.8 *the prophet:* Hebrew "the man of God." ᶜ5.12 *Abana River:* Most Hebrew manuscripts; some Hebrew manuscripts and two ancient translations "Amana River."

Prayer Starter: Make me clean on the inside, dear God. May my mind and spirit be holy.

Memory Verse: Our God says, "Calm down, and learn . . ."
—*Psalm 46.10*

Fiery Horses, Flaming Chariots

Time after time, when the king of Syria was at war against the Israelites, he met with his officers and announced, "I've decided where we will set up camp."

⁹Each time Elisha[a] would send this warning to the king of Israel: "Don't go near there. That's where the Syrian troops have set up camp."[b] ¹⁰So the king would warn the Israelite troops in that place to be on guard.

¹¹The king of Syria was furious when he found out what was happening. He called in his officers and asked, "Which one of you has been telling the king of Israel our plans?"

¹²"None of us, Your majesty," one of them answered. "It's an Israelite named Elisha. He's a prophet, so he can tell his king everything—even what you say in your own room."

¹³"Find out where he is!" the king ordered. "I'll send soldiers to bring him here."

They learned that Elisha was in the town of Dothan,[c] and reported it to the king. ¹⁴He ordered his best troops to go there with horses and chariots. They marched out during the night and surrounded the town.

¹⁵When Elisha's servant got up the next morning, he saw that Syrian troops had the town surrounded. "Sir, what are we going to do?" he asked.

¹⁶"Don't be afraid," Elisha answered. "There are more troops on our side than on theirs." ¹⁷Then he prayed, "LORD, please help him to see." And the LORD let the servant see that the hill[d] was covered with fiery horses and flaming chariots all around Elisha.

¹⁸As the Syrian army came closer, Elisha prayed, "LORD, make those soldiers blind!" And the LORD blinded them with a bright light.

¹⁹Elisha told the enemy troops, "You've taken the wrong road and are in the wrong town. Follow me. I'll lead you to the man you're looking for." Elisha led them straight to the capital city of Samaria.

²⁰When all the soldiers were inside the city, Elisha prayed, "LORD, now let them see again." The LORD let them see that they were standing in the middle of Samaria.

²¹The king of Israel saw them and asked Elisha, "Should I kill them, sir?"

²²"No!" Elisha answered. "You didn't capture these troops in battle, so you have no right to kill them. Instead, give them something to eat and drink and let them return to their leader."

[a]6.9 *Elisha:* Hebrew "the man of God." [b]6.9 *have set up camp:* Or "are going." [c]6.13 *Dothan:* About ten miles north of Samaria. [d]6.17 *the hill:* The hill on which the town was built.

Prayer Starter: Keep your angels around us, heavenly Father. Keep us safe wherever we go.

Memory Verse: Our God says, "Calm down, and learn that I am God! . . ."

—*Psalm 46.10*

Jezebel

Jehu headed toward Jezreel, and when Jezebel heard he was coming, she put on eye shadow and brushed her hair. Then she stood at the window, waiting for him to arrive. [31]As he walked through the city gate, she shouted down to him, "Why did you come here, you murderer? To kill the king? You're no better than Zimri!"[a]

[32]He looked up toward the window and asked, "Is anyone up there on my side?" A few palace workers stuck their heads out of a window, [33]and

Jehu shouted, "Throw her out the window!" They threw her down, and her blood splattered on the walls and on the horses that trampled her body.[b]

³⁴Jehu left to get something to eat and drink. Then he told some workers, "Even though she was evil, she was a king's daughter,[c] so make sure she has a proper burial."

³⁵But when they went out to bury her body, they found only her skull, her hands, and her feet. ³⁶They reported this to Jehu, and he said, "The LORD told Elijah the prophet that Jezebel's body would be eaten by dogs right here in Jezreel. ³⁷And he warned that her bones would be spread all over the ground like manure, so that no one could tell who it was."

[a]9.31 *Zimri:* An Israelite king who killed King Elah and his family so he could become king, but who ruled only seven days. [b]9.33 *horses . . . her body:* Two ancient translations; Hebrew "horses. Then Jehu trampled her body." [c]9.34 *she . . . daughter:* Her father was King Ethbaal of Sidon.

Prayer Starter: Some people are hard and cruel, dear Lord. Help me to leave them in your hands. Make me kind and strong.

Memory Verse: Our God says, "Calm down, and learn that I am God! All nations on earth . . ." —*Psalm 46.10*

Hezekiah Prays

The king of Assyria sent some messengers with this note for Hezekiah:

[10]Don't trust your God or be fooled by his promise to defend Jerusalem against me. [11]You have heard how we Assyrian kings have completely wiped out other nations. What makes you feel so safe?

[14]After Hezekiah had read the note from the king of Assyria, he took it to the temple and spread it out for the LORD to see. [15]He prayed:

LORD God of Israel, your throne is above the winged creatures.[a] You created the heavens and the earth, and you alone rule the kingdoms of this world. [16]But just look how Sennacherib has insulted you, the living God.

[17]It is true, our LORD, that Assyrian kings have turned nations into deserts. [18]They destroyed the idols of wood and stone that the people of those nations had made and worshiped. [19]But you are our LORD and our God! We ask you to keep us safe from the Assyrian king. Then everyone in every kingdom on earth will know that you are the only God.

[35]That same night the LORD sent an angel to the camp of the Assyrians, and he killed one hundred eighty-five thousand of them. And so the next morning, the camp was full of dead bodies. [36]After this King Sennacherib went back to Assyria and lived in the city of Nineveh.

[a]19.15 *winged creatures:* Two creatures made of gold were on the top of the sacred chest and were symbols of the LORD's throne on earth.

Prayer Starter: Protect our nation, dear Lord, and bless our country. Keep us safe from war.

Memory Verse: Our God says, "Calm down, and learn that I am God! All nations on earth will honor me."   —*Psalm 46.10*

Hezekiah's Guests

About this time, Hezekiah got sick and was almost dead. Isaiah the prophet went in and told him, "The LORD says you won't ever get well. You are going to die, so you had better start doing what needs to be done."

²Hezekiah turned toward the wall and prayed. ³"Don't forget that I have been faithful to you, LORD. I have obeyed you with all my heart, and I do whatever you say is right." After this he cried hard.

[7]Then Isaiah said to the king's servants, "Bring some mashed figs and place them on the king's open sore. He will then get well."

[8]Hezekiah asked Isaiah, "Can you prove that the LORD will heal me, so that I can worship in his temple in three days?"

[9]Isaiah replied, "The LORD will prove to you that he will keep his promise. Will the shadow made by the setting sun on the stairway go forward ten steps or back ten steps?"[a]

[10]"It's normal for the sun to go forward," Hezekiah answered. "But how can it go back?"

[11]Isaiah prayed, and the LORD made the shadow go back ten steps on the stairway built for King Ahaz.[b]

[12]Merodach[c] Baladan, the son of Baladan, was now king of Babylonia.[d] And when he learned that Hezekiah had been sick, he sent messengers with letters and a gift for him. [13]Hezekiah welcomed[e] the messengers and showed them all the silver, the gold, the spices, and the fine oils that were in his storehouse. He even showed them where he kept his weapons. Nothing in his palace or in his entire kingdom was kept hidden from them.

[14]Isaiah asked Hezekiah, "Where did these men come from? What did they want?"

"They came all the way from Babylonia," Hezekiah answered.

[15]"What did you show them?" Isaiah asked.

Hezekiah answered, "I showed them everything in my kingdom."

[16]Then Isaiah told Hezekiah:

I have a message for you from the LORD. [17]One day everything you and your ancestors have stored up will be taken to Babylonia. The LORD has promised that nothing will be left. [18]Some of your own sons will be taken to Babylonia, where they will be disgraced and made to serve in the king's palace.

[19]Hezekiah thought, "At least our nation will be at peace for a while." So he told Isaiah, "The message you brought me from the LORD is good."

[a]20.9 *Will . . . steps:* One possible meaning for the difficult Hebrew text. [b]20.11 *the shadow . . . Ahaz:* One possible meaning for the difficult Hebrew text. [c]20.12 *Merodach:* The Hebrew text has "Berodach," another spelling of the name. [d]20.12 *Merodach Baladan . . . Babylonia:* Ruled Babylonia 722–710 and 704–703 B.C. [e]20.13 *welcomed:* Or "listened to."

Prayer Starter: You know the future, Lord. Guide me day by day.

Memory Verse: The LORD is constantly watching . . .
—*2 Chronicles 16.9a*

135

The Book of God's Law

K ing Josiah called together the older leaders of Judah and Jerusalem. [2]Then he went to the LORD's temple, together with the people of Judah and Jerusalem, the priests, and the prophets. Finally, when everybody was there, he read aloud *The Book of God's Law*[a] that had been found in the temple.

[3]After Josiah had finished reading, he stood by one of the columns. He asked the people to promise in the LORD's name to faithfully obey the LORD and to follow his commands. The people agreed to do everything written in the book.

[4]Josiah told Hilkiah the priest, the assistant priests, and the guards at the temple door to go into the temple and bring out the things used to worship Baal, Asherah, and the stars. Josiah had these things burned in Kidron Valley just outside Jerusalem, and he had the ashes carried away to the town of Bethel.

[24]Josiah got rid of every disgusting person and thing in Judah and Jerusalem—including magicians, fortune-tellers, and idols. He did his best to obey every law written in the book that the priest Hilkiah found in the LORD's temple. [25]No other king before or after Josiah tried as hard as he did to obey the Law of Moses.

[a]23.2 *The Book of God's Law:* The Hebrew text has "The Book of God's Agreement." In traditional translations this is called "The Book of the Covenant."

Prayer Starter: Help me to try hard to obey your Word. And give me strength to live a holy life.

Memory Verse: The LORD is constantly watching everyone . . .

—2 Chronicles 16.9a

The Three Warriors

Davia moved to the fortress—that's why it's called the City of David. ⁸He had the city rebuilt, starting at the landfill on the east side.ᵃ Meanwhile, Joab supervised the repairs to the rest of the city.

⁹David became a great and strong ruler, because the LORD All-Powerful was on his side.

¹⁰The LORD had promised that David would become king, and so everyone in Israel gave David their support. Certain warriors also helped keep his kingdom strong.

¹¹The first of these warriors was Jashobeam the son of Hachmoni, the leader of the Three Warriors.ᵇ In one battle he killed three hundred men with his spear.

¹²Another one of the Three Warriors was Eleazar son of Dodo the Aho-

hite. ¹³During a battle against the Philistines at Pas-Dammim, all the Israelites soldiers ran away, ¹⁴except Eleazar, who stayed with David. They took their positions in a nearby barley field and defeated the Philistines! The LORD gave Israel a great victory that day.

¹⁵One time the Three Warriorsᶜ went to meet David among the rocks at Adullam Cave. The Philistine army had set up camp in Rephaim Valley ¹⁶and had taken over Bethlehem. David was in a

fortress, ¹⁷and he said, "I'm very thirsty. I wish I had a drink of water from the well by the gate to Bethlehem."

¹⁸The Three Warriors sneaked through the Philistine camp and got some water from the well near Bethlehem's gate. They took it back to David, but he refused to drink it. Instead, he poured out the water as a sacrifice to the LORD.

ᵃ11.8 *the landfill on the east side:* The Hebrew text has "the Millo," which probably refers to a landfill to strengthen and extend the hill where the city was built. ᵇ11.11 *the Three Warriors:* One ancient translation; Hebrew "the Thirty Warriors." The "Three Warriors" was the most honored group of warriors and may have been part of the "Thirty Warriors." "Three" and "thirty" are spelled almost the same in Hebrew, so there is some confusion in the manuscripts as to which group is being talked about in some places in the following lists. ᶜ11.15 *the Three Warriors:* Hebrew "three of the thirty most important warriors."

Prayer Starter: You are so strong, dear Lord, that I can be brave when you are near me. I love you. I thank you.

Memory Verse: The LORD is constantly watching everyone, and he gives strength . . .
—*2 Chronicles 16.9a*

Solomon's Wealth

Solomon made two hundred gold shields that weighed about seven and a half pounds each. [17]His throne was made of ivory and covered with pure gold. [18]It had a gold footstool attached to it and armrests on each side. There was a statue of a lion on each side of the throne, [19]and there were two lion statues on each of the six steps leading up to the throne. No other throne in the world was like Solomon's.

[20]Solomon's cups and dishes in Forest Hall were made of pure gold, because silver was almost worthless in those days.

[21]Solomon had a lot of seagoing ships.[a] Every three years he sent them out with Hiram's ships to bring back gold, silver, and ivory, as well as monkeys and peacocks.[b]

[22]Solomon was the richest and wisest king in the world. [23-24]Year after year, other kings came to hear the wisdom God had given him. And they brought gifts of silver and gold, as well as clothes, weapons, spices, horses, and mules.

[a]9.21 *seagoing ships:* The Hebrew text has "ships of Tarshish," which may have been a Phoenician city in Spain. "Ships of Tarshish" probably means large, seagoing ships. [b]9.21 *peacocks:* Or "baboons."

Prayer Starter: Keep me from loving money too much, Lord. Teach me to love your Word.

Memory Verse: The LORD is constantly watching everyone, and he gives strength to those who . . . —*2 Chronicles 16.9a*

Jehoshaphat's Ships

Jehoshaphat son of Asa became king and strengthened his defenses against Israel. ²He assigned troops to the fortified cities in Judah, as well as to other towns in Judah and to those towns in Ephraim that his father Asa had captured.

³⁻⁴When Jehoshaphat's father had first become king of Judah, he was faithful to the LORD and refused to worship the god Baal as the kings of Israel did. Jehoshaphat followed his father's example and obeyed and worshiped the LORD. And so the LORD blessed Jehoshaphat ⁵and helped him keep firm control of his kingdom. The people of Judah brought gifts to Jehoshaphat, but even after he became very rich and respected, ⁶he remained completely faithful to the LORD. He destroyed all the local shrinesᵃ in Judah, including the places where the goddess Asherah was worshiped.

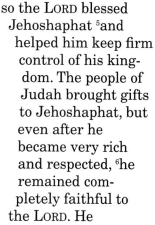

20 Jehoshaphat was thirty-five years old when he became king of Judah, and he ruled from Jerusalem for twenty-five years. His mother was Azubah daughter of Shilhi. ³²Jehoshaphat obeyed the LORD, just as his father Asa had done, ³³but he did not destroy the local shrines.ᵇ So the people still worshiped foreign gods, instead of faithfully serving the God their ancestors had worshiped.

³⁴Everything else Jehoshaphat did while he was king is written in the records of Jehu son of Hanani that are included in *The History of the Kings of Israel.*

ᵃ17.6 *local shrines:* The Hebrew text has "high places," which were local places to worship foreign gods. ᵇ20.33 *local shrines:* The Hebrew text has "high places," which were local places to worship foreign gods.

Prayer Starter: God, I know you are Lord of the winds and waves and storms. Thank you for your mighty power.

Memory Verse: The LORD is constantly watching everyone, and he gives strength to those who faithfully obey him. —*2 Chronicles 16.9a*

The Prophet Micaiah

One day, Jehoshaphat went to visit Ahab in his capital city of Samaria. Ahab slaughtered sheep and cattle and prepared a big feast to honor Jehoshaphat and the officials with him. Ahab talked about attacking the city of Ramoth in Gilead,[a] ³and finally asked, "Jehoshaphat, would you go with me to attack Ramoth?"

"Yes," Jehoshaphat answered. "My army is at your command. ⁴But first let's ask the LORD what to do."

⁵Ahab sent for four hundred prophets and asked, "Should I attack the city of Ramoth?"

"Yes!" the prophets answered. "God will help you capture the city."

⁶But Jehashaphat said, "Just to make sure, is there another of the LORD's prophets we can ask?"

⁷"We could ask Micaiah son of Imlah," Ahab said. "But I hate Micaiah. He always has bad news for me."

"Don't say that!" Jehoshaphat replied. ⁸Then Ahab sent someone to bring Micaiah as soon as possible.

⁹All this time, Ahab and Jehoshaphat were dressed in their royal robes and were seated on their thrones at the threshing place near the gate of Samaria, listening to the prophets tell them what the LORD had said.

¹⁰Zedekiah son of Chenaanah was one of the prophets. He had made some horns out of iron and shouted, "Ahab, the LORD says you will attack the Syrians like a bull with iron horns and wipe them out!"

¹¹All the prophets agreed that Ahab should attack the Syrians at Ramoth and promised that the LORD would help him defeat them.

¹²Meanwhile, the messenger who went to get Micaiah whispered, "Micaiah, all the prophets have good news for Ahab. Now go and say the same thing."

¹³"I'll say whatever the living LORD my God tells me to say," Micaiah replied.

¹⁴Then Micaiah went up to Ahab, who asked, "Micaiah, should we attack Ramoth?"

"Yes!" Micaiah answered. "The LORD will help you capture the city."

¹⁵Ahab shouted, "Micaiah, I've told you over and over to tell me the truth! What does the LORD really say?"

¹⁶Micaiah answered, "In a vision[b] I saw Israelite soldiers wandering around, lost in the hills like sheep without a shepherd. The LORD said, 'These troops have no leader. They should go home and not fight.'"

¹⁷Ahab turned to Jehoshaphat and said, "I told you he would bring me bad news!"

a18.2 *attacking the city of Ramoth in Gilead:* The Syrians had taken control of Ramoth. b18.16 *vision:* In ancient times, prophets often told about future events from what they had seen in visions or dreams.

Prayer Starter: Help me to be truthful, God. Make me honest, and keep me from telling lies.

Joash was only seven years old when he became king of Judah, and he ruled forty years from Jerusalem. His mother Zibiah was from the town of Beersheba.

²While Jehoiada the priest was alive, Joash obeyed the LORD by doing right. ³Jehoiada even chose two women for Joash to marry so he could have a family.

⁴Some time later, Joash decided it was time to repair the temple. ⁵He called together the priests and Levites and said, "Go everywhere in Judah and collect the annual tax from the people. I want this done right away—we need that money to repair the temple."

But the Levites were in no hurry to follow the king's orders. ⁶So he sent for Jehoiada the high priest and asked, "Why didn't you send the Levites to collect the taxes? The LORD's servant Moses and the people agreed long ago that this tax would be collected and used to pay for the upkeep of the sacred tent. ⁷And now we need it to repair the temple because the sons of that evil woman Athaliah came in and wrecked it. They even used some of the sacred objects to worship the god Baal."

⁸Joash gave orders for a wooden box to be made and had it placed outside, near the gate of the temple. ⁹He then sent letters everywhere in

Judah and Jerusalem, asking everyone to bring their taxes to the temple, just as Moses had required their ancestors to do.

[10]The people and their leaders agreed, and they brought their money to Jerusalem and placed it in the box. [11]Each day, after the Levites took the box into the temple, the king's secretary and the high priest's assistant would dump out the money and count it. Then the empty box would be taken back outside.

This happened day after day, and soon a large amount of money was collected. [12]Joash and Jehoiada turned the money over to the men who were supervising the repairs to the temple. They used the money to hire stonecutters, carpenters, and experts in working with iron and bronze.

[13]These workers went right to work repairing the temple, and when they were finished, it looked as good as new. [14]They did not use all the tax money for the repairs, so the rest of it was handed over to Joash and Jehoiada, who then used it to make dishes and other gold and silver objects for the temple.

Sacrifices to please the LORD[a] were offered regularly in the temple for as long as Jehoiada lived. [15]He died at the ripe old age of one hundred thirty years, [16]and he was buried in the royal tombs in Jerusalem, because he had done so much good for the people of Israel, for God, and for the temple.

[a]24.14 *Sacrifices to please the* LORD: These sacrifices have traditionally been called "whole burnt offerings," because the whole animal was burned on the altar. A main purpose of such sacrifices was to please the LORD with the smell of the sacrifice, and so in the CEV they are often called "sacrifices to please the LORD."

Prayer Starter: Thank you for our church, dear Lord. Please give wise and godly hearts to our church leaders.

Memory Verse: LORD God of heaven, you are great . . .
—*Nehemiah 1.5*

Uzziah

After the death of King Amaziah, the people of Judah crowned his son Uzziah[a] king, even though he was only sixteen at the time. Uzziah ruled fifty-two years from Jerusalem, the hometown of his mother Jecoliah. During his rule, he recaptured and rebuilt the town of Elath.

[15]God helped Uzziah become more and more powerful, and he was famous all over the world.

[16]Uzziah became proud of his power, and this led to his downfall.

One day, Uzziah disobeyed the LORD his God by going into the temple and burning incense as an offering to him.[b] [17]Azariah the priest and eighty other brave priests followed Uzziah into the temple [18]and said, "Your Majesty, this isn't right! You are not allowed to burn incense to the LORD. That must be done only by priests who are descendants of Aaron. You will have to leave! You have sinned against the LORD, and so he will no longer bless you."

[19]Uzziah, who was standing next to the incense altar at the time, was holding the incense burner, ready to offer incense to the LORD. He became very angry when he heard Azariah's warning, and leprosy[c] suddenly appeared on his forehead! [20]Azariah and the other priests saw it and immediately told him to leave the temple. Uzziah realized that the LORD had punished him, so he hurried to get outside.

[a]26.1-3 *Uzziah:* In the parallel passages, he is called "Azariah." One of these names was probably his birth name, while the other was his name after he became king. [b]26.16 *going into the temple and burning incense as an offering to him:* This was to be done only by priests. [c]26.19 *leprosy:* The word translated "leprosy" was used for many different kinds of skin diseases.

Prayer Starter: Keep me from becoming proud and thinking too highly of myself. May I always put you first.

Memory Verse: LORD God of heaven, you are great and fearsome. . . .
　　　　　　　　　　　　　　　　　　　　　　　　—Nehemiah 1.5

Ahaz Locks the Temple Doors

Ahaz was nothing like his ancestor David. Ahaz disobeyed the LORD ²and was as sinful as the kings of Israel. He made idols of the god Baal, ³and he offered sacrifices in Hinnom Valley. ⁴Ahaz offered sacrifices at the local shrines,ᵃ as well as on every hill and in the shade of large trees.

²²Even after all these terrible things happened to Ahaz, he sinned against the LORD even worse than before. ²³He said to himself, "The Syrian gods must have helped their kings defeat me. Maybe if I offer sacrifices to those gods, they will help me." That was the sin that finally led to the downfall of Ahaz, as well as to the destruction of Judah.

²⁴Ahaz collected all the furnishings of the temple and smashed them to pieces. Then he locked the doors to the temple and set up altars to foreign gods on every street corner in Jerusalem.

ᵃ28.4 *local shrines:* The Hebrew text has "high places," which were local places to worship foreign gods.

Prayer Starter: The doors of my heart are open to you, O Lord. Never let them close.

Memory Verse: LORD God of heaven, you are great and fearsome. And you faithfully keep your promises . . .   *—Nehemiah 1.5*

Nehemiah Before the King

During the month of Nisan[a] in the twentieth year that Artaxerxes was king, I served him his wine, as I had done before. But this was the first time I had ever looked depressed. ²So the king said, "Why do you look so sad? You're not sick. Something must be bothering you."

Even though I was frightened, ³I answered, "Your Majesty, I hope you live forever! I feel sad because the city where my ancestors are buried is in ruins, and its gates have been burned down."

⁴The king asked, "What do you want me to do?"

I prayed to the God who rules from heaven. ⁵Then I told the king, "Sir, if it's all right with you, please send me back to Judah, so that I can rebuild the city where my ancestors are buried."

⁶The queen was sitting beside the king when he asked me, "How long will it take, and when will you be back?" The king agreed to let me go, and I told him when I would return.

⁷Then I asked, "Your Majesty, would you be willing to give me letters to the governors of the provinces west of the Euphrates River, so that I can travel safely to Judah? ⁸I will need timber to rebuild the gates of the fortress near the temple and more timber to construct the city wall and to build a place for me to live. And so, I would appreciate a letter to Asaph, who is in charge of the royal forces." God was good to me, and the king did everything I asked.

[a]2.1 *Nisan:* Or Abib, the first month of the Hebrew calendar, from about mid-March to mid-April.

Prayer Starter: Lord God of heaven, you are great, and you faithfully keep your promises.

Memory Verse: LORD God of heaven, you are great and fearsome. And you faithfully keep your promises to everyone who loves you.

—Nehemiah 1.5

Rebuilding Jerusalem's Walls

Three days after arriving in Jerusalem, ¹²I got up during the night and left my house. I took some men with me, without telling anyone what I thought God wanted me to do for the city. The only animal I took was the donkey I rode on. ¹³I went through Valley Gate on the west, then south past Dragon Spring, before coming to Garbage Gate. As I rode along, I took a good look at the crumbled walls of the city and the gates that had been torn down and burned. ¹⁴On the east side of the city, I headed north to Fountain Gate and King's Pool, but then the trail became too narrow for my donkey. ¹⁵So I went down to Kidron Valley and looked at the wall from there. Then before daylight I returned to the city through Valley Gate.

¹⁶None of the city officials knew what I had in mind. And I had not even told any of the Jews—not the priests, the leaders, the officials, or any other Jews who would be helping in the work. ¹⁷But when I got back, I said to them, "Jerusalem is truly in a mess! The gates have been torn down and burned, and everything is in ruins. We must rebuild the city wall so that we can again take pride in our city."

¹⁸Then I told them how kind God had been and what the king had said.

Immediately, they replied, "Let's start building now!" So they got everything ready.

Prayer Starter: Make me a hard worker, dear Lord.

Memory Verse: Surrender your heart to God . . .   *—Job 11.13–14*

Queen Esther

Mordecai had a very beautiful cousin named Esther, whose Hebrew name was Hadassah. He had raised her as his own daughter, after her father and mother died. [8]When the king ordered the search for beautiful women, many were taken to the king's palace in Susa, and Esther was one of them.

Hegai was put in charge of all the women, [9]and from the first day, Esther was his favorite. He began her beauty treatments at once. He also gave her plenty of food and seven special maids from the king's palace, and they had the best rooms.

[10]Mordecai had warned Esther not to tell anyone that she was a Jew, and she obeyed him. [11]He was anxious to see how Esther was getting along and to learn what had happened to her. So each day he would walk back and forth in front of the court where the women lived.

[12]The young women were given beauty treatments for one whole year. The first six months their skin was rubbed with olive oil and myrrh, and the last six months it was treated with perfumes and cosmetics. Then each of them spent the night alone with King Xerxes.

[15-16]Xerxes had been king for seven years when Esther's turn came to go to him during Tebeth,[a] the tenth month of the year. Everyone liked Esther. The king's personal servant Hegai was in charge of the women, and Esther trusted Hegai and asked him what she ought to take with her.[b]

[17]Xerxes liked Esther more than he did any of the other young women. None of them pleased him as much as she did, and right away he fell in love with her and crowned her queen in place of Vashti. [18]In honor of Esther he gave a big dinner for his leaders and officials. Then he declared a holiday everywhere in his kingdom and gave expensive gifts.

[a]2.15,16 *Tebeth:* The tenth month of the Hebrew calendar, from about mid-December to mid-January. [b]2.15,16 *her:* The Hebrew text adds, "Esther was the daughter of Abihail and was the cousin of Mordecai, who had adopted her after her parents died."

Prayer Starter: Heavenly Father, I believe you guide world rulers even when they don't know it. Bless our nation and our leaders today.

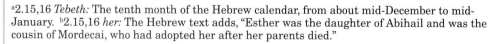

Memory Verse: Surrender your heart to God, turn to him in prayer . . .
— *Job 11.13–14*

Save My People

Mordecai gave Hathach a copy of the orders for the murder of the Jews and told him that these had been read in Susa. He said, "Show this to Esther and explain what it means. Ask her to go to the king and beg him to have pity on her people, the Jews!"

⁹Hathach went back to Esther and told her what Mordecai had said. ¹⁰She answered, "Tell Mordecai ¹¹there is a law about going in to see the king, and all his officials and his people know about this law. Anyone who goes in to see the king without being invited by him will be put to death. The only way that anyone can be saved is for the king to hold out the gold scepter to that person.

5 Three days later, Esther dressed in her royal robes and went to the inner court of the palace in front of the throne. The king was sitting there, facing the open doorway. ²He was happy to see Esther, and he held out the gold scepter to her.

7 The king and Haman were dining with Esther ²and drinking wine during the second dinner, when the king again said, "Esther, what can I do for you? Just ask, and I will give you as much as half of my kingdom!"

³Esther answered, "Your Majesty, if you really care for me and are willing to help, you can save me and my people. That's what I really want, ⁴because a reward has been promised to anyone who kills my people. Your Majesty, if we were merely going to be sold as slaves, I would not have bothered you."ᵃ

⁵"Who would dare to do such a thing?" the king asked.

⁶Esther replied, "That evil Haman is the one out to get us!"

Haman was terrified, as he looked at the king and the queen.

⁷The king was so angry that he got up, left his wine, and went out into the palace garden.

Haman realized that the king had already decided what to do with him, and he stayed and begged Esther to save his life.

ᵃ7.4 *I would . . . bothered you:* One possible meaning for the difficult Hebrew text.

Prayer Starter: Please help me to do the right thing always, especially during times when I am afraid.

Memory Verse: Surrender your heart to God, turn to him in prayer, and give up your sins . . .
—*Job 11.13–14*

Job Loses Everything

Many years ago, a man named Job lived in the land of Uz.[a] He was a truly good person, who respected God and refused to do evil.

[2]Job had seven sons and three daughters. [3]He owned seven thousand sheep, three thousand camels, five hundred pair of oxen, five hundred donkeys, and a large number of servants. He was the richest person in the East.

2 When the angels[b] gathered around the LORD again, Satan[c] was there with them, [2]and the LORD asked, "Satan, where have you been?"

Satan replied, "I have been going all over the earth."

[3]Then the LORD asked, "What do you think of my servant Job? No one on earth is like him—he is a truly good person, who respects me and refuses to do evil. And he hasn't changed, even though you persuaded me to destroy him for no reason."

[4]Satan answered, "There's no pain like your own.[d] People will do anything to stay alive. [5]Try striking Job's own body with pain, and he will curse you to your face."

[6]"All right!" the LORD replied. "Make Job suffer as much as you want, but just don't kill him." [7]Satan left and caused painful sores to break out all over Job's body—from head to toe.

[8]Then Job sat on the ash-heap to show sorrow. And while he was scraping his sores with a broken piece of pottery, [9]his wife asked, "Why do you still trust God? Why don't you curse him and die?"

[10]Job replied, "Don't talk like a fool! If we accept blessings from God, we must accept trouble as well." In all that happened, Job never once said anything against God.

---

[a]1.1 *Uz:* The exact location of this place is unknown, though it was possibly somewhere in northwest Arabia. [b]2.1 *angels:* The angels and others who gather to discuss matters with God. [c]2.1 *Satan:* Hebrew "the accuser." [d]2.4 *There's no pain like your own:* The Hebrew text has "Skin for skin," which was probably a popular saying.

Prayer Starter: Keep me from being a complainer, Lord. Give me a good attitude in everything.

Memory Verse: Surrender your heart to God, turn to him in prayer, and give up your sins—even those you do . . .   *—Job 11.13–14*

**God Speaks
from a
Storm**

From out of a storm, the LORD said to Job:
² Why do you talk so much
　　　when you know so little?
³ 　　Now get ready to face me!
　Can you answer the questions I ask?
⁴ How did I lay the foundation for the earth?
　　　Were you there?

⁵ Doubtless you know who decided its length and width.
⁶ What supports the foundation? Who placed the cornerstone,
⁷   while morning stars sang, and angels rejoiced?

⁸ When the ocean was born, I set its boundaries
⁹   and wrapped it in blankets of thickest fog.
¹⁰ Then I built a wall around it, locked the gates, ¹¹and said,
    "Your powerful waves stop here! They can go no farther."

¹² Did you ever tell the sun to rise?
    And did it obey?

¹⁶ Job, have you ever walked on the ocean floor?

³¹ Can you arrange stars in groups
    such as Orion and the Pleiades?
³² Do you control the stars or set in place the Big Dipper
    and the Little Dipper?
³³ Do you know the laws
that govern the heavens,
    and can you make them rule
    the earth?
³⁴ Can you order the clouds
to send a downpour,
³⁵   or will lightning flash
    at your command?
³⁶ Did you teach birds to know
that rain or floods
    are on their way?[a]
³⁷ Can you count the clouds or pour out their water
³⁸   on the dry, lumpy soil?

40 Job said to the LORD:
⁴Who am I to answer you?

[a]38.36 *way:* One possible meaning for the difficult Hebrew text of verse 36.

Prayer Starter: Thank you for thunder and lightning and wind and storms—signs of your power, dear Lord.

Memory Verse: Surrender your heart to God, turn to him in prayer, and give up your sins—even those you do in secret.   *—Job 11.13–14*

153

> W hy are you far away, Lord?
>   Why do you hide yourself
>   when I am in trouble?
> 2 Proud and brutal people hunt down the poor.
>   But let them get caught
>   by their own evil plans!

Do Something, Lord

3 The wicked brag about their deepest desires.
  Those greedy people hate and curse you, Lord.
4 The wicked are too proud to turn to you
  or even think about you.
5 They are always successful,
  though they can't understand your teachings,
    and they keep sneering at their enemies.

⁶ In their hearts they say, "Nothing can hurt us!
    We'll always be happy and free from trouble."
⁷ They curse and tell lies, and all they talk about
    is how to be cruel or how to do wrong.

⁸ They hide outside villages,
    waiting to strike and murder some innocent victim.
⁹ They are hungry lions hiding in the bushes,
    hoping to catch some helpless passerby.
They trap the poor in nets and drag them away.
¹⁰ They crouch down and wait to grab a victim.
¹¹   They say, "God can't see! He's got on a blindfold."

¹² Do something, LORD God,
    and use your powerful arm to help those in need.
¹³ The wicked don't respect you.
    In their hearts they say, "God won't punish us!"

¹⁴ But you see the trouble and the distress,
    and you will do something.
The poor can count on you, and so can orphans.
¹⁵ Now break the arms of all merciless people.
    Punish them for doing wrong and make them stop.

¹⁶ Our LORD, you will always rule,
    but nations will vanish from the earth.
¹⁷ You listen to the longings of those who suffer.
You offer them hope,
    and you pay attention to their cries for help.
¹⁸ You defend orphans and everyone else in need,
    so that no one on earth can terrify others again.

Prayer Starter: Do something, Lord God, to help those in need.

Memory Verse: You, LORD, are my shepherd. . . .   — *Psalm 23.1–2*

My Shepherd

Yºu, Lᴏʀᴅ, are my shepherd.
I will never be in need.
2   You let me rest in fields of green grass.
You lead me to streams of peaceful water,
3   and you refresh my life.

You are true to your name,
and you lead me along the right paths.
4 I may walk through valleys as dark as death,
but I won't be afraid.
You are with me,
and your shepherd's rodª makes me feel safe.

5 You treat me to a feast, while my enemies watch.
You honor me as your guest,
and you fill my cup until it overflows.

6 Your kindness and love will always be with me
each day of my life,
and I will live forever in your house, Lᴏʀᴅ.

ª23.4 *shepherd's rod:* The Hebrew text mentions two objects carried by the shepherd: a club to defend against wild animals and a long pole to guide and control the sheep.

Prayer Starter: Thank you for being my shepherd, O Lord. May your kindness and love always be with me.

Memory Verse: You, Lᴏʀᴅ, are my shepherd. I will never be in need. . . .
— Psalm 23.1–2

We Worship
You, Lord

Our God, you bless everyone
whose sins you forgive and wipe away.
² You bless them by saying,
"You told me your sins, without trying to hide them,
and now I forgive you."

³ Before I confessed my sins, my bones felt limp,
and I groaned all day long.
⁴ Night and day your hand weighed heavily on me,
and my strength was gone as in the summer heat.

⁵ So I confessed my sins and told them all to you.
I said, "I'll tell the LORD each one of my sins."
Then you forgave me and took away my guilt.

⁶ We worship you, Lord, and we should always pray
whenever we find out that we have sinned.ᵃ
Then we won't be swept away by a raging flood.
⁷ You are my hiding place! You protect me from trouble,
and you put songs in my heart
because you have saved me.

⁸ You said to me, "I will point out the road
    that you should follow.
I will be your teacher and watch over you.
⁹ Don't be stupid like horses and mules
    that must be led with ropes to make them obey."

¹⁰ All kinds of troubles will strike the wicked,
    but your kindness shields those who trust you, LORD.
¹¹ And so your good people should celebrate and shout.

ᵃ32.6 *whenever . . . sinned:* Hebrew "at a time of finding only."

Prayer Starter: Forgive my sins today, O Lord, and wipe them away. Show me the road that I should follow.

Memory Verse: You, LORD, are my shepherd. I will never be in need. You let me rest . . .
    — Psalm 23.1–2

Thirsty for God

A s a deer gets thirsty for streams of water,
     I truly am thirsty for you, my God.
2 In my heart, I am thirsty for you, the living God.
     When will I see your face?
3 Day and night my tears are my only food,
     as everyone keeps asking, "Where is your God?"

4 Sorrow floods my heart, when I remember
leading the worshipers to your house.[a]
     I can still hear them shout their joyful praises.
5 Why am I discouraged? Why am I restless?
I trust you! And I will praise you again
     because you help me, 6and you are my God.

I am deeply discouraged as I think about you
from where the Jordan begins at Mount Hermon
     and from Mount Mizar.[b]
7 Your vicious waves have swept over me
     like an angry ocean
     or a roaring waterfall.

8 Every day, you are kind,
and at night
you give me a song
     as my prayer to you,
     the living LORD God.

9 You are my mighty rock.[c] Why have you forgotten me?
     Why must enemies mistreat me and make me sad?
10 Even my bones are in pain,
while all day long my enemies sneer and ask,
     "Where is your God?"

11 Why am I discouraged? Why am I restless?
I trust you! And I will praise you again
     because you help me, and you are my God.

[a]42.4 *leading . . . house:* One possible meaning for the difficult Hebrew text. [b]42.6 *Mount Mizar:* The location is not known. [c]42.9 *mighty rock:* The Hebrew text has "rock," which is sometimes used in poetry to compare the Lord to a mountain where his people can run for protection from their enemies.

Prayer Starter: Make me thirsty for you, Lord, like a deer by streams of water.

Memory Verse: You, LORD, are my shepherd. I will never be in need. You let me rest in fields of green grass. . . .   — *Psalm 23.1–2*

You Send
Showers
of Rain

Our God, you deserve[a] praise in Zion,
      where we keep our promises to you.
2 Everyone will come to you
      because you answer prayer.
3   Our terrible sins get us down,
         but you forgive us.
4 You bless your chosen ones, and you invite them
      to live near you in your temple.
We will enjoy your house, the sacred temple.

5 Our God, you save us, and your fearsome deeds
      answer our prayers for justice!
You give hope to people everywhere on earth,
      even those across the sea.
6 You are strong,
      and your mighty power put the mountains in place.
7 You silence the roaring waves
      and the noisy shouts of the nations.
8 People far away marvel
      at your fearsome deeds,
and all who live under the sun
      celebrate and sing
      because of you.

9 You take care of the earth
and send rain
      to help the soil grow all kinds of crops.
Your rivers never run dry,
      and you prepare the earth to produce much grain.
10 You water all of its fields and level the lumpy ground.
You send showers of rain to soften the soil
      and help the plants sprout.
11 Wherever your footsteps touch the earth,
      a rich harvest is gathered.
12 Desert pastures blossom, and mountains celebrate.
13 Meadows are filled with sheep and goats;
         valleys overflow with grain
         and echo with joyful songs.

[a]65.1 *deserve:* One possible meaning for the difficult Hebrew text.

Prayer Starter: I praise you, Father, for hearing and answering my prayers and meeting all my needs.

Memory Verse: You, LORD, are my shepherd. I will never be in need. You let me rest in fields of green grass. You lead me to streams of peaceful water.
                                                              — *Psalm 23.1–2*

His Love
Never Fails

With all my heart I praise the LORD,
and with all that I am
I praise his holy name!
² With all my heart I praise the LORD!
I will never forget how kind he has been.

³ The LORD forgives our sins,
heals us when we are sick,
⁴ and protects us from death.
His kindness and love are a crown on our heads.
⁵ Each day that we live,ᵃ he provides for our needs.
and gives us the strength of a young eagle.

⁶ For all who are mistreated, the LORD brings justice.
⁷ He taught his Law to Moses
and showed all Israel what he could do.

⁸ The LORD is merciful! He is kind and patient,
and his love never fails.
⁹ The LORD won't always be angry and point out our sins;
¹⁰ he doesn't punish us as our sins deserve.

¹¹ How great is God's love for all who worship him?
Greater than the distance between heaven and earth!
¹² How far has the LORD taken our sins from us?
Farther than the distance from east to west!

¹³ Just as parents are kind to their children,
the LORD is kind to all who worship him,
¹⁴ because he knows we are made of dust.
¹⁵ We humans are like grass
or wild flowers that quickly bloom.
¹⁶ But a scorching wind blows,
and they quickly wither
to be forever forgotten.

¹⁷ The LORD is always kind
to those who worship him,
and he keeps his promises to their descendants
¹⁸ who faithfully obey him.

ᵃ103.5 *Each . . . live:* One possible meaning for the difficult Hebrew text.

Prayer Starter: With all my heart I praise you, Lord, and with all that I am I praise your holy name.

Memory Verse: With all my heart . . .
—Psalm 103.1

**Teach Me
Your Laws**

O ur LORD, you bless everyone
  who lives right and obeys your Law.
² You bless all of those
  who follow your commands
    from deep in their hearts
³   and who never do wrong or turn from you.
⁴ You have ordered us always
  to obey your teachings;
⁵   I don't ever want to stray from your laws.
⁶ Thinking about your commands
  will keep me from doing some foolish thing.
⁷ I will do right and praise you
  by learning to respect your perfect laws.

⁸ I will obey all of them!
  Don't turn your back on me.

⁹ Young people can live a clean life
  by obeying your word.
¹⁰ I worship you with all my heart.
  Don't let me walk away
    from your commands.
¹¹ I treasure your word above all else;
  it keeps me from sinning against you,
¹² I praise you, LORD! Teach me your laws.
¹³ With my own mouth,
  I tell others the laws that you have spoken.
¹⁴ Obeying your instructions brings as much happiness
  as being rich.
¹⁵ I will study your teachings and follow your footsteps.
¹⁶ I will take pleasure in your laws and remember your words.

¹⁷ Treat me with kindness, LORD,
  so that I may live and do what you say.
¹⁸ Open my mind
  and let me discover the wonders of your Law.
¹⁹ I live here as a stranger.
  Don't keep me from knowing your commands.
²⁰ What I want most of all and at all times
  is to honor your laws.
²⁴ Your laws are my greatest joy! I follow their advice.

Prayer Starter: Lord, enable me to treasure your words above all else, so that I will not sin against you.

Memory Verse: With all my heart I praise the LORD . . .   *—Psalm 103.1*

**Come Praise
the Lord**

Shout praises to the LORD!
   Shout the LORD's praise
   in the highest heavens.
² All of you angels, and all who serve him above,
   come and offer praise.

³ Sun and moon, and all of you bright stars,
   come and offer praise.
⁴ Highest heavens,
   and the water above the highest heavens,ᵃ
   come and offer praise.

⁵ Let all things praise the name of the LORD,
   because they were created at his command.
⁶ He made them to last forever,
   and nothing can change what he has done.ᵇ
⁷ All creatures on earth, you obey his commands,

so come praise the LORD!

8 Sea monsters and the deep sea, fire and hail,
   snow and frost, and every stormy wind,
      come praise the LORD!

9 All mountains and hills, fruit trees and cedars,
10 every wild and tame animal, all reptiles and birds,
      come praise the LORD!

11 Every king and every ruler, all nations on earth,
12 every man and every woman, young people and old,
      come praise the LORD!

a148.4 *the water . . . heavens:* It was believed that the earth and the heavens were surrounded by water. b148.6 *nothing . . . done:* Or "his laws will never change."

Prayer Starter: Thank you, Lord, that the sun, moon, and stars display your majesty and power.

Memory Verse: With all my heart I praise the LORD, and with all . . .
                                                              —*Psalm 103.1*

Celebrate and Worship

Shout praises to the LORD!
Sing him a new song of praise
    when his loyal people meet.
² People of Israel, rejoice because of your Creator.
    People of Zion, celebrate because of your King.
³ Praise his name by dancing
    and playing music on harps and tambourines.
⁴ The LORD is pleased with his people,
    and he gives victory to those who are humble.
⁵ All of you faithful people, praise our glorious Lord!
    Celebrate and worship.
⁶ Praise God with songs on your lips
    and a sword in your hand.
⁷ Take revenge and punish the nations.
⁸   Put chains of iron on their kings and rulers.
⁹ Punish them as they deserve;
    this is the privilege of God's faithful people.
Shout praises to the LORD!

150 Shout praises to the LORD! Praise God in his temple.
    Praise him in heaven, his mighty fortress.
² Praise our God!
    His deeds are wonderful, too marvelous to describe.

³ Praise God with trumpets and all kinds of harps.
⁴ Praise him with tambourines and dancing,
    with stringed instruments and woodwinds.
⁵ Praise God with cymbals, with clashing cymbals.
⁶ Let every living creature praise the LORD.
    Shout praises to the LORD!

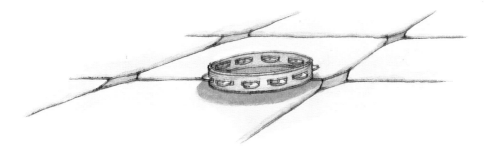

Prayer Starter: I praise you, God, for your deeds are wonderful, too marvelous to describe.

Memory Verse: With all my heart I praise the LORD, and with all that I am . . .
    —Psalm 103.1

The Proverbs of Solomon

These are the proverbs of King Solomon
   of Israel, the son of David.
² Proverbs will teach you wisdom and self-control
      and how to understand sayings
      with deep meanings.
³ You will learn what is right and honest and fair.
⁴ From these, an ordinary person
      can learn to be smart,
and young people can gain knowledge and good sense.

⁵ If you are already wise, you will become even wiser.
   And if you are smart, you will learn to understand
⁶   proverbs and sayings, as well as words of wisdom
      and all kinds of riddles.
⁷ Respect and obey the LORD!
   This is the beginning of knowledge.ᵃ
      Only a fool rejects wisdom and good advice.

8 My child, obey the teachings of your parents,
9 and wear their teachings as you would a lovely hat
    or a pretty necklace.
10 Don't be tempted by sinners or listen [11]when they say,
    "Come on! Let's gang up and kill somebody,
        just for the fun of it!
12 They're well and healthy now,
    but we'll finish them off once and for all.
13 We'll take their valuables
    and fill our homes with stolen goods.
14 If you join our gang, you'll get your share."

15 Don't follow anyone like that or do what they do.
16 They are in a big hurry to commit some crime,
    perhaps even murder.
17 They are like a bird that sees the bait,
    but ignores the trap.[b]
18 They gang up to murder someone,
    but they are the victims.
19 The wealth you get from crime robs you of your life.

3 My child, remember my teachings and instructions
    and obey them completely.
2 They will help you live a long and prosperous life.
3 Let love and loyalty always show like a necklace,
    and write them in your mind.
4 God and people will like you and consider you a success.

5 With all your heart you must trust the LORD
    and not your own judgment.
6 Always let him lead you,
    and he will clear the road for you to follow.
7 Don't ever think that you are wise enough,
    but respect the LORD and stay away from evil.

[a]1.7 *the beginning of knowledge:* Or "what knowledge is all about." [b]1.17 *They are . . . trap:* Or "Be like a bird that won't go for the bait, if it sees the trap."

Prayer Starter: Cause us to respect and obey you Lord, that we may be wise.

Memory Verse: With all my heart I praise the LORD, and with all that I am I praise his holy name! —*Psalm 103.1*

Nuggets
of
Wisdom

Cheating to get rich is a foolish dream
    and no less than suicide.[a]

[7] You destroy yourself by being cruel and violent
    and refusing to live right.

[8] All crooks are liars,
    but anyone who is innocent will do right.

[9] It's better to stay outside
        on the roof of your house
than to live inside with a nagging wife.

[10] Evil people want to do wrong,
    even to their friends.

[11] An ignorant fool learns
    by seeing others punished;
        a sensible person learns by being instructed.

[12] God is always fair! He knows what the wicked do
    and will punish them.

¹³ If you won't help the poor, don't expect to be heard
     when you cry out for help.
¹⁴ A secret bribe will save you from someone's fierce anger.
¹⁵ When justice is done, good citizens are glad
     and crooks are terrified.
¹⁶ If you stop using good sense,
     you will find yourself in the grave.
¹⁷ Heavy drinkers and others who live only for pleasure
     will lose all they have.

¹⁸ God's people will escape,
     but all who are wicked will pay the price.
¹⁹ It's better out in the desert
     than at home with a nagging, complaining wife.
²⁰ Be sensible and store up precious treasures—
     don't waste them like a fool.
²¹ If you try to be kind and good,
     you will be blessed with life and goodness and honor.
²² One wise person can defeat a city full of soldiers
     and capture their fortress.
²³ Watching what you say can save you a lot of trouble.
²⁴ If you are proud and conceited,
     everyone will say, "You're a snob!"

²⁵ If you want too much and are too lazy to work,
     it could be fatal.
²⁶ But people who obey God are always generous.

[a]21.6 *and ... suicide:* One possible meaning for the difficult Hebrew text.

Prayer Starter: Remind me to help the poor, and to be concerned about those in need.

Memory Verse: Charm can be deceiving . . .   —*Proverbs 31.30*

Use Your Best Manners

W hen you are invited to eat with a king,
use your best manners.
² Don't go and stuff yourself!
That would be just the same
as cutting your throat.
³ Don't be greedy for all of that fancy food!
It may not be so tasty.

⁴ Give up trying so hard
to get rich.
⁵ Your money flies away
before you know it,
just like an eagle
suddenly taking off.

⁶ Don't accept
an invitation to eat
a selfish person's food,
no matter how good
it is.
⁷ People like that
take note
of how much
you eat.ᵃ
They say, "Take all
you want!"
But they don't
mean it.
⁸ Each bite
will come back up,
and all your kind words
will be wasted.

⁹ Don't talk to fools—they will just make fun.

¹⁰ Don't move a boundary markerᵇ
or take the land that belongs to orphans.
¹¹ God All-Powerful is there to defend them against you.

ᵃ23.7 *People . . . eat:* One possible meaning for the difficult Hebrew text. ᵇ23.10 *marker:* In ancient Israel boundary lines were sacred because all property was a gift from the Lord.

Prayer Starter: Lord, help me to use good manners wherever I am.

Memory Verse: Charm can be deceiving, and beauty fades away . . .
—*Proverbs 31.30*

The Most Precious Treasure

A truly good wife is the most precious treasure
a man can find!
¹¹ Her husband depends on her,
and she never lets him down.
¹² She is good to him every day of her life,
¹³ and with her own hands she gladly makes clothes.

¹⁴ She is like a sailing ship
that brings food from across the sea.
¹⁵ She gets up before daylight to prepare food
for her family and for her servants.[a]
¹⁶ She knows how to buy land
and how to plant a vineyard,
¹⁷ and she always works hard.
¹⁸ She knows when to buy or sell,
and she stays busy until late at night.
¹⁹ She spins her own cloth,
²⁰ and she helps the poor and the needy.
²¹ Her family has warm clothing,
and so she doesn't worry when it snows.
²² She does her own sewing,
and everything she wears is beautiful.

²⁴ She makes clothes to sell to the shop owners.
²⁵ She is strong and graceful,[b]
as well as cheerful about the future.
²⁶ Her words are sensible,
and her advice is thoughtful.
²⁷ She takes good care of her family and is never lazy.
²⁸ Her children praise her,
and with great pride her husband says,
²⁹ "There are many good women, but you are the best!"

³⁰ Charm can be deceiving, and beauty fades away,
but a woman who honors the LORD
deserves to be praised.
³¹ Show her respect—
praise her in public for what she has done.

[a]31.15 *and . . . servants:* Or "and to tell her servants what to do." [b]31.25 *She . . . graceful:* Or "The clothes she makes are attractive and of good quality."

Prayer Starter: Teach me, Lord, that loving you is more important than being beautiful.

Memory Verse: Charm can be deceiving, and beauty fades away, but a woman who honors the LORD . . .   *—Proverbs 31.30*

Friends

God makes everything happen at the right time, yet none of us can ever fully understand all he has done, and he puts questions in our minds about the past and the future. [12]I know the best thing we can do is to always enjoy life, [13]because God's gift to us is the happiness we get from our food and drink and from the work we do. [14]Everything God has done will last forever; nothing he does can ever be changed. God has done all this, so that we will worship him.

[15] Everything that happens has happened before,
   and all that will be has already been—
      God does everything over and over again.[a]

4 You are better off to have a friend than to be all alone, because then you will get more enjoyment out of what you earn. [10]If you fall, your friend can help you up. But if you fall without having a friend nearby, you are really in trouble. [11]If you sleep alone, you won't have anyone to keep you warm on a cold night. [12]Someone might be able to beat up one of you, but not both of you. As the saying goes, "A rope made from three strands of cord is hard to break."

[13]You may be poor and young. But if you are wise, you are better off than a foolish old king who won't listen to advice. [14]Even if you were not born into the royal family and have been a prisoner and poor, you can still be king.

[a]3.15 *God does . . . again:* One possible meaning for the difficult Hebrew text.

Prayer Starter: Thank you for being my best friend, dear Lord. Help me to be a good friend to others.

Memory Verse: Charm can be deceiving, and beauty fades away, but a woman who honors the LORD deserves . . .   —*Proverbs 31.30*

Solomon's Beautiful Song

This is Solomon's most beautiful song.

She Speaks:
2 Kiss me tenderly! Your love is better than wine,
3   and you smell so sweet.
All the young women adore you;
    the very mention of your name
is like spreading perfume.
4 Hurry, my king! Let's hurry. 5Take me to your home.

The Young Women Speak:
We are happy for you! And we praise your love
    even more than wine.

She Speaks:
Young women of Jerusalem, it is only right
    that you should adore him.
My skin is dark and beautiful, like a tent in the desert
    or like Solomon's curtains.
6 Don't stare at me just because the sun
    has darkened my skin.
My brothers were angry with me;
they made me work in the vineyard,
    and so I neglected my complexion.

Don't let the other shepherds think badly of me.[a]
7 I'm not one of those women
    who shamelessly follow after shepherds.[b]
My darling, I love you!
Where do you feed your sheep
    and let them rest at noon?

He Speaks:
15 My darling, you are lovely, so very lovely—
    your eyes are those of a dove.

[a]1.6 *Don't . . . me:* One possible meaning for the difficult Hebrew text. [b]1.7 *I'm . . . shepherds:* One possible meaning for the difficult Hebrew text.

Prayer Starter: Thank you for loving me, Lord. And for helping me to love others.

Memory Verse: Charm can be deceiving, and beauty fades away, but a woman who honors the LORD deserves to be praised.
—*Proverbs 31.30*

> **A Lily Among Thorns**

She Speaks:
¹ I am merely a rose[a] from the land of Sharon,
     a lily from the valley.

He Speaks:
² My darling, when compared
     with other young women,
       you are a lily among thorns

She Speaks:
³ And you, my love, are an apple tree
     among trees of the forest.
Your shade brought me pleasure;
     your fruit was sweet.
⁴ You led me to your banquet room
     and showered me with love.
⁵ Refresh and strengthen me
with raisins and apples.
     I am hungry for love!
⁶ Put your left hand under my head
     and embrace me with your right arm.

⁷ Young women of Jerusalem,
promise me by the power of deer and gazelles[b]
     never to awaken love before it is ready.

She Speaks:
⁸ I hear the voice of the one I love,
     as he comes leaping over mountains and hills
⁹   like a deer or a gazelle.
Now he stands outside our wall,
     looking through the window ¹⁰and speaking to me.

He Speaks:
     My darling, I love you! Let's go away together.
¹¹ Winter is past, the rain has stopped;
¹²   flowers cover the earth, it's time to sing.[c]
The cooing of doves is heard in our land.

---

[a]2.1 *rose:* The traditional translation. The exact variety of the flower is not known, though it may have been a crocus. [b]2.7 *deer and gazelles:* Deer and gazelles were sacred animals in some religions of Old Testament times, and they were thought to have special powers. [c]2.12 *sing:* Or "trim the vines."

Prayer Starter: Lord, you are as beautiful to me as a rose from Sharon, as a lily from the valley. I love you.

Isaiah's Message

I am Isaiah, the son of Amoz.
And this is the message[a] that I was given about Judah and Jerusalem when Uzziah, Jotham, Ahaz, and Hezekiah were the kings of Judah:[b]

² The LORD has said, "Listen, heaven and earth!
    The children I raised have turned against me.
³ Oxen and donkeys know who owns
and feeds them,
        but my people
        won't ever learn."

⁴ Israel, you are a sinful nation
        loaded down with guilt.
    You are wicked and corrupt
        and have turned
        from the LORD,
        the holy God of Israel.
⁵ Why be punished more?
    Why not give up your sin?
        Your head
        is badly bruised,
        and you are weak
        all over.
⁶ From your head to your toes
        there isn't a healthy spot.
    Bruises, cuts, and open sores
    go without care
        or oil to ease the pain.

⁷ Your country lies in ruins;
        your towns are in ashes.
    Foreigners and strangers
    take and destroy your land
        while you watch.
⁸ Enemies surround Jerusalem,
    alone like a hut
        in a vineyard[c]
        or in a cucumber field.
⁹ Zion would have disappeared like Sodom and Gomorrah,[d]
    if the LORD All-Powerful had not let a few
        of its people survive.

¹⁵ "No matter how much you pray, I won't listen.
        You are too violent.

¹⁶ Wash yourselves clean!
> I am disgusted with your filthy deeds.
> Stop doing wrong ¹⁷and learn to live right.
> See that justice is done. Defend widows and orphans
>   and help those in need."^e

¹⁸ I, the LORD, invite you to come and talk it over.
> Your sins are scarlet red,
>   but they will be whiter than snow or wool.

^a1.1 *message:* Or "vision." ^b1.1 *kings of Judah:* Uzziah (783–742 B.C.); Jotham (742–735 B.C.); Ahaz (735–715 B.C.); Hezekiah (715–687 B.C.). ^c1.8 *a hut in a vineyard:* When it was almost time for grapes to ripen, farmers would put up a temporary shelter or hut in the field or vineyard and stay there to keep thieves and wild animals away. ^d1.9 *Sodom and Gomorrah:* Two ancient cities of Palestine that God destroyed because the people were so wicked. ^e1.17 *and help those in need:* Or "and punish cruel people."

Prayer Starter: Heavenly Father, thank you for Jesus who died on the cross that my sins could become whiter than snow.

Memory Verse: I, the LORD, invite you to come and talk it over. . . .
—*Isaiah 1.18*

Holy, Holy, Holy

In the year that King Uzziah died,[a] I had a vision of the LORD. He was on his throne high above, and his robe filled the temple. ²Flaming creatures with six wings each were flying over him. They covered their faces with two of their wings and their bodies with two more. They used the other two wings for flying, ³as they shouted,

"Holy, holy, holy, LORD All-Powerful!
The earth is filled with your glory."

⁴As they shouted, the doorposts of the temple shook, and the temple was filled with smoke. ⁵Then I cried out, "I'm doomed! Everything I say is sinful, and so are the words of everyone around me. Yet I have seen the King, the LORD All-Powerful."

⁶One of the flaming creatures flew over to me with a burning coal that it had taken from the altar with a pair of metal tongs. ⁷It touched my lips with the hot coal and said, "This has touched your lips. Your sins are forgiven, and you are no longer guilty."

⁸After this, I heard the LORD ask, "Is there anyone I can send? Will someone go for us?"

"I'll go," I answered. "Send me!"

⁹Then the LORD told me to go and speak this message to the people:

"You will listen and listen, but never understand.
You will look and look, but never see."

The LORD also said,

¹⁰ "Make these people stubborn! Make them stop up their ears,
cover their eyes, and fail to understand.
Don't let them turn to me and be healed."

¹¹Then I asked the LORD, "How long will this last?"

The LORD answered:

Until their towns are destroyed and their houses are deserted, until their fields are empty, ¹²and I have sent them far away, leaving their land in ruins. ¹³If only a tenth of the people are left, even they will be destroyed. But just as stumps remain after trees have been cut down,[b] some of my chosen ones will be left.

---

[a]6.1 *the year that King Uzziah died:* Probably 742 B.C. [b]6.13 *But just . . . down:* One possible meaning for the difficult Hebrew text.

Prayer Starter: You are holy, O Lord, and the whole earth is filled with your glory.

Memory Verse: I, the LORD, invite you to come and talk it over. Your sins are scarlet red . . .
                                                        —*Isaiah 1.18*

> **A Child Has Been Born**

A child has been born for us.
We have been given a son
who will be our ruler.
His names will be Wonderful Advisor
and Mighty God,
Eternal Father and Prince of Peace.
⁷ His power will never end; peace will last forever.
He will rule David's kingdom and make it grow strong.
He will always rule with honesty and justice.
The LORD All-Powerful will make certain
that all of this is done.

⁸The Lord had warned the people of Israel, ⁹and all of them knew it, including everyone in the capital city of Samaria. But they were proud and stubborn and said,

¹⁰ "Houses of brick and sycamore have fallen to the ground,
but we will build houses with stones and cedar."

¹¹The LORD made their enemies[a] attack them. ¹²He sent the Arameans from the east and the Philistines from the west, and they swallowed up Israel. But even this did not stop him from being angry, so he kept on punishing them.[b] ¹³The people of Israel still did not turn back to the LORD All-Powerful and worship him. ¹⁴In one day he cut off their head and tail, their leaves and branches. ¹⁵Their rulers and leaders were the head, and the lying prophets were the tail. ¹⁶They had led the nation down the wrong path, and the people were confused. ¹⁷The Lord was angry with his people and kept punishing them, because they had turned against him.[c] They were evil and spoke foolishly. That's why he did not have pity on their young people or on their widows and orphans.

[a]9.11 *their enemies:* Hebrew "the enemies of Rezin." [b]9.12 *so . . . them:* Or "but he hasn't given up on them yet." [c]9.17 *and kept . . . against him:* Or "but even though they had turned against him, he still had not given up on them."

Prayer Starter: Dear heavenly Father, thank you for sending us your Son, Jesus.

Memory Verse: I, the LORD, invite you to come and talk it over. Your sins are scarlet red, but they will be whiter . . . —*Isaiah 1.18*

A Branch from David's Family

L ike a branch that sprouts from a stump,
  someone from David's family[a]
  will someday be king.
2 The Spirit of the LORD will be with him
  to give him understanding, wisdom,
  and insight.
He will be powerful, and he will know
  and honor the LORD.
3 His greatest joy will be to obey the LORD.

This king won't judge by appearances or listen to rumors.
4 The poor and the needy will be treated with fairness
  and with justice.
His word will be law everywhere in the land,
  and criminals will be put to death.
5 Honesty and fairness will be his royal robes.

6 Leopards will lie down with young goats,
  and wolves will rest with lambs.
Calves and lions will eat together
  and be cared for by little children.
7 Cows and bears will share the same pasture;
  their young will rest side by side.
  Lions and oxen will both eat straw.

8 Little children will play near snake holes.
They will stick their hands into dens of poisonous snakes
  and never be hurt.

9 Nothing harmful will take place
  on the LORD's holy mountain.
Just as water fills the sea,
  the land will be filled with people
  who know and honor the LORD.

10The time is coming when one of David's descendants[b] will be the signal for the people of all nations to come together. They will follow his advice, and his own nation will become famous.

[a]11.1 *David's family:* Hebrew "Jesse's family." Jesse was the father of King David. [b]11.10 *David's descendants:* Hebrew "Jesse's descendants."

Prayer Starter: Thank you for giving us understanding, wisdom, and insight. Keep me reading your Word.

Memory Verse: I, the LORD, invite you to come and talk it over. Your sins are scarlet red, but they will be whiter than snow or wool. —*Isaiah 1.18*

The Fallen Star

You, the bright morning star,
    have fallen from the sky!
You brought down other nations;
    now you are brought down.
13 You said to yourself, "I'll climb to heaven
    and place my throne above the highest stars.
I'll sit there with the gods far away in the north.
14 I'll be above the clouds, just like God Most High."

15 But now you are deep in the world of the dead.
16 Those who see you will stare and wonder,
  "Is this the man who made the world tremble
  and shook up kingdoms?
17 Did he capture every city and make earth a desert?
  Is he the one who refused to let prisoners go home?"

18 When kings die, they are buried
    in glorious tombs.
19 But you will be left unburied,
    just another dead body
      lying underfoot like a broken branch.
You will be one of many killed in battle
      and gone down to the deep rocky pit.[a]
20 You won't be buried with kings;
you ruined your country and murdered your people.

You evil monster! We hope that your family
  will be forgotten forever.

24 The LORD All-Powerful has made this promise:
  Everything I have planned will happen just as I said.
25 I will wipe out every Assyrian in my country,
  and I will crush those on my mountains.
I will free my people from slavery to the Assyrians.
26 I have planned this for the whole world,
  and my mighty arm controls every nation.
27 I, the LORD All-Powerful, have made these plans.
  No one can stop me now!

a14.19 *deep rocky pit:* The world of the dead.

Prayer Starter: O Lord our God, you have planned the future, and we are trusting you to keep your promises.

Memory Verse: The LORD All-Powerful . . .   *—Isaiah 14.24*

Egypt Punished

This is a message about Egypt:
The LORD comes to Egypt,
        riding swiftly on a cloud.
    The people are weak from fear.
Their idols tremble as he approaches and says,
2 "I will punish Egypt with civil war—
        neighbors, cities, and kingdoms
        will fight each other.

3 "Egypt will be discouraged when I confuse their plans.
They will try to get advice from their idols,
        from the spirits of the dead, and from fortunetellers.
4 I will put the Egyptians under the power
of a cruel, heartless king.
        I, the LORD All-Powerful, have promised this."

5 The Nile River will dry up and become parched land.
6 Its streams will stink, Egypt will have no water,
        and the reeds and tall grass will dry up.
7 Fields along the Nile
will be completely barren;
        every plant will disappear.

8 Those who fish in the Nile
        will be discouraged
        and mourn.
9 None of the cloth makers[a]
will know what to do,
        and they will turn pale.[b]
10 Weavers will be confused;
        paid workers will cry and mourn.

11 The king's officials in Zoan[c] are foolish themselves
        and give stupid advice.
How can they say to him, "We are very wise,
        and our families go back to kings of long ago"?
12 Where are those wise men now? If they can, let them say
        what the LORD All-Powerful intends for Egypt.

[a]19.9 *cloth makers:* Cloth was made from several kinds of plants that grew in the fields along the Nile. [b]19.9 *turn pale:* One possible meaning for the difficult Hebrew text. [c]19.11 *Zoan:* The city of Tanis in the Nile delta.

Prayer Starter: Help me, Lord, to turn off television programs that you don't want me to watch.

Memory Verse: The LORD All-Powerful has made this promise . . .
—*Isaiah 14.24*

The Glorious King

But there will be rewards for those who live right
and tell the truth,
for those who refuse to take money by force
or accept bribes,
for all who hate murder and violent crimes.
16 They will live in a fortress high on a rocky cliff,
where they will have food and plenty of water.

17 With your own eyes you will see the glorious King;
you will see his kingdom reaching far and wide.
18 Then you will ask yourself,
"Where are those officials
who terrified us and forced us
to pay such heavy taxes?"
19 You will never again have to see
the proud people
who spoke a strange
and foreign language
you could not understand.

20 Look to Mount Zion where we celebrate
our religious festivals.
You will see Jerusalem, secure as a tent
with pegs that cannot be pulled up
and fastened with ropes that can never be broken.
21 Our wonderful LORD will be with us!
There will be deep rivers and wide streams
safe from enemy ships.[a]

22 The LORD is our judge and our ruler;
the LORD is our king and will keep us safe.
23 But your nation[b] is a ship with its rigging loose,
its mast shaky, and its sail not spread.

Someday even you that are lame
will take everything you want from your enemies.
24 The LORD will forgive your sins,
and none of you will say, "I feel sick."

Prayer Starter: Thank you, Lord, for the wonderful future you've promised those who love you.

Memory Verse: The LORD All-Powerful has made this promise: Everything I have planned . . .
—*Isaiah 14.24*

Hezekiah's Sickness

About this time, Hezekiah got sick and was almost dead. So I went in and told him, "The LORD says you won't ever get well. You are going to die, and so you had better start doing what needs to be done."

²Hezekiah turned toward the wall and prayed, ³"Don't forget that I have been faithful to you, LORD. I have obeyed you with all my heart, and I do whatever you say is right." After this, he cried hard.

⁴Then the LORD sent me ⁵with this message for Hezekiah:

I am the LORD God, who was worshiped by your ancestor David. I heard you pray, and I saw you cry. I will let you live fifteen years more, ⁶while I protect you and your city from the king of Assyria.

⁷Now I will prove to you that I will keep my promise. ⁸Do you see the shadow made by the setting sun on the stairway built for King Ahaz? I will make the shadow go back ten steps.

Then the shadow went back ten steps.ᵃ

⁹This is what Hezekiah wrote after he got well:

¹⁰ I thought I would die during my best years
    and stay as a prisoner forever in the world of the dead.

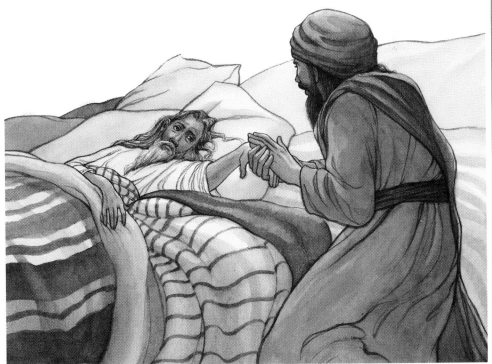

¹¹ I thought I would never again see you, my LORD,
>   or any of the people who live on this earth.
¹² My life was taken from me
>   like the tent that a shepherd pulls up and moves.
>   You cut me off like thread from a weaver's loom;
>   you make a wreck of me day and night.

¹³ Until morning came, I thought you would crush my bones
>   just like a hungry lion;
>   both night and day you make a wreck of me.ᵇ
¹⁴ I cry like a swallow; I mourn like a dove.
>   My eyes are red from looking to you, LORD.
>   I am terribly abused. Please come and help me.ᶜ
¹⁵ There's nothing I can say in answer to you,
>   since you are the one who has done this to me.ᵈ
>   My life has turned sour; I will limp until I die.

¹⁶ Your words and your deeds bring life to everyone,
>   including me.ᵉ Please make me healthy and strong again.
¹⁷ It was for my own good that I had such hard times.
>   But your love protected me from doom in the deep pit,ᶠ
>   and you turned your eyes away from my sins.

¹⁸ No one in the world of the dead can thank you
>   or praise you;
>   none of those in the deep pit can hope for you
>   to show them how faithful you are.
¹⁹ Only the living can thank you, as I am doing today.
>   Each generation tells the next about your faithfulness.ᵍ

²⁰ You, LORD, will save me, and every day that we live
>   we will sing in your temple
>   to the music of stringed instruments.

ᵃ38.8 *steps:* One possible meaning for the difficult Hebrew text of verse 8. ᵇ38.13 *of me:* One possible meaning for the difficult Hebrew text of verse 13. ᶜ38.14 *help me:* One possible meaning for the difficult Hebrew text of verse 14. ᵈ38.15 *There's . . . me:* One possible meaning for the difficult Hebrew text. ᵉ38.16 *Your . . . me:* One possible meaning for the difficult Hebrew text. ᶠ38.17 *deep pit:* The world of the dead, as in verse 18. ᵍ38.19 *about your faithfulness:* One possible meaning for the difficult Hebrew text.

Prayer Starter: May I praise you, heavenly Father, every day that I live.

Memory Verse: The LORD All-Powerful has made this promise: Everything I have planned will happen . . .   —*Isaiah 14.24*

Household Idols

*T*he LORD said:

⁹ Those people who make idols
    are nothing themselves,
        and the idols they treasure
    are just as worthless.
    Worshipers of idols are blind, stupid, and foolish.

¹⁰   Why make an idol or an image
    that can't do a thing?

¹³ Some woodcarver measures a piece of wood,
    then draws an outline.
The idol is carefully carved with each detail exact.
At last it looks like a person
    and is placed in a temple.

¹⁴ Either cedar, cypress, oak, or
any tree from the forest
    may be chosen.
Or even a pine tree planted
by the woodcarver
    and watered by the rain.

¹⁵ Some of the wood is used to make a fire for heating
    or for cooking.
One piece is made into an idol,
    then the woodcarver bows down and worships it.

¹⁶ He enjoys the warm fire and the meat that was roasted
    over the burning coals.

¹⁷ Afterwards, he bows down to worship the wooden idol.
    "Protect me!" he says. "You are my god."

¹⁸ Those who worship idols are stupid and blind! ¹⁹They don't have enough sense to say to themselves, "I made a fire with half of the wood and cooked my bread and meat on it. Then I made something worthless with the other half. Why worship a block of wood?"

²⁰ How can anyone be stupid enough to trust something that can be burned to ashes?[a] No one can save themselves like that. Don't they realize that the idols they hold in their hands are not really gods?

[a]44.20 *How . . . ashes?:* One possible meaning for the difficult Hebrew text.

Prayer Starter: You are the Lord my God. May nothing in my life be more important to me than you are.

> ### God Chooses Jeremiah

My name is Jeremiah. I am a priest, and my father Hilkiah and everyone wise in my family are from Anathoth in the territory of the Benjamin tribe. This book contains the things that the LORD told me to say. ²The LORD first spoke to me in the thirteenth year that Josiah[a] was king of Judah, ³and he continued to speak to me during the rule of Josiah's son Jehoiakim.[b] The last time the LORD spoke to me was in the fifth month[c] of the eleventh year that Josiah's son Zedekiah[d] was king. That was also when the people of Jerusalem were taken away as prisoners.

⁴The LORD said:

⁵"Jeremiah, I am your Creator, and before you were born,
    I chose you to speak for me to the nations."

⁶I replied, "I'm not a good speaker, LORD, and I'm too young."

⁷"Don't say you're too young," the LORD answered. "If I tell you to go and speak to someone, then go! And when I tell you what to say, don't leave out a word! ⁸I promise to be with you and keep you safe, so don't be afraid."

⁹The LORD reached out his hand, then he touched my mouth and said, "I am giving you the words to say, ¹⁰and I am sending you with authority to speak to the nations for me. You will tell them of doom and destruction, and of rising and rebuilding again."

¹¹The LORD showed me something in a vision. Then he asked, "What do you see, Jeremiah?"

I answered, "A branch of almonds that ripen early."

¹²"That's right," the LORD replied, "and I always rise early[e] to keep a promise."

¹³Then the LORD showed me something else and asked, "What do you see now?"

I answered, "I see a pot of boiling water in the north, and it's about to spill out toward us."

¹⁴The LORD said:

I will pour out destruction all over the land.
¹⁵   Just watch while I send for the kings of the north.
They will attack and capture Jerusalem and other towns,
    then set up their thrones at the gates of Jerusalem.

---

[a]1.2 *Josiah:* Ruled 640–609 B.C. [b]1.3 *Jehoiakim:* Ruled 609–598 B.C. [c]1.3 *fifth month:* Ab, the fifth month of the Hebrew calendar, from about mid-July to mid-August. [d]1.3 *Zedekiah:* Ruled 598–586 B.C. [e]1.11,12 *almonds . . . rise early:* In Hebrew "almonds that ripen early" sounds like "always rise early."

Prayer Starter: You always rise early to keep your promises, Lord. Help me to trust every one of them.

Memory Verse: With your wisdom . . .   *—Jeremiah 10.12*

Linen Shorts

The LORD told me, "Go and buy a pair of linen shorts. Wear them for a while, but don't wash them." [2]So I bought a pair of shorts and put them on.

[3]Then the LORD said, [4]"Take off the shorts. Go to Parah[a] and hide the shorts in a crack between some large rocks." [5]And that's what I did.

[6]Some time later the LORD said, "Go back and get the shorts." [7]I went back and dug the shorts out of their hiding place, but the cloth had rotted, and the shorts were ruined.

[8]Then the LORD said:

[9]Jeremiah, I will use Babylonia to[b] destroy the pride of the people of Judah and Jerusalem. [10]The people of Judah are evil and stubborn. So instead of listening to me, they do whatever they want and even worship other gods. When I am finished with these people, they will be good for nothing, just like this pair of shorts.

[11]These shorts were tight around your waist, and that's how tightly I held onto the kingdoms of Israel and Judah. I wanted them to be my people. I wanted to make them famous, so that other nations would praise and honor me, but they refused to obey me.

[15] People of Judah, don't be too proud to listen
　　to what the LORD has said.
[16] You hope for light, but God is sending darkness.
　　Evening shadows already deepen in the hills.
　So return to God and confess your sins to him
　　before you trip and fall.

[a]13.4 *Parah:* Or "the Euphrates River." Parah was a village about five and a half miles northeast of Jerusalem.　[b]13.9 *I will use Babylonia to:* Or "that's how I'm going to."

Prayer Starter: Thank you for giving me a school to attend, Lord. Help me to study hard and do well. Bless my teachers.

Memory Verse: With your wisdom and power . . .　　*—Jeremiah 10.12*

The Prophet's Scroll

During the fourth year that Jehoiakim[a] son of Josiah[b] was king of Judah, the LORD said to me, "Jeremiah, [2]since the time Josiah was king, I have been speaking to you about Israel, Judah, and the other nations. Now, get a scroll[c] and write down everything I have told you, [3]then read it to the people of Judah. Maybe they will stop sinning when they hear what terrible things I plan for them. And if they turn to me, I will forgive them."

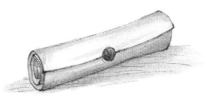

[4]I sent for Baruch son of Neriah and asked him to help me. I repeated everything the LORD had told me, and Baruch wrote it all down on a scroll. [5]Then I said,

Baruch, the officials refuse to let me go into the LORD's temple, [6]so you must go instead. Wait for the next holy day when the people of Judah come to the temple to pray and to go without eating.[d] Then take this scroll to the temple and read it aloud. [7]The LORD is furious, and if the people hear how he is going to punish them, maybe they will ask to be forgiven.

8-10In the ninth month[e] of the fifth year that Jehoiakim was king, the leaders set a day when everyone who lived in Jerusalem or who was visiting here had to pray and go without eating. So Baruch took the scroll to the upper courtyard of the temple. He went over to the side of the courtyard and stood in a covered area near New Gate, where he read the scroll aloud.

16After they heard what was written on the scroll, they were worried and said to each other, "The king needs to hear this!" Turning to Baruch, they asked, 17"Did someone tell you what to write on this scroll?"

18"Yes, Jeremiah did," Baruch replied. "I wrote down just what he told me."

19The officials said, "You and Jeremiah must go into hiding, and don't tell anyone where you are."

20-22The officials put the scroll in Elishama's room and went to see the king, who was in one of the rooms where he lived and worked during the winter. It was the ninth month[f] of the year, so there was a fire burning in the fireplace,[g] and the king was sitting nearby. After the officials told the king about the scroll, he sent Jehudi to get it. Then Jehudi started reading the scroll to the king and his officials. 23-25But every time Jehudi finished reading three or four columns, the king would tell him to cut them off with his penknife and throw them in the fire. Elnathan, Delaiah, and Gemariah begged the king not to burn the scroll, but he ignored them, and soon there was nothing left of it.

The king and his servants listened to what was written on the scroll, but they were not afraid, and they did not tear their clothes in sorrow.[h]

[a]36.1 *Jehoiakim:* Ruled 609–598 B.C. [b]36.1 *Josiah:* Ruled 640–609 B.C. [c]36.2 *scroll:* A roll of paper or special leather used for writing on. [d]36.6 *to go without eating:* As a way of asking for God's help. [e]36.8-10 *ninth month:* Chislev, the ninth month of the Hebrew calendar, from about mid-November to mid-December. [f]36.20-22 *ninth month:* Chislev, the ninth month of the Hebrew calendar, from about mid-November to mid-December. [g]36.20-22 *fireplace:* Probably a large metal or clay pot on a movable stand, with the fire burning inside. [h]36.23-25 *they did not tear their clothes in sorrow:* Such actions would have shown that they were sorry for disobeying the LORD and were turning back to him.

Prayer Starter: Help me to always respect your Word, dear Lord. May I read it each day and obey it.

Memory Verse: With your wisdom and power you created . . .
—Jeremiah 10.12

Jeremiah Rescued

One day, Shephatiah, Gedaliah, Jehucal,[a] and Pashhur[b] heard me tell the people of Judah ²⁻³that the LORD said, "If you stay here in Jerusalem, you will die in battle or from disease or hunger, and the Babylonian army will capture the city anyway. But if you surrender to the Babylonians, they will let you live."

⁴So the four of them went to the king and said, "You should put Jeremiah to death, because he is making the soldiers and everyone else lose hope. He isn't trying to help our people; he's trying to harm them."

⁵Zedekiah replied, "Do what you want with him. I can't stop you."

⁶Then they took me back to the courtyard of the palace guards and let me down with ropes into the well that belonged to Malchiah, the king's son. There was no water in the well, and I sank down in the mud.

⁷⁻⁸Ebedmelech from Ethiopia[c] was an official at the palace, and he heard what they had done to me. So he went to speak with King Zedekiah, who was holding court at Benjamin Gate. ⁹Ebedmelech said, "Your Majesty, Jeremiah is a prophet, and those men were wrong to throw him into a well. And when Jerusalem runs out of food, Jeremiah will starve to death down there."

¹⁰Zedekiah answered, "Take thirty[d] of my soldiers and pull Jeremiah out before he dies."

¹¹Ebedmelech and the soldiers went to the palace and got some rags from the room under the treasury. He used ropes to lower them into the well. ¹²Then he said, "Put these rags under your arms so the ropes won't hurt you." After I did, ¹³the men pulled me out. And from then on, I was kept in the courtyard of the palace guards.

---

[a]38.1 *Jehucal:* The Hebrew text has "Jucal," another form of the name. [b]38.1 *Shephatiah, Gedaliah, Jehucal, and Pashhur:* Hebrew "Shephatiah son of Mattan, Gedaliah son of Pashhur, Jucal son of Shelemiah, and Pashhur son of Malchiah." [c]38.7,8 *Ethiopia:* The Hebrew text has "Cush," a region south of Egypt that included parts of the present countries of Ethiopia and Sudan. [d]38.10 *thirty:* Most Hebrew manuscripts; one Hebrew manuscript "three."

Prayer Starter: Protect your people all over the world, dear Lord. Keep us safe from those who would like to hurt us because of our faith in you.

Memory Verse: With your wisdom and power you created the earth . . .
—*Jeremiah 10.12*

Jerusalem Captured

In Zedekiah's ninth year as king, on the tenth day of the tenth month,[a] King Nebuchadnezzar of Babylonia led his entire army to attack Jerusalem. The troops set up camp outside the city and built ramps up to the city walls.

[5-6]After a year and a half,[b] all the food in Jerusalem was gone. Then on the ninth day of the fourth month,[c] [7]the Babylonian troops broke through the city wall. That same night, Zedekiah and his soldiers tried to escape through the gate near the royal garden, even though they knew the enemy had the city surrounded. They headed toward the Jordan River valley, [8]but the Babylonian troops caught up with them near Jericho. The Babylonians arrested Zedekiah, but his soldiers scattered in every direction. [9]Zedekiah was taken to Riblah in the land of Hamath, where Nebuchadnezzar put him on trial and found him guilty. [10]Zedekiah's sons and the officials of Judah were killed while he watched, [11]then his eyes were poked out. He was put in chains, then dragged off to Babylon and kept in prison until he died.

[12]Jerusalem was captured during Nebuchadnezzar's nineteenth year as king of Babylonia.

About a month later,[d] Nebuchadnezzar's officer in charge of the guards arrived in Jerusalem. His name was Nebuzaradan, [13]and he burned down the LORD's temple, the king's palace, and every important building in the city, as well as all the houses. [14]Then he ordered the Babylonian soldiers to break down the walls around Jerusalem. [15]He led away the people left in the city, including everyone who had become loyal to

Nebuchadnezzar, the rest of the skilled workers,ᵉ and even some of the poor people of Judah. ¹⁶Only the very poorest were left behind to work the vineyards and the fields.

ᵃ52.4 *tenth month:* Tebeth, the tenth month of the Hebrew calendar, from about mid-December to mid-January. ᵇ52.5,6 *After a year and a half:* Jerusalem was captured in 586 B.C. ᶜ52.5,6 *fourth month:* Tammuz, the fourth month of the Hebrew calendar, from about mid-June to mid-July. ᵈ52.12 *About a month later:* Hebrew "On the seventh day of the fifth month." ᵉ52.15 *the rest of the skilled workers:* Nebuchadnezzar had taken away some of the skilled workers eleven years before.

Prayer Starter: It is so important to obey your commands, dear Lord. Help me and my friends to serve you.

Memory Verse: With your wisdom and power you created the earth and spread out the heavens.   *—Jeremiah 10.12*

Ezekiel Eats a Scroll

The LORD said, "Ezekiel, son of man, after you eat this scroll, go speak to the people of Israel." [2-3]He handed me the scroll and said, "Eat this and fill up on it." So I ate the scroll, and it tasted sweet as honey.

[4]The LORD said:

Ezekiel, I am sending you to your own people. [5-6]They are Israelites, not some strangers who speak a foreign language you can't understand. If I were to send you to foreign nations, they would listen to you. [7]But the people of Israel will refuse to listen, because they have refused to listen to me. All of them are stubborn and hardheaded, [8]so I will make you as stubborn as they are. [9]You will be so determined to speak my message that nothing will stop you. I will make you hard like a diamond, and you'll have no reason to be afraid of those arrogant rebels.

[10]Listen carefully to everything I say and then think about it. [11]Then go to the people who were brought here to Babylonia with you and tell them you have a message from me, the LORD God. Do this, whether they listen to you or not.

[12]The Spirit[a] lifted me up, and as the glory of the LORD started to leave,[b] I heard a loud, thundering noise behind me. [13]It was the sound made by the creatures' wings as they brushed against each other, and by the rumble of the wheels beside them. [14]Then the Spirit carried me away.

[a]3.12 *The Spirit:* Or "A wind." [b]3.12 *as the glory of the LORD started to leave:* One possible meaning for the difficult Hebrew text.

Prayer Starter: Help me to tell others about you, dear Lord. May I never be ashamed of Jesus.

Memory Verse: Our God, your name . . .   *—Daniel 2.20*

Dry Bones

Some time later, I felt the LORD's power take control of me, and his Spirit carried me to a valley full of bones. ²The LORD showed me all around, and everywhere I looked I saw bones that were dried out. ³He said, "Ezekiel, son of man, can these bones come back to life?"

I replied, "LORD God, only you can answer that."

⁴He then told me to say:

Dry bones, listen to what the LORD is saying to you, ⁵"I, the LORD God, will put breath in you, and once again you will live. ⁶I will wrap you with muscles and skin and breathe life into you. Then you will know that I am the LORD."

⁷I did what the LORD said, but before I finished speaking, I heard a rattling noise. The bones were coming together! ⁸I saw muscles and skin cover the bones, but they had no life in them.

⁹The LORD said:

Ezekiel, now say to the wind,ᵃ "The LORD God commands you to blow from every direction and to breathe life into these dead bodies, so they can live again."

¹⁰As soon as I said this, the wind blew among the bodies, and they came back to life! They all stood up, and there were enough to make a large army.

¹¹The LORD said:

Ezekiel, the people of Israel are like dead bones. They complain that they are dried up and that they have no hope for the future. ¹²So tell them, "I, the LORD God, promise to open your graves and set you free. I will bring you back to Israel, ¹³and when that happens, you will realize that I am the LORD. ¹⁴My Spirit will give you breath, and you will live again. I will bring you home, and you will know that I have kept my promise. I, the LORD, have spoken."

¹⁵The LORD said:

¹⁶Ezekiel, son of man, get a stick and write on it, "The kingdom of Judah." Then get another stick and write on it, "The kingdom of Israel."ᵇ ¹⁷Hold these two sticks end to end, so they look like one stick. ¹⁸And when your people ask you what this means, ¹⁹tell them that I, the LORD, will join together the stick of Israel and the stick of Judah. I will hold them in my hand, and they will become one.

²⁰Hold these two sticks where they can be seen by everyone ²¹and then say:

I, the LORD God, will gather the people of Israel and bring them home from the foreign nations where they now live. ²²I will make them into one nation and let them once again live in the land of Israel. Only one king will rule them, and they will never again be divided into two nations.

ᵃ37.9 *wind:* Or "breath." The Hebrew word may mean either. ᵇ37.16 *Israel:* The Hebrew text has "Joseph, that is, Ephraim," the leading tribe in the northern kingdom.

Prayer Starter: Keep me from saying the wrong thing today, Lord. Give me good words to speak.

Memory Verse: Our God, your name will be praised . . .

—Daniel 2.20

The Flaming Furnace	

King Nebuchadnezzar was furious. So he sent for the three young men and said, [14]"I hear that you refuse to worship my gods and the gold statue I have set up. [15]Now I am going to give you one more chance. If you bow down and worship the statue when you hear the music, everything will be all right. But if you don't, you will at once be thrown into a flaming furnace. "No god can save you from me."

[16]The three men replied, "Your Majesty, we don't need to defend ourselves. [17]The God we worship can save us from you and your flaming furnace. [18]But even if he doesn't, we still won't worship your gods and the gold statue you have set up."

[19]Nebuchadnezzar's face twisted with anger at the three men. And he ordered the furnace to be heated seven times hotter than usual. [20]Next, he commanded some of his strongest soldiers to tie up the men and throw them into the flaming furnace. [21-23]The king wanted it done at that very moment. So the soldiers tied up Shadrach, Meshach, and Abednego and threw them into the flaming furnace with all of their clothes still on, including their turbans. The fire was so hot that flames leaped out and killed the soldiers.

[24]Suddenly the king jumped up and shouted, "Weren't only three men tied up and thrown into the fire?"

"Yes, Your Majesty," the people answered.

[25]"But I see four men walking around in the fire," the king replied. "None of them is tied up or harmed, and the fourth one looks like a god."[a]

[a]3.25 *a god:* Aramaic "a son of the gods."

Prayer Starter: Our God, your name will be praised forever and ever. You are all-powerful, and you know everything.

Memory Verse: Our God, your name will be praised forever and forever. . . .
—*Daniel 2.20*

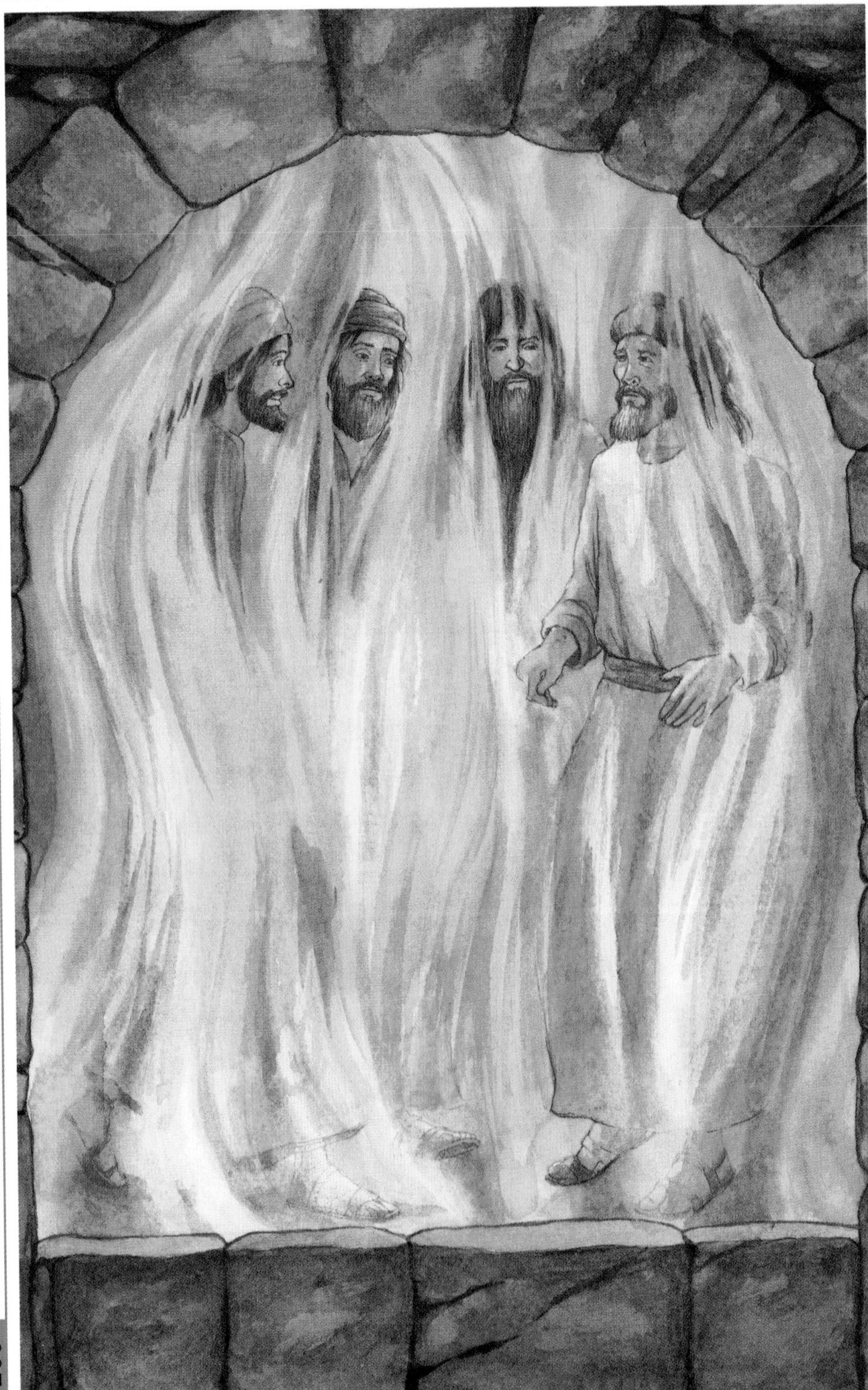

Nebuchad-nezzar Eats Grass

About twelve months later, I was walking on the flat roof of my royal palace and admiring the beautiful city of Babylon, when these things started happening to me. I was saying to myself, "Just look at this wonderful capital city that I have built by my own power and for my own glory!"

³¹But before I could finish speaking, a voice from heaven interrupted:

King Nebuchadnezzar, this kingdom is no longer yours. ³²You will be forced to live with the wild animals, away from people. For seven years[a] you will eat grass, as though you were an ox, until you learn that God Most High is in control of all earthly kingdoms and that he is the one who chooses their rulers.

³³This was no sooner said than done—I was forced to live like a wild animal; I ate grass and was unprotected from the dew. As time went by, my hair grew longer than eagle feathers, and my fingernails looked like the claws of a bird.

³⁴Finally, I prayed to God in heaven, and my mind was healed. Then I said:

"I praise and honor God Most High.
He lives forever,
    and his kingdom will never end.

[a]4.32 *years:* Aramaic "times."

Prayer Starter: Thank you for ruling over the nations, dear Lord. You are King of kings and Lord of lords. And I love you.

Memory Verse: Our God, your name will be praised forever and forever. You are all-powerful . . . —*Daniel 2.20*

Writing on the Wall

One evening, King Belshazzar gave a great banquet for a thousand of his highest officials, and he drank wine with them. ²He got drunk and ordered his servants to bring in the gold and silver cups his father Nebuchadnezzar° had taken from the temple in Jerusalem. Belshazzar wanted the cups, so that he and all his wives and officials could drink from them.

³⁻⁴When the gold cups were brought in, everyone at the banquet drank from them and praised their idols made of gold, silver, bronze, iron, wood, and stone.

⁵Suddenly a human hand was seen writing on the plaster wall of the palace. The hand was just behind the lampstand, and the king could see it writing. ⁶He was so frightened that his face turned pale, his knees started shaking, and his legs became weak.

⁸All of King Belshazzar's highest officials came in, but not one of them could read the writing or tell what it meant, ⁹and they were completely puzzled. Now the king was more afraid than ever before, and his face turned white as a ghost.

¹⁷Daniel answered:

Your Majesty, I will read the writing and tell you what it means. But you may keep your gifts or give them to someone else.

²⁵⁻²⁸The words written there are *mene,* which means "numbered," *tekel,* which means "weighed," and *parsin,*ᵇ which means "divided." God has numbered the days of your kingdom and has brought it to an end. He has weighed you on his balance scales, and you fall short of what it takes to be king. So God has divided your kingdom between the Medes and the Persians.

²⁹Belshazzar gave a command for Daniel to be made the third most powerful man in his kingdom and to be given a purple robe and a gold chain.

³⁰That same night, the king was killed. ³¹Then Darius the Mede, who was sixty-two years old, took over his kingdom.

ᵃ5.2 *his father Nebuchadnezzar:* Belshazzar was actually the son of King Nabonidus, who was from another family. But in ancient times, it was possible to refer to a previous king as the "father" of the present king. ᵇ5.25-28 *mene . . . tekel . . . parsin:* In the Aramaic text of verse 25, the words "mene, tekel, parsin," are used, and in verses 26-28 the words "mene, tekel, peres" (the singular of "parsin") are used. "Parsin" means "divided," but "peres" can mean either "divided" or "Persia."

Prayer Starter: Help me to be respectful to my teachers, Father. May they know that I am one of your children.

Memory Verse: Our God, your name will be praised forever and forever. You are all-powerful, and you know everything.   —*Daniel 2.20*

The Lions' Den

The men then told the king, "That Jew named Daniel, who was brought here as a captive, refuses to obey you or the law that you ordered to be written. And he still prays to his god three times a day." ¹⁴The king was really upset to hear about this, and for the rest of the day he tried to think how he could save Daniel.

¹⁵At sunset the men returned and said, "Your Majesty, remember that no written law of the Medes and Persians can be changed, not even by the king."

¹⁶So Darius ordered Daniel to be brought out and thrown into a pit of lions. But he said to Daniel, "You have been faithful to your God, and I pray that he will rescue you."

¹⁷A stone was rolled over the pit, and it was sealed. Then Darius and his officials stamped the seal to show that no one should let Daniel out. ¹⁸All night long the king could not sleep. He did not eat anything, and he would not let anyone come in to entertain him.

¹⁹At daybreak the king got up and ran to the pit. ²⁰He was anxious and shouted, "Daniel, you were faithful and served your God. Was he able to save you from the lions?"

²¹Daniel answered, "Your Majesty, I hope you live forever! ²²My God knew that I was innocent, and he sent an angel to keep the lions from eating me. Your Majesty, I have never done anything to hurt you."

²³The king was relieved to hear Daniel's voice, and he gave orders for him to be taken out of the pit. Daniel's faith in his God had kept him from being harmed.

Prayer Starter: May I be as faithful in praying each day as Daniel was, dear Lord.

The Ram and the Goat

Daniel wrote:

In the third year of King Belshazzar of Babylonia,[a] I had a second vision [2]in which I was in Susa, the chief city of Babylonia's Elam Province. I was beside the Ulai River,[b] [3]when I looked up and saw a ram standing there with two horns on its head—both of them were long, but the second one was longer than the first. [4]The ram went charging toward the west, the north, and the south. No other animals were strong enough to oppose him, and nothing could save them from his power. So he did as he pleased and became even more powerful.

[5]I kept on watching and saw a goat come from the west and charge across the entire earth, without even touching the ground. Between his eyes was a powerful horn,[c] [6]and with tremendous anger the goat started toward the ram that I had seen beside the river.[d] [7]The goat was so fierce that its attack broke both horns of the ram, leaving him powerless. Then the goat stomped on the ram, and no one could do anything to help. [8]After this, the goat became even more powerful. But at the peak of his power, his mighty horn was broken, and four other mighty horns took its place—one pointing to the north and one to the east, one to the south and one to the west.

[27]After this, I was so worn out and weak that it was several days before I could get out of bed and go about my duties for the king. I was disturbed by this vision that made no sense to me.

[a]8.1 *third year . . . Babylonia:* 552 B.C., two years after the first vision. [b]8.2 *River:* Or "Gate."
[c]8.5 *powerful horn:* Hebrew "horn of vision." [d]8.6 *river:* Or "Gate."

Prayer Starter: Keep us safe while traveling, Lord. Watch over us when we are in the car, on planes, on boats, or just crossing the street.

Memory Verse: I command everyone in my kingdom . . .

—*Daniel 6.26a*

Daniel's Vision

In the third year[a] of Cyrus the king of Persia, a message came to Daniel[b] from God, and it was explained in a vision. The message was about a horrible war, and it was true. [2]Daniel wrote:

For three weeks I was in sorrow. [3]I ate no fancy food or meat, I drank no wine, and I put no olive oil on my face or hair.[c] [4]Then, on the twenty-fourth day of the first month,[d] I was standing on the banks of the great Tigris River, [5]when I looked up and saw someone dressed in linen and wearing a solid gold belt.[e] [6]His body was like a precious stone,[f] his face like lightning, his eyes like flaming fires, his arms and legs like polished bronze, and his voice like the roar of a crowd. [7]Although the people who were with me did not see the vision, they became so frightened that they scattered and hid. [8]Only I saw this great vision. I became weak and pale, [9]and at the sound of his voice, I fell facedown in a deep sleep.

[10]He raised me to my hands and knees [11]and then said, "Daniel, your God thinks highly of you, and he has sent me. So stand up and pay close attention." I stood trembling, while the angel said:

¹²Daniel, don't be afraid! God has listened to your prayers since the first day you humbly asked for understanding, and he has sent me here. ¹³But the guardian angelᵍ of Persia opposed me for twenty-one days. Then Michael, who is one of the strongest guardian angels,ʰ came to rescue me from the kings of Persia.ⁱ ¹⁴Now I have come here to give you another vision about what will happen to your people in the future.

¹⁵While this angel was speaking to me, I stared at the ground, speechless. ¹⁶Then he appeared in human form and touched my lips. I said, "Sir, this vision has brought me great pain and has drained my strength. ¹⁷I am merely your servant. How can I possibly speak with someone so powerful, when I am almost too weak to get my breath?"

¹⁸⁻¹⁹The angel touched me a second time and said, "Don't be frightened! God thinks highly of you, and he intends this for your good, so be brave and strong."

ᵃ10.1 *third year:* 536 B.C. ᵇ10.1 *Daniel:* Aramaic "Daniel whose name was Belteshazzar." ᶜ10.3 *olive oil . . . hair:* On special occasions, it was the custom to put olive oil on one's face and hair. ᵈ10.4 *first month:* Nisan (also known as Abib), the first month of the Hebrew calendar, from about mid-March to mid-April. ᵉ10.5 *solid gold belt:* Hebrew "belt of gold from Uphaz." ᶠ10.6 *a precious stone:* The Hebrew text has "beryl," which is green or bluish-green. ᵍ10.13 *guardian angel:* Hebrew "prince." ʰ10.13 *one of the strongest guardian angels:* Hebrew "chief prince." ⁱ10.13 *came . . . Persia:* One possible meaning for the difficult Hebrew text.

Prayer Starter: I believe you control human events, Lord. You give rulers their power and take it away. No one is like you.

Memory Verse: I command everyone in my kingdom to worship and honor . . .
—*Daniel 6.26a*

Hosea
and Gomer

I am Hosea son of Beeri. When Uzziah, Jotham, Ahaz, and Hezekiah were the kings of Judah, and when Jeroboam son of Jehoash[a] was king of Israel,[b] the LORD spoke this message to me.

²The LORD said, "Hosea, Israel has betrayed me like an unfaithful wife.[c] Marry such a woman and have children by her." ³So I married Gomer the daughter of Diblaim, and we had a son.

⁴Then the LORD said, "Hosea, name your son Jezreel,[d] because I will soon punish the descendants of King Jehu of Israel for the murders he committed in Jezreel Valley.[e] I will destroy his kingdom, ⁵and in Jezreel Valley I will break the power of Israel."

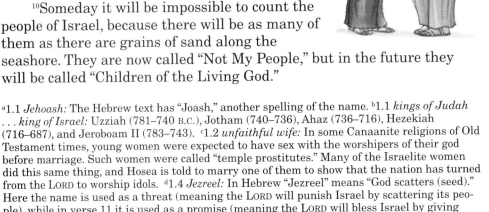

⁶Later, Gomer had a daughter, and the LORD said, "Name her Lo-Ruhamah,[f] because I will no longer have mercy and forgive Israel. ⁷But I am the LORD God of Judah, and I will have mercy and save Judah by my own power—not by wars and arrows or swords and cavalry."

⁸After Gomer had stopped nursing Lo-Ruhamah, she had another son. ⁹Then the LORD said, "Name him Lo-Ammi,[g] because these people are not mine, and I am not their God."

¹⁰Someday it will be impossible to count the people of Israel, because there will be as many of them as there are grains of sand along the seashore. They are now called "Not My People," but in the future they will be called "Children of the Living God."

[a]1.1 *Jehoash:* The Hebrew text has "Joash," another spelling of the name. [b]1.1 *kings of Judah . . . king of Israel:* Uzziah (781–740 B.C.), Jotham (740–736), Ahaz (736–716), Hezekiah (716–687), and Jeroboam II (783–743). [c]1.2 *unfaithful wife:* In some Canaanite religions of Old Testament times, young women were expected to have sex with the worshipers of their god before marriage. Such women were called "temple prostitutes." Many of the Israelite women did this same thing, and Hosea is told to marry one of them to show that the nation has turned from the LORD to worship idols. [d]1.4 *Jezreel:* In Hebrew "Jezreel" means "God scatters (seed)." Here the name is used as a threat (meaning the LORD will punish Israel by scattering its people), while in verse 11 it is used as a promise (meaning the LORD will bless Israel by giving their nation many people, just as a big harvest comes when many seeds are scattered in a field). [e]1.4 *murders . . . Valley:* Jehu murdered the wife and relatives of King Ahab. [f]1.6 *Lo-Ruhamah:* In Hebrew "Lo-Ruhamah" means "No Mercy." [g]1.9 *Lo-Ammi:* In Hebrew "Lo-Ammi" means "Not My People."

Prayer Starter: Lord, so many people are homeless. Please have mercy on them, and show us who we can help.

Memory Verse: I command everyone in my kingdom to worship and honor the God of Daniel. . . .   —*Daniel 6.26a*

Swarms of Locusts

I am Joel the son of Pethuel.
And this is the message
  the LORD gave to me.

2 Listen, you leaders and everyone else
  in the land.
    Has anything like this
    ever happened before?
3 Tell our children! Let it be told to our grandchildren
  and their children too.

4 Swarm after swarm of locusts[a] has attacked our crops,
  eating everything in sight.
5 Sober up, you drunkards! Cry long and loud;
  your wine supply is gone.
6 A powerful nation[b] with countless troops
    has invaded our land.
  They have the teeth and jaws of powerful lions.
7 Our grapevines and fig trees are stripped bare;
  only naked branches remain.

8 Grieve like a young woman
    mourning for the man she was to marry.
9 Offerings of grain and wine
    are no longer brought to the LORD's temple.
  His servants, the priests, are deep in sorrow.
10 Barren fields mourn;
    grain, grapes, and olives are scorched and shriveled.

[a]1.4 *Swarm . . . locusts:* The Hebrew text lists either four kinds of locusts or locusts in four stages of their development. Locusts are a type of grasshopper that comes in swarms and causes great damage to plant life. [b]1.6 *A powerful nation:* The swarms of locusts.

Prayer Starter: Thank you for insects, Lord. Especially for lightning bugs, lady bugs, and caterpillars.

Memory Verse: I command everyone in my kingdom to worship and honor the God of Daniel. He is the living God. *—Daniel 6.26a*

**Women
of Samaria**

*T*he LORD said:
　　You women of Samaria are fat cows!ᵃ
　You mistreat and abuse the poor and needy,
　　　then you say to your husbands,
　　　"Bring us more drinks!"
² I, the LORD God, have sworn by my own name
　　　that your time is coming.
Not one of you will be left—
　　you will be taken away by sharp hooks.ᵇ
³ You will be dragged through holes in your city walls,
　　and you will be thrown toward Harmon.ᶜ
I, the LORD, have spoken!

The LORD *said:*
⁴ Come to Bethel and Gilgal.ᵈ Sin all you want!
　Offer sacrifices the next morning
　　　and bring a tenth of your crops on the third day.ᵉ
⁵ Bring offerings to show me how thankful you are.
　　Gladly bring more offerings than I have demanded.

You really love to do this.
I, the LORD God, have spoken!

⁶ I, the LORD, took away the food
from every town and village,
but still you rejected me.
⁷ Three months before harvest, I kept back the rain.
Sometimes I would let it fall on one town or field
but not on another, and pastures dried up.
⁸ People from two or three towns would go to a town
that still had water, but it wasn't enough.
Even then you rejected me.
I, the LORD, have spoken!

⁹ I dried up your grain fields;
your gardens and vineyards turned brown.
Locusts^f ate your fig trees and olive orchards,
but even then you rejected me.
I, the LORD, have spoken!

ᵃ4.1 *fat cows:* The Hebrew text has "cows of Bashan," a fertile plain famous for its rich pastures
and well-fed cattle. ᵇ4.2 *taken . . . hooks:* One possible meaning for the difficult Hebrew text.
ᶜ4.3 *Harmon:* Hebrew; some manuscripts of one ancient translation "Mount Hermon," a mountain in the north of Palestine, on the way to Assyria. ᵈ4.4 *Bethel and Gilgal:* These were two of
the most important centers of worship in northern Israel. ᵉ4.4 *Offer . . . day:* Or "Offer sacrifices each morning and bring a tenth of your crops every three days." In verses 4,5 God is con-
demning the people for meaningless acts of worship. ᶠ4.9 *Locusts:* A type of grasshopper that
comes in swarms and causes great damage to plant life.

Prayer Starter: Lord, help me to always be concerned for the poor and needy.

Memory Verse: Others may follow . . .   *—Micah 4.5*

A Basket of Fruit

The LORD God showed me a basket of ripe fruit [2]and asked, "Amos, what do you see?"

"A basket of ripe fruit," I replied.

Then he said,

"This is the end[a] for my people Israel.
    I won't forgive them again.
[3] Instead of singing in the temple,
        they will cry and weep.
    Dead bodies will be everywhere. So keep silent!
        I, the LORD, have spoken!"

The LORD said:
[4] You people crush those in need and wipe out the poor.
[5] You say to yourselves, "How much longer before the end
        of the New Moon Festival?
    When will the Sabbath[b] be over?
        Our wheat is ready, and we want to sell it now.
    We can't wait to cheat
    and charge high prices for the grain we sell.
        We will use dishonest scales [6]and mix dust in the grain.
    Those who are needy and poor don't have any money,
    We will make them our slaves
        for the price of a pair of sandals."

[7] I, the LORD, won't forget any of this,
        though you take great pride in your ancestor Jacob.[c]
[8] Your country will tremble, and you will mourn.
    It will be like the Nile River that rises and overflows,
        then sinks back down.

[9] On that day, I, the LORD God,
    will make the sun go down at noon,
        and I will turn daylight into darkness.

[a]8.2 *end:* In Hebrew "ripe fruit" and "end" sound alike.   [b]8.5 *New Moon Festival . . . Sabbath:* Selling grain at these times was forbidden by the Law of Moses.   [c]8.7 *though . . . Jacob:* Or "though I am the God that Jacob proudly worshiped."

Prayer Starter: Father, bless those who work in homeless shelters and among the poor around the world.

Memory Verse: Others may follow their gods, but . . .   *—Micah 4.5*

Jonah and the Fish

One day the LORD told Jonah, the son of Amittai, ²to go to the great city of Nineveh[a] and say to the people, "The LORD has seen your terrible sins. You are doomed!"

³Instead, Jonah ran from the LORD. He went to the seaport of Joppa and bought a ticket on a ship that was going to Spain. Then he got on the ship and sailed away to escape.

⁴But the LORD made a strong wind blow, and such a bad storm came up that the ship was about to be broken to pieces. ⁵The sailors were frightened, and they all started praying to their gods. They even threw the ship's cargo overboard to make the ship lighter.

All this time, Jonah was down below deck, sound asleep. ⁶The ship's captain went to him and said, "How can you sleep at a time like this? Get up and pray to your God! Maybe he will have pity on us and keep us from drowning."

⁷Finally, the sailors got together and said, "Let's ask our gods to show us[b] who caused all this trouble." It turned out to be Jonah.

¹⁵Then they threw Jonah overboard, and the sea calmed down. ¹⁶The sailors were so terrified that they offered a sacrifice to the LORD and made all kinds of promises.

¹⁷The LORD sent a big fish to swallow Jonah, and Jonah was inside the fish for three days and three nights.

[a]1.2 *Nineveh:* Capital city of Assyria, a hated enemy of Israel. [b]1.7 *ask . . . show us:* The Hebrew text has "cast lots," which were pieces of wood or stone used to find out how and when to do something. In this case, the lots would show who was the guilty person.

Prayer Starter: I want to serve you with my whole heart, dear Lord, and with my whole life.

Memory Verse: Others may follow their gods, but we will . . .
—Micah 4.5

Angry Enough to Die

Once again the LORD told Jonah ²to go to that great city of Nineveh and preach his message of doom.

³Jonah obeyed the LORD and went to Nineveh. The city was so big that it took three days just to walk through it. ⁴After walking for a day, Jonah warned the people, "Forty days from now, Nineveh will be destroyed!"

⁵They believed God's message and set a time when they would go without eating to show their sorrow. Then everyone in the city, no matter who they were, dressed in sackcloth.

¹⁰When God saw that the people had stopped doing evil things, he had pity and did not destroy them as he had planned.

4 Jonah was really upset and angry. ²So he prayed:
Our LORD, I knew from the very beginning that you wouldn't destroy Nineveh. That's why I left my own country and headed for Spain. You are a kind and merciful God, and you are very patient. You always show love, and you don't like to punish anyone, not even foreigners.

³Now let me die! I'd be better off dead.

⁴The LORD replied, "What right do you have to be angry?"

⁵Jonah then left through the east gate of the city and made a shelter to protect himself from the sun. He sat under the shelter, waiting to see what would happen to Nineveh.

⁶The LORD made a vine grow up to shade Jonah's head and protect him from the sun. Jonah was very happy to have the vine, ⁷but early the next morning the LORD sent a worm to chew on the vine, and the vine dried up. ⁸During the day the LORD sent a scorching wind, and the sun beat down on Jonah's head, making him feel faint. Jonah was ready to die, and he shouted, "I wish I were dead!"

⁹But the LORD asked, "Jonah, do you have the right to be angry about the vine?"

"Yes, I do," he answered, "and I'm angry enough to die."

¹⁰But the LORD said:

You are concerned about a vine that you did not plant or take care of, a vine that grew up in one night and died the next. ¹¹In that city of Nineveh there are more than a hundred twenty thousand people who cannot tell right from wrong, and many cattle are also there. Don't you think I should be concerned about that big city?

Prayer Starter: Lord, help me be concerned about the needs of all the people and animals you have made.

Memory Verse: Others may follow their gods, but we will always follow the LORD . . .
—Micah 4.5

Micah's Warning

I am Micah from Moresheth.[a] And this is the message about Samaria and Jerusalem[b] that the LORD gave me when Jotham, Ahaz, and Hezekiah[c] were the kings of Judah.

² Listen, all of you!
Earth and everything on it, pay close attention.
The LORD God accuses you from his holy temple.[d]
³ And he will come down to crush underfoot
  every pagan altar.
⁴ Mountains will melt beneath his feet
  like wax beside a fire.
Valleys will vanish like water rushing down a ravine.
⁵ This will happen because of the terrible sins of Israel,
  the descendants of Jacob.
Samaria has led Israel to sin,
  and pagan altars at Jerusalem have made Judah sin.

⁶ So the LORD will leave Samaria in ruins—
  merely an empty field where vineyards are planted.
He will scatter its stones and destroy its foundations.
⁷   Samaria's idols will be smashed,
and the wages of temple prostitutes[e]
  will be destroyed by fire.
Silver and gold from those idols will then be used
  by foreigners as payment for prostitutes.

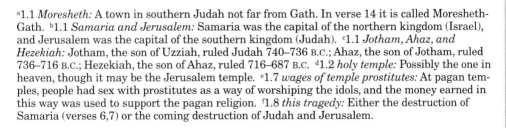

⁸ Because of this tragedy,[f] I go barefoot and naked.
My crying and weeping sound like howling wolves
  or ostriches.
⁹ The nation is fatally wounded. Judah is doomed.
  Jerusalem will fall.

---

[a]1.1 *Moresheth:* A town in southern Judah not far from Gath. In verse 14 it is called Moresheth-Gath. [b]1.1 *Samaria and Jerusalem:* Samaria was the capital of the northern kingdom (Israel), and Jerusalem was the capital of the southern kingdom (Judah). [c]1.1 *Jotham, Ahaz, and Hezekiah:* Jotham, the son of Uzziah, ruled Judah 740–736 B.C.; Ahaz, the son of Jotham, ruled 736–716 B.C.; Hezekiah, the son of Ahaz, ruled 716–687 B.C. [d]1.2 *holy temple:* Possibly the one in heaven, though it may be the Jerusalem temple. [e]1.7 *wages of temple prostitutes:* At pagan temples, people had sex with prostitutes as a way of worshiping the idols, and the money earned in this way was used to support the pagan religion. [f]1.8 *this tragedy:* Either the destruction of Samaria (verses 6,7) or the coming destruction of Judah and Jerusalem.

Prayer Starter: Bless our nation, God. Turn it to you.

Memory Verse: Others may follow their gods, but we will always follow the LORD our God.   —*Micah 4.5*

In the Future

In the future, the mountain
with the LORD's temple
will be the highest of all.
It will reach above the hills,
and every nation will rush to it.
² People of many nations will come and say,
"Let's go up to the mountain
of the LORD God of Jacob
and worship in his temple."

The LORD will teach us his Law from Jerusalem,
and we will obey him.
³ He will settle arguments
between distant and
powerful nations.
They will pound their swords
and their spears
into rakes and shovels;
they will never again
make war
or attack one another.

⁴ Everyone will find rest
beneath their own fig trees or grape vines,
and they will live in peace.
This is a solemn promise of the LORD All-Powerful.

⁵ Others may follow their gods,
but we will always follow the LORD our God.

⁶The LORD said:
At that time I will gather my people—
the lame and the outcasts,
and all into whose lives I have brought sorrow.
⁷ Then the lame and the outcasts will belong to my people
and become a strong nation.
I, the LORD, will rule them from Mount Zion forever.
⁸ Mount Zion in Jerusalem, guardian of my people,
you will rule again.

Prayer Starter: Others may follow their gods, but we will always follow you, O Lord.

Memory Verse: The LORD . . .   —*Nahum 1.7*

The Coming Shepherd

Bethlehem Ephrathah, you are one of the smallest towns
in the nation of Judah.
But the LORD will choose one of your people
to rule the nation—
someone whose family goes back
to ancient times.[a]

3 The LORD will abandon Israel only until this ruler is born,
and the rest of his family returns to Israel.
4 Like a shepherd taking care of his sheep,
this ruler will lead and care for his people
by the power and glorious name of the LORD his God.
His people will live securely,
and the whole earth will know his true greatness,
5 because he will bring peace.

6 What offering should I bring when I bow down to worship
the LORD God Most High?
Should I try to please him[b] by sacrificing calves a year old?
7 Will thousands of sheep or rivers of olive oil
make God satisfied with me?
Should I sacrifice to the LORD my first-born child
as payment for my terrible sins?
8 The LORD God has told us what is right and what he demands:
"See that justice is done,
let mercy be your first concern,
and humbly obey your God."

7 *The people said:*
Our God, no one is like you.
We are all that is left of your chosen people,
and you freely forgive our sin and guilt.
You don't stay angry forever; you're glad to have pity
19 and pleased to be merciful.
You will trample on our sins
and throw them in the sea.

[a]5.2 *family . . . times:* Or "kingdom is eternal." [b]6.6 *try to please him:* This refers to what are traditionally called "burnt sacrifices," which were offered as a way of pleasing the LORD.

Prayer Starter: Thank you for being God. No one is like you!

Memory Verse: The LORD is good. . . .   —*Nahum 1.7*

I am Nahum from Elkosh.[a] And this is the message[b] that I wrote down about Nineveh.[c]

2 The LORD God demands loyalty.
In his anger, he takes revenge on his enemies.
3   The LORD is powerful, yet patient;
he makes sure that the guilty are always punished.
He can be seen in storms and in whirlwinds;
clouds are the dust from his feet.

4 At the LORD's command, oceans and rivers dry up.
Bashan, Mount Carmel, and Lebanon[d] wither,
and their flowers fade.
5 At the sight of the LORD,
mountains and hills tremble and melt;
the earth and its people shudder and shake.
6 Who can stand the heat of his furious anger?
It flashes out like fire and shatters stones.

7 The LORD is good. He protects those who trust him
in times of trouble.
8 But like a roaring flood, the LORD chases his enemies
into dark places and destroys them.

[a]1.1 *Elkosh:* The location of Elkosh is not known. [b]1.1 *message:* Or "vision." [c]1.1 *Nineveh:* The capital of Assyria, the hated enemy of Israel. [d]1.4 *Bashan, Mount Carmel, and Lebanon:* Three regions noted for their trees and flowers.

Prayer Starter: You are so good, dear Lord. Protect me in times of trouble.

Memory Verse: The LORD is good. He protects . . .   —*Nahum 1.7*

Feet of a Deer

This is my prayer.[a]
² I know your reputation, LORD,
and I am amazed at what you have done.
Please turn from your anger and be merciful;
do for us what you did for our ancestors.

³ You are the same Holy God
who came from Teman and Paran[b] to help us.
The brightness of your glory covered the heavens,
and your praises were heard everywhere on earth.
⁴ Your glory shone like the sun,
and light flashed from our hands,
hiding your mighty power.

⁹ You split the earth apart with rivers and streams;
¹⁰ mountains trembled at the sight of you;
rain poured from the clouds;
ocean waves roared and rose.
¹¹ The sun and moon stood still,
while your arrows and spears flashed like lightning.

¹⁴ His troops had come like a storm,
hoping to scatter us and glad to gobble us down.

¹⁷ Fig trees may no longer bloom,
or vineyards produce grapes;
olive trees may be fruitless,
and harvest time a failure;
sheep pens may be empty,
and cattle stalls vacant—
¹⁸ but I will still celebrate
because the LORD God saves me.
¹⁹ The LORD gives me strength.
He makes my feet as sure as those of a deer,
and he helps me stand on the mountains.[c]

[a]3.1 *prayer:* The Hebrew text adds "according to the shiginoth," which may mean a prayer of request or a prayer to be accompanied by a special musical instrument. [b]3.3 *Teman . . . Paran:* Teman is a district in Edom, but the name is sometimes used of the whole country of Edom; Paran is the hill country along the western border of the Gulf of Aqaba. [c]3.19 *stand on the mountains:* One possible meaning for the difficult Hebrew text.

Prayer Starter: Father, give me strength every day to do what is right.

Memory Verse: The LORD is good. He protects those who trust him . . .
—*Nahum 1.7*

I am the prophet Zechariah, the son of Berechiah and the grandson of Iddo.

The Prophet Zechariah

2 This time I saw someone holding a measuring line, ²and I asked, "Where are you going?"

"To measure Jerusalem," was the answer. "To find out how wide and long it is."

³The angel who had spoken to me was leaving, when another angel came up to him ⁴and said, "Hurry! Tell that man with the measuring line that Jerusalem won't have any boundaries. It will be too full of people and animals even to have a wall. ⁵The LORD himself has promised to be a protective wall of fire surrounding Jerusalem, and he will be its shining glory in the heart of the city."

⁶The LORD says to his people, "Run! Escape from the land in the north, where I scattered you to the four winds. ⁷Leave Babylonia and hurry back to Zion."

⁸Then the glorious LORD All-Powerful ordered me to say to the nations that had raided and robbed Zion:

Zion is as precious to the LORD as are his eyes. Whatever you do to Zion, you do to him. ⁹And so, he will put you in the power of your slaves, and they will raid and rob you. Then you will know that I am a prophet of the LORD All-Powerful.

¹⁰City of Zion, sing and celebrate! The LORD has promised to come and live with you. ¹¹When he does, many nations will turn to him and become his people. At that time you will know that I am a prophet of the LORD All-Powerful. ¹²Then Judah will be his part of the holy land, and Jerusalem will again be his chosen city.

¹³ Everyone, be silent! The LORD is present and moving about in his holy place.

Prayer Starter: Thank you for making this day. I celebrate your goodness.

Memory Verse: The LORD is good. He protects those who trust him in times of trouble.   —*Nahum 1.7*

**Zechariah's
Four
Chariots**

Finally, I looked up and saw four chariots coming from between two bronze mountains. ²The first chariot was pulled by red horses, and the second by black horses; ³the third chariot was pulled by white horses, and the fourth by spotted gray horses.

⁴"Sir," I asked the angel. "What do these stand for?"

⁵Then he explained, "These are the four winds ᵃ of heaven, and now they are going out, after presenting themselves to the Lord of all the earth. ⁶The chariot with black horses goes toward the

north, the chariot with white horses goes toward the west,[b] and the one with spotted horses goes toward the south."

[7]The horses came out eager to patrol the earth, and the angel told them, "Start patrolling the earth."

When they had gone on their way, [8]he shouted to me, "Those that have gone to the country in the north will do what the LORD's Spirit[c] wants them to do there."

[9]The LORD said to me:

[10-11]Heldai, Tobijah, and Jedaiah have returned from Babylonia. Collect enough silver and gold from them to make a crown.[d] Then go with them to the house of Josiah son of Zephaniah and put the crown on the head of the high priest Joshua son of Jehozadak.[e] [12-13]Tell him that I, the LORD All-Powerful, say, "Someone will reach out from here like a branch and build a temple for me. I will name him 'Branch,' and he will rule with royal honors. A priest will stand beside his throne,[f] and the two of them will be good friends. [14]This crown will be kept in my temple as a reminder and will be taken care of by Heldai,[g] Tobijah, Jedaiah, and Josiah."[h]

[15]When people from distant lands come and help build the temple of the LORD All-Powerful, you will know that the LORD is the one who sent me. And this will happen, if you truly obey the LORD your God.

---

[a]6.5 *winds:* Or "spirits." The Hebrew word may mean either. [b]6.6 *goes toward the west:* Or "follows behind." [c]6.8 *LORD's Spirit:* Or "LORD." [d]6.10,11 *a crown:* Two ancient translations; Hebrew "some crowns." [e]6.10,11 *Heldai . . . Jehozadak:* Or "Go to the house of Josiah son of Zephaniah, where you will find Heldai, Tobijah, and Jedaiah, who have returned from Babylonia. Collect enough silver and gold from them to make a crown. Then put it on the head of the high priest Joshua son of Jehozadak." [f]6.12,13 *stand beside his throne:* Or "sit on a throne." [g]6.14 *Heldai:* One ancient translation; Hebrew "Helem." [h]6.14 *Josiah:* One ancient translation; Hebrew "Hen."

Prayer Starter: You watch over all the earth, Lord. Help the world be at peace.

Memory Verse: Then after her baby . . .   *—Matthew 1.21*

The Unending Day

The LORD will have his day. And when it comes, everything that was ever taken from Jerusalem will be returned and divided among its people. [2]But first, he will bring many nations to attack Jerusalem—homes will be robbed . . . and half of the population dragged off, though the others will be allowed to remain.

[3]The LORD will attack those nations like a warrior fighting in battle. [4]He will take his stand on the Mount of Olives east of Jerusalem, and the mountain will split in half, forming a wide valley that runs from east to west. [5]Then you people will escape from the LORD's mountain, through this valley, which reaches to Azal.[a] You will run in all directions, just as everyone did when the earthquake struck in the time of King Uzziah of Judah. Afterwards, the LORD my God will appear with his holy angels.

[6]It will be a bright day that won't turn cloudy.[b] [7]And the LORD has decided when it will happen—this time of unending day.

[8]In both summer and winter, life-giving streams will flow from Jerusalem, half of them to the Dead Sea in the east and half to the Mediterranean Sea in the west. [9]Then there will be only one LORD who rules as King and whose name is worshiped everywhere on earth.

[10-11]From Geba down to Rimmon[c] south of Jerusalem, the entire country will be turned into flatlands, with Jerusalem still towering above. Then the city will be full of people, from Benjamin Gate, Old Gate Place, and Hananel Tower in the northeast part of the city over to Corner Gate in the northwest and down to King's Wine Press in the south. Jerusalem will always be secure and will never again be destroyed.

[a]14.5 *to Azal:* One possible meaning for the difficult Hebrew text. The location of Azal is unknown. [b]14.6 *a bright . . . cloudy:* One possible meaning for the difficult Hebrew text. [c]14.10,11 *From Geba down to Rimmon:* Approximately the northern and southern borders of Judah before the exile; Geba is about ten miles north of Jerusalem, and Rimmon is about ten miles north of Beersheba.

Prayer Starter: Father, thank you for Jesus, who is coming back to earth.

Memory Verse: Then after her baby is born . . .   *—Matthew 1.21*

The Entire Ten Percent

Descendants of Jacob, I am the LORD All-Powerful, and I never change. That's why you haven't been wiped out, ⁷even though you have ignored and disobeyed my laws ever since the time of your ancestors. But if you return to me, I will return to you. And yet you ask, "How can we return?"

⁸You people are robbing me, your God. And, here you are, asking, "How are we robbing you?"

You are robbing me of the offerings and of the ten percent that belongs to me.ᵃ ⁹That's why your whole nation is under a curse. ¹⁰I am the LORD All-Powerful, and I challenge you to put me to the test. Bring the entire ten percent into the storehouse, so there will be food in my house. Then I will open the windows of heaven and flood you with blessing after blessing.ᵇ ¹¹I will also stop locustsᶜ from destroying your crops and keeping your vineyards from producing. ¹²Everyone of every nation will talk about how I have blessed you and about your wonderful land. I, the LORD All-Powerful, have spoken!

¹⁶All those who truly respected the LORD and honored his name started discussing these things, and when God saw what was happening, he had their namesᵈ written as a reminder in his book.

¹⁷Then the LORD All-Powerful said:

You people are precious to me, and when I come to bring justice, I will protect you, just as parents protect an obedient child. ¹⁸Then everyone will once again see the difference between those who obey me by doing right and those who reject me by doing wrong.

ᵃ3.8 *the ten percent . . . to me:* The people of Israel were supposed to give a tenth of their harvests and of their flocks and herds to the LORD. ᵇ3.10 *open the windows . . . blessing:* This may refer to rain, since there seems to have been a terrible drought at this time. ᶜ3.11 *locusts:* A kind of grasshopper that comes in swarms and causes great damage to plant life. ᵈ3.16 *names:* Or "deeds."

Prayer Starter: Make me generous, Lord, in giving my money to your work.

Memory Verse: Then after her baby is born, name him Jesus . . .
—*Matthew 1.21*

Wise Men from the East

When Jesus was born in the village of Bethlehem in Judea, Herod was king. During this time some wise men[a] from the east came to Jerusalem ²and said, "Where is the child born to be king of the Jews? We saw his star in the east[b] and have come to worship him."

³When King Herod heard about this, he was worried, and so was everyone else in Jerusalem. ⁴Herod brought together the chief priests and the teachers of the Law of Moses and asked them, "Where will the Messiah be born?"

⁵They told him, "He will be born in Bethlehem, just as the prophet wrote.

⁹The wise men listened to what the king said and then left. And the star they had seen in the east went on ahead of them until it stopped over the place where the child was. ¹⁰They were thrilled and excited to see the star.

¹¹When the men went into the house and saw the child with Mary, his mother, they knelt down and worshiped him. They took out their gifts of gold, frankincense, and myrrh[c] and gave them to him. ¹²Later they were warned in a dream not to return to Herod, and they went back home by another road.

[a]2.1 *wise men:* People famous for studying the stars. [b]2.2 *his star in the east:* Or "his star rise."
[c]2.11 *frankincense, and myrrh:* Frankincense was a valuable powder that was burned to make a sweet smell. Myrrh was a valuable sweet-smelling powder often used in perfume.

Prayer Starter: Thank you for Jesus, born on Christmas Day.

Memory Verse: Then after her baby is born, name him Jesus, because he will save his people . . .   —*Matthew 1.21*

Hiding in Egypt

After the wise men had gone, an angel from the Lord appeared to Joseph in a dream and said, "Get up! Hurry and take the child and his mother to Egypt! Stay there until I tell you to return, because Herod is looking for the child and wants to kill him."

¹⁴That night, Joseph got up and took his wife and the child to Egypt, ¹⁵where they stayed until Herod died. So the Lord's promise came true, just as the prophet had said, "I called my son out of Egypt."

¹⁶When Herod found out that the wise men from the east had tricked him, he was very angry. He gave orders for his men to kill all the boys who lived in or near Bethlehem and were two years old and younger. This was based on what he had learned from the wise men.

¹⁷So the Lord's promise came true, just as the prophet Jeremiah had said,

18 "In Ramah a voice was heard
      crying and weeping loudly.
    Rachel was mourning for her children,
    and she refused to be comforted,
        because they were dead."

19After King Herod died, an angel from the Lord appeared in a dream to Joseph while he was still in Egypt. 20The angel said, "Get up and take the child and his mother back to Israel. The people who wanted to kill him are now dead."

21Joseph got up and left with them for Israel. 22But when he heard that Herod's son Archelaus was now ruler of Judea, he was afraid to go there. Then in a dream he was told to go to Galilee, 23and they went to live there in the town of Nazareth. So the Lord's promise came true, just as the prophet had said, "He will be called a Nazarene."[a]

[a]2.23 *He will be called a Nazarene:* The prophet who said this is not known.

Prayer Starter: Lord, help the people of Israel and Egypt and all the other nations to know and love Jesus Christ.

Memory Verse: Then after her baby is born, name him Jesus, because he will save his people from their sins. *—Matthew 1.21*

Jesus Tested by Satan

The Holy Spirit led Jesus into the desert, so that the devil could test him. ²After Jesus had gone without eating[a] for forty days and nights, he was very hungry. ³Then the devil came to him and said, "If you are God's Son, tell these stones to turn into bread."

⁴Jesus answered, "The Scriptures say:

'No one can live only on food.
People need every word that God has spoken.'"

⁵Next, the devil took Jesus to the holy city and had him stand on the highest part of the temple. ⁶The devil said, "If you are God's son, jump off. The Scriptures say:

'God will give his angels orders about you.
They will catch you in their arms,
and you won't hurt your feet on the stones.'"

⁷Jesus answered, "The Scriptures also say, 'Don't try to test the Lord your God!'"

⁸Finally, the devil took Jesus up on a very high mountain and showed him all the kingdoms on earth and their power. ⁹The devil said to him, "I will give all this to you, if you will bow down and worship me."

¹⁰Jesus answered, "Go away Satan! The Scriptures say:

'Worship the Lord your God
and serve only him.'"

¹¹Then the devil left Jesus, and angels came to help him.

[a]4.2 *went without eating:* The Jewish people sometimes went without eating (also called "fasting") to show their love for God or to show sorrow for their sins.

Prayer Starter: Keep us safe from the devil's traps, Lord. Deliver us from evil.

Memory Verse: But more than anything else . . . —*Matthew 6.33*

The Sermon on the Mount

Large crowds followed Jesus from Galilee and the region around the ten cities known as Decapolis.[a] They also came from Jerusalem, Judea, and from across the Jordan River.

5 When Jesus saw the crowds, he went up on the side of a mountain and sat down.[b]

Jesus' disciples gathered around him, [2]and he taught them:

[3] God blesses those people who depend only on him.
> They belong to the kingdom of heaven![c]
[4] God blesses those people who grieve.
> They will find comfort!
[5] God blesses those people who are humble.
> The earth will belong to them!
[6] God blesses those people who want to obey him[d]
more than to eat or drink.
> They will be given what they want!
[7] God blesses those people who are merciful.
> They will be treated with mercy!
[8] God blesses those people whose hearts are pure.
> They will see him!
[9] God blesses those people who make peace.
> They will be called his children!

[10] God blesses those people who are treated badly for doing right.
> They belong to the kingdom of heaven.[e]

[11]God will bless you when people insult you, mistreat you, and tell all kinds of evil lies about you because of me. [12]Be happy and excited! You will have a great reward in heaven. People did these same things to the prophets who lived long ago.

[a]4.25 *the ten cities known as Decapolis:* A group of ten cities east of Samaria and Galilee, where the people followed the Greek way of life. [b]5.1 *sat down:* Teachers in the ancient world, including Jewish teachers, usually sat down when they taught. [c]5.3 *They belong to the kingdom of heaven:* Or "The kingdom of heaven belongs to them." [d]5.6 *who want to obey him:* Or "who want to do right" or "who want everyone to be treated right." [e]5.10 *They belong to the kingdom of heaven:* Or "The kingdom of heaven belongs to them."

Prayer Starter: Lord, bless us. May we depend only on you.

Memory Verse: But more than anything else, put God's work first . . .
> —*Matthew 6.33*

When You Pray

When you pray, don't be like those show-offs who love to stand up and pray in the meeting places and on the street corners. They do this just to look good. I can assure you that they already have their reward.

⁶When you pray, go into a room alone and close the door. Pray to your Father in private. He knows what is done in private, and he will reward you.

⁷When you pray, don't talk on and on as people do who don't know God. They think God likes to hear long prayers. ⁸Don't be like them. Your Father knows what you need before you ask.

⁹You should pray like this:

Our Father in heaven
help us to honor your name.
¹⁰ Come and set up your kingdom,
so that everyone on earth
will obey you,
as you are obeyed in heaven.
¹¹ Give us our food for today.ᵃ
¹² Forgive us for doing wrong,
as we forgive others.
¹³ Keep us from being tempted
and protect us from evil.ᵇ

¹⁴If you forgive others for the wrongs they do to you, your Father in heaven will forgive you. ¹⁵But if you don't forgive others, your Father will not forgive your sins.

¹⁶When you go without eating,ᶜ don't try to look gloomy as those show-offs do when they go without eating. I can assure you that they already have their reward. ¹⁷Instead, comb your hair and wash your face. ¹⁸Then others won't know that you are going without eating. But your Father sees what is done in private, and he will reward you.

ᵃ6.11 *our food for today:* Or "the food that we need" or "our food for the coming day." ᵇ6.13 *evil:* Or "the evil one," that is, the devil. Some manuscripts add, "the kingdom, the power, and the glory are yours forever. Amen." ᶜ6.16 *without eating:* The Jewish people sometimes went without eating (also called "fasting") to show their love for God or to show sorrow for their sins.

Prayer Starter: Our father in heaven, help us to honor your name.

Memory Verse: But more than anything else, put God's work first and do what he wants. . . .
—*Matthew 6.33*

Look at the Birds

You cannot be the slave of two masters! You will like one more than the other or be more loyal to one than the other. You cannot serve both God and money.

²⁵I tell you not to worry about your life. Don't worry about having something to eat, drink, or wear. Isn't life more than food or clothing? ²⁶Look at the birds in the sky! They don't plant or harvest. They don't even store grain in barns. Yet your Father in heaven takes care of them. Aren't you worth more than birds?

²⁷Can worry make you live longer?[a] ²⁸Why worry about clothes? Look how the wild flowers grow. They don't work hard to make their clothes. ²⁹But I tell you that Solomon with all his wealth[b] wasn't as well clothed as one of them. ³⁰God gives such beauty to everything that grows in the fields, even though it is here today and thrown into a fire tomorrow. He will surely do even more for you! Why do you have such little faith?

³¹Don't worry and ask yourselves, "Will we have anything to eat? Will we have anything to drink? Will we have any clothes to wear?" ³²Only people who don't know God are always worrying about such things. Your Father in heaven knows that you need all of these. ³³But more than anything else, put God's work first and do what he wants. Then the other things will be yours as well.

[a]6.27 *live longer:* Or "grow taller." [b]6.29 *Solomon with all his wealth:* The Jewish people thought that Solomon was the richest person who had ever lived.

Prayer Starter: Keep me from worry, dear Lord, for I know you love and care for me.

Memory Verse: But more than anything else, put God's work first and do what he wants. Then the other things . . .   —*Matthew 6.33*

Jesus Walks on Water

Right away, Jesus made his disciples get into a boat and start back across the lake.[a] But he stayed until he had sent the crowds away. ²³Then he went up on a mountain where he could be alone and pray. Later that evening, he was still there.

²⁴By this time the boat was a long way from the shore. It was going against the wind and was being tossed around by the waves. ²⁵A little while before morning, Jesus came walking on the water toward his disciples. ²⁶When they saw him, they thought he was a ghost. They were terrified and started screaming.

²⁷At once, Jesus said to them, "Don't worry! I am Jesus. Don't be afraid."

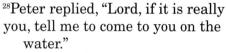

²⁸Peter replied, "Lord, if it is really you, tell me to come to you on the water."

²⁹"Come on!" Jesus said. Peter then got out of the boat and started walking on the water toward him. ³⁰But when Peter saw how strong the wind was, he was afraid and started sinking, "Save me, Lord!" he shouted.

³¹Right away, Jesus reached out his hand. He helped Peter up and said, "You surely don't have much faith. Why do you doubt?"

³²When Jesus and Peter got into the boat, the wind died down. ³³The men in the boat worshiped Jesus and said, "You really are the Son of God!"

³⁴Jesus and his disciples crossed the lake and came to shore near the town of Gennesaret. ³⁵The people found out that he was there, and they sent word to everyone who lived in that part of the country. So they brought all the sick people to Jesus. ³⁶They begged him just to let them touch his clothes, and everyone who did was healed.

ᵃ14.22 *back across the lake:* To the west side.

Prayer Starter: Give me a stronger faith, dear Lord.

Memory Verse: But more than anything else, put God's work first and do what he wants. Then the other things will be yours as well.
—*Matthew 6.33*

235

Who Is Jesus?

When Jesus and his disciples were near the town of Caesarea Philippi, he asked them, "What do people say about the Son of Man?"

[14]The disciples answered, "Some people say you are John the Baptist or maybe Elijah[a] or Jeremiah or some other prophet."

[15]Then Jesus asked them, "But who do you say I am?"

[16]Simon Peter spoke up, "You are the Messiah, the Son of the living God."

[17]Jesus told him:

Simon, son of Jonah, you are blessed! You didn't discover this on your own. It was shown to you by my Father in heaven. [18]So I will call you Peter, which means "a rock." On this rock I will build my church, and death itself will not have any power over it. [19]I will give you the keys to the kingdom of heaven, and God in heaven will allow whatever you allow on earth. But he will not allow anything that you don't allow.

[20]Jesus told his disciples not to tell anyone that he was the Messiah.

[21]From then on, Jesus began telling his disciples what would happen to him. He said, "I must go to Jerusalem. There the nation's leaders, the chief priests, and the teachers of the Law of Moses will make me suffer terribly. I will be killed, but three days later I will rise to life."

[24]Then Jesus said to his disciples:

If any of you want to be my followers, you must forget about yourself. You must take up your cross and follow me.

[a]16.14 *Elijah:* Many of the Jewish people expected the prophet Elijah to come and prepare the way for the Messiah.

Prayer Starter: I praise you for Jesus, the Messiah, Son of the living God.

Memory Verse: Hooray for the Son of David! . . .   —*Matthew 21.9*

My Own Dear Son

Six days later Jesus took Peter and the brothers James and John with him. They went up on a very high mountain where they could be alone. ²There in front of the disciples, Jesus was completely changed. His face was shining like the sun, and his clothes became white as light.

³All at once Moses and Elijah were there talking with Jesus. ⁴So Peter said to him, "Lord, it is good for us to be here! Let us make three shelters, one for you, one for Moses, and one for Elijah."

⁵While Peter was still speaking, the shadow of a bright cloud passed over them. From the cloud a voice said, "This is my own dear Son, and I am pleased with him. Listen to what he says!" ⁶When the disciples heard the voice, they were so afraid that they fell flat on the ground. ⁷But Jesus came over and touched them. He said, "Get up and don't be afraid!" ⁸When they opened their eyes, they saw only Jesus.

⁹On their way down from the mountain, Jesus warned his disciples not to tell anyone what they had seen until after the Son of Man had been raised from death.

¹⁰The disciples asked Jesus, "Don't the teachers of the Law of Moses say that Elijah must come before the Messiah does?"

¹¹Jesus told them, "Elijah certainly will come and get everything ready. ¹²In fact, he has already come. But the people did not recognize him and treated him just as they wanted to. They will soon make the Son of Man suffer in the same way." ¹³Then the disciples understood that Jesus was talking to them about John the Baptist.

Prayer Starter: I love your Word, Lord. Thank you for every verse in the Bible.

Memory Verse: Hooray for the Son of David! God bless . . .

—*Matthew 21.9*

Jesus Enters Jerusalem

hen Jesus and his disciples came near Jerusalem, he went to Bethphage on the Mount of Olives and sent two of them on ahead. ²He told them, "Go into the next village, where you will at once find a donkey and her colt. Untie the two donkeys and bring them to me. ³If anyone asks why you are doing that, just say, 'The Lord[a] needs them.' Right away he will let you have the donkeys."

⁴So God's promise came true, just as the prophet had said,

⁵ "Announce to the people of Jerusalem:
    'Your king is coming to you!
He is humble and rides on a donkey.
    He comes on the colt of a donkey.'"

⁶The disciples left and did what Jesus had told them to do. ⁷They brought the donkey and its colt and laid some clothes on their backs. Then Jesus got on.

⁸Many people spread clothes in the road, while others put down branches[b] which they had cut from trees. ⁹Some people walked ahead of Jesus and others followed behind. They were all shouting,

"Horray[c] for the Son of David![d]
God bless the one who comes in the name of the Lord.
    Horray for God in heaven above!"

¹⁰When Jesus came to Jerusalem, everyone in the city was excited and asked, "Who can this be?"

¹¹The crowd answered, "This is Jesus, the prophet from Nazareth in Galilee."

[a]21.3 *The Lord:* Or "The master of the donkeys." [b]21.8 *spread clothes . . . put down branches:* This was one way that the Jewish people welcomed a famous person. [c]21.9 *Hooray:* This translates a word that can mean "please save us." But it is most often used as a shout of praise to God. [d]21.9 *Son of David:* The Jewish people expected the Messiah to be from the family of King David, and for this reason the Messiah was often called the "Son of David."

Prayer Starter: Hooray for the Son of David! Hooray for Jesus!

Memory Verse: Hooray for the Son of David! God bless the one who comes . . .
    —*Matthew 21.9*

Peter Denies Christ

After Jesus had been arrested, he was led off to the house of Caiaphas the high priest. The nation's leaders and the teachers of the Law of Moses were meeting there. ⁵⁸But Peter followed along at a distance and came to the courtyard of the high priest's palace. He went in and sat down with the guards to see what was going to happen.

⁵⁹The chief priests and the whole council wanted to put Jesus to death. So they tried to find some people who would tell lies about him in court.ᵃ

⁶⁹While Peter was sitting out in the courtyard, a servant girl came up to him and said, "You were with Jesus from Galilee."

⁷⁰But in front of everyone Peter said, "That isn't so! I don't know what you are talking about!"

⁷¹When Peter had gone out to the gate, another servant girl saw him and said to some people there, "This man was with Jesus from Nazareth."

⁷²Again Peter denied it, and this time he swore, "I don't even know that man!"

⁷³A little while later some people standing there walked over to Peter and said, "We know that you are one of them. We can tell it because you talk like someone from Galilee."

⁷⁴Peter began to curse and swear, "I don't know that man!"

Right then a rooster crowed.

ᵃ26.59 *some people who would tell lies about him in court:* The Law of Moses taught that two witnesses were necessary before a person could be put to death.

Prayer Starter: Keep me from ever being ashamed of being a Christian, Lord.

Memory Verse: Hooray for the Son of David! God bless the one who comes in the name of the Lord. . . .   —*Matthew 21.9*

Pilate

During Passover the governor always freed a prisoner chosen by the people. [16]At that time a well-known terrorist named Jesus Barabbas[a] was in jail. [17]So when the crowd came together, Pilate asked them, "Which prisoner do you want me to set free? Do you want Jesus Barabbas or Jesus who is called the Messiah?" [18]Pilate knew that the leaders had brought Jesus to him because they were jealous.

[19]While Pilate was judging the case, his wife sent him a message. It said, "Don't have anything to do with that innocent man. I have had nightmares because of him."

[20]But the chief priests and the leaders convinced the crowds to ask for Barabbas to be set free and for Jesus to be killed. [21]Pilate asked the crowd again, "Which of these two men do you want me to set free?"

"Barabbas!" they replied.

[22]Pilate asked them, "What am I to do with Jesus, who is called the Messiah?"

They all yelled, "Nail him to a cross!"

[23]Pilate answered, "But what crime has he done?"

"Nail him to a cross!" they yelled even louder.

[24]Pilate saw that there was nothing he could do and that the people were starting to riot. So he took some water and washed his hands[b] in front of them and said, "I won't have anything to do with killing this man. You are the ones doing it!"

[25]Everyone answered, "We and our descendants will take the blame for his death!"

[26]Pilate set Barabbas free. Then he ordered his soldiers to beat Jesus with a whip and nail him to a cross.

[a]27.16 *Jesus Barabbas:* Here and in verse 17 many manuscripts have "Barabbas." [b]27.24 *washed his hands:* To show that he was innocent.

Prayer Starter: How can I ever thank you enough for the Lord Jesus Christ?

Memory Verse: Hooray for the Son of David! God bless the one who comes in the name of the Lord. Hooray for God in heaven above!
—Matthew 21.9

Jesus Heals the Sick

Everyone was amazed at his teaching. He taught with authority, and not like the teachers of the Law of Moses. ²³Suddenly a man with an evil spiritᵃ in him entered the meeting place and yelled. ²⁴"Jesus from Nazareth, what do you want with us? Have you come to destroy us? I know who you are! You are God's Holy One."

²⁵Jesus told the evil spirit, "Be quiet and come out of the man!" ²⁶The spirit shook him. Then it gave a loud shout and left.

²⁷Everyone was completely surprised and kept saying to each other, "What is this? It must be some new kind of powerful teaching! Even the evil spirits obey him." ²⁸News about Jesus quickly spread all over Galilee.

²⁹As soon as Jesus left the meeting place with James and John, they went home with Simon and Andrew. ³⁰When they got there, Jesus was told that Simon's mother-in-law was sick in bed with fever. ³¹Jesus went to her. He took hold of her hand and helped her up. The fever left her, and she served them a meal.

³²That evening after sunset,ᵇ all who were sick or had demons in them were brought to Jesus. ³³In fact, the whole town gathered around the door of the house. ³⁴Jesus healed all kinds of terrible diseases and forced out a lot of demons. But the demons knew who he was, and he did not let them speak.

ᵃ1.23 *evil spirit:* A Jewish person who had an evil spirit was considered "unclean" and was not allowed to eat or worship with other Jewish people. ᵇ1.32 *after sunset:* The Sabbath was over, and a new day began at sunset.

Prayer Starter: Help me to tell the good news about Jesus to someone this week.

Memory Verse: Let the children come to me! . . . —*Mark 10.14b*

Lots of Evil Spirits

Jesus and his disciples crossed Lake Galilee and came to shore near the town of Gerasa.[a] [2]When he was getting out of the boat, a man with an evil spirit quickly ran to him [3]from the graveyard[b] where he had been living. No one was able to tie the man up anymore, not even with a chain. [4]He had often been put in chains and leg irons, but he broke the chains and smashed the leg irons. No one could control him. [5]Night and day he was in the graveyard or on the hills, yelling and cutting himself with stones.

[6]When the man saw Jesus in the distance, he ran up to him and knelt down. [7]He shouted, "Jesus, Son of God in heaven, what do you want with me? Promise me in God's name that you won't torture me!" [8]The man said this because Jesus had already told the evil spirit to come out of him.

[9]Jesus asked, "What is your name?"

The man answered, "My name is Lots, because I have 'lots' of evil spirits." [10]He then begged Jesus not to send them away.

[11]Over on the hillside a large herd of pigs was feeding. [12]So the evil spirits begged Jesus, "Send us into those pigs! Let us go into them." [13]Jesus let them go, and they went out of the man and into the pigs. The whole herd of about two thousand pigs rushed down the steep bank into the lake and drowned.

[a]5.1 *Gerasa:* Some manuscripts have "Gadara," and others have "Gergesa." [b]5.3 *graveyard:* It was thought that demons and evil spirits lived in graveyards.

Prayer Starter: You are stonger than the devil and all the demons, God. You are Lord over all the earth.

Memory Verse: Let the children come to me! Don't try to stop them. . . .
                                                                —*Mark 10.14b*

Once again Jesus got into the boat and crossed Lake Galilee.[a] Then as he stood on the shore, a large crowd gathered around him. [22]The person in charge of the Jewish meeting place was also there. His name was Jairus, and when he saw Jesus, he went over to him. He knelt at Jesus' feet [23]and started begging him for help. He said, "My daughter is about to die! Please come and touch her, so she will get well and live." [24]Jesus went with Jairus. Many people followed along and kept crowding around.

[35]While Jesus was still speaking, some men came from Jairus' home and said, "Your daughter has died! Why bother the teacher anymore?"

[36]Jesus heard[b] what they said, and he said to Jairus, "Don't worry. Just have faith!"

[37]Jesus did not let anyone go with him except Peter and the two brothers, James and John. [38]They went home with Jairus and saw the people crying and making a lot of noise.[c] [39]Then Jesus went inside and said to them, "Why are you crying and carrying on like this? The child isn't dead. She is just asleep." [40]But the people laughed at him.

After Jesus had sent them all out of the house, he took the girl's father and mother and his three disciples and went to where she was. [41-42]He took the twelve-year-old girl by the hand and said, "Talitha, koum!"[d] which means, "Little girl, get up!" The girl got right up and started walking around.

[a]5.21 *crossed Lake Galilee:* To the west side. [b]5.36 *heard:* Or "ignored." [c]5.38 *crying and making a lot of noise:* The Jewish people often hired mourners for funerals. [d]5.41,42 *Talitha, koum:* These words are in Aramaic, a language spoken in Palestine during the time of Jesus.

Prayer Starter: Keep me from worry. Give me faith instead of fear.

Memory Verse: Let the children come to me! Don't try to stop them. People who are like . . .   —*Mark 10.14b*

Jesus Feeds Five Thousand

After the apostles returned to Jesus,[a] they told him everything they had done and taught. [31]But so many people were coming and going that Jesus and the apostles did not even have a chance to eat. Then Jesus said, "Let's go to a place[b] where we can be alone and get some rest." [32]They left in a boat for a place where they could be alone. [33]But many people saw them leave and figured out where they were going. So people from every town ran on ahead and got there first.

[34]When Jesus got out of the boat, he saw the large crowd that was like sheep without a shepherd. He felt sorry for the people and started teaching them many things.

[35]That evening the disciples came to Jesus and said, "This place is like a desert, and it is already late. [36]Let the crowds leave, so they can go to the farms and villages near here and buy something to eat."

[37]Jesus replied, "You give them something to eat."

But they asked him, "Don't you know that it would take almost a year's wages[c] to buy all of these people something to eat?"

[38]Then Jesus said, "How much bread do you have? Go and see!"

They found out and answered, "We have five small loaves of bread[d] and two fish." [39]Jesus told his disciples to have the people sit down on the green grass. [40]They sat down in groups of a hundred and groups of fifty.

[41]Jesus took the five loaves and the two fish. He looked up toward heaven and blessed the food. Then be broke the bread and handed it to his disciples to give to the people. He also divided the two fish, so that everyone could have some.

[42]After everyone had eaten all they wanted, [43]Jesus' disciples picked up twelve large baskets of leftover bread and fish.

[44]There were five thousand men who ate the food.

[a]6.30 *the apostles returned to Jesus:* From the mission on which he had sent them. [b]6.31 *a place:* This was probably northeast of Lake Galilee. [c]6.37 *almost a year's wages:* The Greek text has "two hundred silver coins." Each coin was the average day's wage for a worker. [d]6.38 *loaves of bread:* These would have been flat and round or in the shape of a bun.

Prayer Starter: Thank you, Lord, for fish and bread and pizzas and cherry pies, and for all good things to eat.

Memory Verse: Let the children come to me! Don't try to stop them. People who are like these little children . . .   —*Mark 10.14b*

Jesus Blesses Children

Some Pharisees wanted to test Jesus. So they came up to him and asked if it was right for a man to divorce his wife. ³Jesus asked them, "What does the Law of Moses say about that?"

⁴They answered, "Moses allows a man to write out divorce papers and send his wife away."

⁵Jesus replied, "Moses gave you this law because you are so heartless. ⁶But in the beginning God made a man and a woman. ⁷That's why a man leaves his father and mother and gets married. ⁸He becomes like one person with his wife. Then they are no longer two people, but one. ⁹And no one should separate a couple that God has joined together."

¹⁰When Jesus and his disciples were back in the house, they asked him about what he had said. ¹¹He told them, "A man who divorces his wife and marries someone else is unfaithful to his wife. ¹²A woman who divorces her husband[a] and marries again is also unfaithful."

¹³Some people brought their children to Jesus so that he could bless them by placing his hands on them. But his disciples told the people to stop bothering him.

¹⁴When Jesus saw this, he became angry and said, "Let the children come to me! Don't try to stop them. People who are like these little children belong to the kingdom of God.[b] ¹⁵I promise you that you cannot get into God's kingdom, unless you accept it the way a child does." ¹⁶Then Jesus took the children in his arms and blessed them by placing his hands on them.

[a]10.12 *A woman who divorces her husband:* Roman law let a woman divorce her husband, but Jewish law did not let a woman do this. [b]10.14 *People who are like these little children belong to the kingdom of God:* Or "The kingdom of God belongs to people who are like these little children."

Prayer Starter: Thank you, Lord, for loving me. Thank you for blessing me.

Memory Verse: Let the children come to me! Don't try to stop them. People who are like these little children belong to the kingdom of God.
—*Mark 10.14b*

The Lord's Supper

It was the first day of the Festival of Thin Bread, and the Passover lambs were being killed. Jesus' disciples asked him, "Where do you want us to prepare the Passover meal?"

[13]Jesus said to two of the disciples, "Go into the city, where you will meet a man carying a jar of water.[a] Follow him, [14]and when he goes into a house, say to the owner, 'Our teacher wants to know if you have room where he can eat the Passover meal with his disciples.' [15]The owner will take you upstairs and show you a large room furnished and ready for you to use. Prepare the meal there."

[16]The two disciples went into the city and found everything just as Jesus had told them. So they prepared the Passover meal.

[17-18]While Jesus and the twelve disciples were eating together that evening, he said, "The one who will betray me is now eating with me."

[19]This made the disciples sad, and one after another they said to Jesus, "You surely don't mean me!"

[20]He answered, "It is one of you twelve men who is eating from this dish with me. [21]The Son of Man will die, just as the Scriptures say. But it is going to be terrible for the one who betrays me. That man would be better off if he had never been born."

[22]During the meal Jesus took some bread in his hands. He blessed the bread and broke it. Then he gave it to his disciples and said, "Take this. It is my body."

[23]Jesus picked up a cup of wine and gave thanks to God. He gave it to his disciples, and they all drank some. [24]Then he said, "This is my blood, which is poured out for many people, and with it God makes his agreement. [25]From now on I will not drink any wine, until I drink new wine in God's kingdom." [26]Then they sang a hymn and went out to the Mount of Olives.

[a]14.13 *a man carrying a jar of water:* A male slave carrying water could mean that the family was rich.

Prayer Starter: How precious is the body and blood of my Lord Jesus.

**Nail Him
to a Cross**

Early the next morning the chief priests, the nation's leaders, and the teachers of the Law of Moses met together with the whole Jewish council. They tied up Jesus and led him off to Pilate.

²He asked Jesus, "Are you the king of the Jews?"

"Those are your words," Jesus answered.

³The chief priests brought many charges against Jesus. ⁴Then Pilate questioned him again, "Don't you have anything to say? Don't you hear what crimes they say you have done?" ⁵But Jesus did not answer, and Pilate was amazed.

⁶During Passover, Pilate always freed one prisoner chosen by the people. ⁷And at that time there was a prisoner named Barabbas. He and some others had been arrested for murder during a riot. ⁸The crowd now came and asked Pilate to set a prisoner free, just as he usually did.

⁹Pilate asked them, "Do you want me to free the king of the Jews?" ¹⁰Pilate knew that the chief priests had brought Jesus to him because they were jealous.

¹¹But the chief priests told the crowd to ask Pilate to free Barabbas.

¹²Then Pilate asked the crowd, "What do you want me to do with this man you say isᵃ the king of the Jews?"

¹³They yelled, "Nail him to a cross!"

¹⁴Pilate asked, "But what crime has he done?"

"Nail him to a cross!" they yelled even louder.

¹⁵Pilate wanted to please the crowd. So he set Barabbas free. Then he ordered his soldiers to beat Jesus with a whip and nail him to a cross.

ᵃ15.12 *this man you say is:* These words are not in some manuscripts.

Prayer Starter: I love the one who suffered for me on his way to the cross.

Memory Verse: Nothing is . . . —*Luke 1.37*

Soldiers Make Fun of Jesus

The soldiers led Jesus inside the courtyard of the fortress[a] and called together the rest of the troops. [17]They put a purple robe[b] on him, and on his head they placed a crown that they had made out of thorn branches. [18]They made fun of Jesus and shouted, "Hey, you king of the Jews!" [19]Then they beat him on the head with a stick. They spit on him and knelt down and pretended to worship him.

[20]When the soldiers had finished making fun of Jesus, they took off the purple robe. They put his own clothes back on him and led him off to be nailed to a cross. [21]Simon from Cyrene happened to be coming in from a farm, and they forced him to carry Jesus' cross. Simon was the father of Alexander and Rufus.

[22]The soldiers took Jesus to Golgotha, which means "Place of a Skull."[c] [23]There they gave him some wine mixed with a drug to ease the pain, but he refused to drink it.

[24]They nailed Jesus to a cross and gambled to see who would get his clothes. [25]It was about nine o'clock in the morning when they nailed him to the cross.

[26]On it was a sign that told why he was nailed there. It read, "This is the King of the Jews." [27-28]The soldiers also nailed two criminals on crosses, one to the right of Jesus and the other to his left.[d]

[a]15.16 *fortress:* The place where the Roman governor stayed. It was probably at Herod's palace west of Jerusalem, though it may have been Fortress Antonia, north of the temple, where the Roman troops were stationed. [b]15.17 *purple robe:* This was probably a Roman soldier's robe. [c]15.22 *Place of a Skull:* The place was probably given this name because it was near a large rock in the shape of a human skull. [d]15.27,28 *left:* Some manuscripts add, "So the Scriptures came true which say, 'He was accused of being a criminal.'"

Prayer Starter: Thank you, Lord, thank you for Christ Jesus.

Memory Verse: Nothing is impossible . . .   *—Luke 1.37*

An Angel Visits Mary

God sent the angel Gabriel to the town of Nazareth in Galilee ²⁷with a message for a virgin named Mary. She was engaged to Joseph from the family of King David. ²⁸The angel greeted Mary and said, "You are truly blessed! The Lord is with you."

²⁹Mary was confused by the angel's words and wondered what they meant. ³⁰Then the angel told Mary, "Don't be afraid! God is pleased with you, ³¹and you will have a son. His name will be Jesus. ³²He will be great and will be called the Son of God Most High. The Lord God will make him king, as his ancestor David was. ³³He will rule the people of Israel forever, and his kingdom will never end."

³⁴Mary asked the angel, "How can this happen? I am not married!"

³⁵The angel answered, "The Holy Spirit will come down to you, and God's power will come over you. So your child will be called the holy Son of God. ³⁶Your relative Elizabeth is also going to have a son, even though she is old. No one thought she could ever have a baby, but in three months she will have a son. ³⁷Nothing is impossible for God!"

³⁸Mary said, "I am the Lord's servant! Let it happen as you have said." And the angel left her.

Prayer Starter: I am your servant, Lord. Use me.

Memory Verse: Nothing is impossible for . . .   —Luke 1.37

Mary and Elizabeth

A short time later Mary hurried to a town in the hill country of Judea. ⁴⁰She went into Zechariah's home, where she greeted Elizabeth. ⁴¹When Elizabeth heard Mary's greeting, her baby moved within her.

The Holy Spirit came upon Elizabeth. ⁴²Then in a loud voice she said to Mary:

God has blessed you more than any other woman! He has also blessed the child you will have. ⁴³Why should the mother of my Lord come to me? ⁴⁴As soon as I heard your greeting, my baby became happy and moved within me. ⁴⁵The Lord has blessed you because you believed that he will keep his promise.

⁴⁶Mary said:

With all my heart ⁴⁷I praise the Lord,
    and I am glad because of God my Savior.
⁴⁸ God cares for me, his humble servant.
From now on, all people will say
    God has blessed me.
⁴⁹ God All-Powerful has done great things for me,
    and his name is holy.
⁵⁰ He always shows mercy
    to everyone who worships him.
⁵¹ The Lord has used his powerful arm
    to scatter those who are proud.
⁵² God drags strong rulers from their thrones
    and puts humble people in places of power.
⁵³ God gives the hungry good things to eat,
and sends the rich away
    with nothing.
⁵⁴ God helps his servant Israel
    and is always merciful to his people.
⁵⁵ The Lord made this promise to our ancestors,
    to Abraham and his family forever!

⁵⁶Mary stayed with Elizabeth about three months. Then she went back home.

Prayer Starter: With all my heart, I praise the Lord.

Memory Verse: Nothing is impossible for God!   *—Luke 1.37*

Simeon and Anna

At this time a man named Simeon was living in Jerusalem. Simeon was a good man. He loved God and was waiting for God to save the people of Israel. God's Spirit came to him [26]and told him that he would not die until he had seen Christ the Lord.

[27]When Mary and Joseph brought Jesus to the temple to do what the Law of Moses says should be done for a new baby, the Spirit told Simeon to go into the temple. [28]Simeon took the baby Jesus in his arms and praised God,

[29] "Lord, I am your servant,
and now I can die in peace,
because you have kept your promise to me.
[30] With my own eyes I have seen
what you have done to save your people,
[31] and foreign nations will also see this.
[32] Your mighty power is a light for all nations,
and it will bring honor to your people Israel."

[33]Jesus' parents were surprised at what Simeon had said. [34]Then he blessed them and told Mary, "This child of yours will cause many people in Israel to fall and others to stand. The child will be like a warning sign. Many people will reject him, [35]and you, Mary, will suffer as though you had been stabbed by a dagger. But all this will show what people are really thinking."

[36]The prophet Anna was also there in the temple. She was the daughter of Phanuel from the tribe of Asher, and she was very old. In her youth she had been married for seven years, but her husband died. [37]And now she was eighty-four years old.[a] Night and day she served God in the temple by praying and often going without eating.[b]

[38]At that time Anna came in and praised God. She spoke about the child Jesus to everyone who hoped for Jerusalem to be set free.

[a]2.37 *And now she was eighty-four years old:* Or "And now she had been a widow for eighty-four years." [b]2.37 *without eating:* The Jewish people sometimes went without eating (also called "fasting") to show their love for God or to show sorrow for their sins.

Prayer Starter: Lord, your mighty power is a light for all the nations.

Memory Verse: Jesus became wise . . .   —*Luke 2.52*

The Child Jesus

After Joseph and Mary had done everything that the Law of the Lord commands, they returned home to Nazareth in Galilee. ⁴⁰The child Jesus grew. He became strong and wise, and God blessed him.

⁴¹Every year Jesus' parents went to Jerusalem for Passover. ⁴²And when Jesus was twelve years old, they all went there as usual for the celebration. ⁴³After Passover his parents left, but they did not know that Jesus had stayed on in the city. ⁴⁴They thought he was traveling with some other people, and they went a whole day before they started looking for him. ⁴⁵When they could not find him with their relatives and friends, they went back to Jerusalem and started looking for him there.

⁴⁶Three days later they found Jesus sitting in the temple, listening to the teachers and asking them questions. ⁴⁷Everyone who heard him was surprised at how much he knew and at the answers he gave.

⁴⁸When his parents found him, they were amazed. His mother said, "Son, why have you done this to us? Your father and I have been very worried, and we have been searching for you!"

⁴⁹Jesus answered, "Why did you have to look for me? Didn't you know that I would be in my Father's house?"ᵃ ⁵⁰But they did not understand what he meant.

⁵¹Jesus went back to Nazareth with his parents and obeyed them. His mother kept on thinking about all that had happened.

⁵²Jesus became wise, and he grew strong. God was pleased with him and so were the people.

ᵃ2.49 *in my Father's house:* Or "doing my Father's work."

Prayer Starter: May I be like Jesus, dear Father. Make me wise and strong.

Memory Verse: Jesus became wise, and he grew strong. . . .

—*Luke 2.52*

John the Baptist

For fifteen years[a] Emperor Tiberius had ruled that part of the world. Pontius Pilate was governor of Judea, and Herod[b] was the ruler of Galilee. Herod's brother, Philip, was the ruler in the countries of Iturea and Trachonitis, and Lysanias was the ruler of Abilene. [2]Annas and Caiaphas were the Jewish high priests.[c]

At that time God spoke to Zechariah's son John, who was living in the desert. [3]So John went along the Jordan Valley, telling the people, "Turn back to God and be baptized! Then your sins will be forgiven." [4]Isaiah the prophet wrote about John when he said,

> "In the desert someone is shouting,
> 'Get the road ready for the Lord!
>   Make a straight path for him.
> [5] Fill up every valley and level every mountain and hill.
>   Straighten the crooked paths
>   and smooth out the rough roads.
> [6] Then everyone will see the saving power of God.'"

[15]Everyone became excited and wondered, "Could John be the Messiah?"

[16]John said, "I am just baptizing with water. But someone more powerful is going to come, and I am not good enough even to untie his sandals.[d] He will baptize you with the Holy Spirit and with fire.

[21]While everyone else was being baptized, Jesus himself was baptized. Then as he prayed, the sky opened up, [22]and the Holy Spirit came down upon him in the form of a dove. A voice from heaven said, "You are my own dear Son, and I am pleased with you."

---

[a]3.1 *For fifteen years:* This was either A.D. 28 or 29, and Jesus was about thirty years old. [b]3.1 *Herod:* Herod Antipas, the son of Herod the Great. [c]3.2 *Annas and Caiaphas . . . high priests:* Annas was high priest from A.D. 6 until 15. His son-in-law Caiaphas was high priest from A.D. 18 until 37. [d]3.16 *untie his sandals:* This was the duty of a slave.

Prayer Starter: Lord, you are well pleased with your son Jesus. Be pleased with me, too.

Memory Verse: Jesus became wise, and he grew strong. God was pleased . . .
—Luke 2.52

Jesus Heals a Servant

Jesus and his apostles went down from the mountain and came to some flat, level ground. Many other disciples were there to meet him. Large crowds of people from all over Judea, Jerusalem, and the coastal cities of Tyre and Sidon were there too. ¹⁸These people had come to listen to Jesus and to be healed of their diseases.

7 After Jesus had finished teaching the people, he went to Capernaum. ²In that town an army officer's servant was sick and about to die. The officer liked this servant very much. ³And when he heard about Jesus, he sent some Jewish leaders to ask him to come and heal the servant.

⁴The leaders went to Jesus and begged him to do something. They said, "This man deserves your help! ⁵He loves our nation and even built us a meeting place." ⁶So Jesus went with them.

When Jesus wasn't far from the house, the officer sent some friends to tell him, "Lord, don't go to any trouble for me! I am not good enough for you to come into my house. ⁷And I am certainly not worthy to come to you. Just say the word, and my servant will get well. ⁸I have officers who give orders to me, and I have soldiers who take orders from me. I can say to one of them, 'Go!' and he goes. I can say to another, 'Come!' and he comes. I can say to my servant, 'Do this!' and he will do it."

⁹When Jesus heard this, he was so surprised that he turned and said to the crowd following him, "In all of Israel I've never found anyone with this much faith!"

¹⁰The officer's friends returned and found the servant well.

Prayer Starter: Give me faith like the officer in this story, O God.

Memory Verse: Jesus became wise, and he grew strong. God was pleased with him . . .
                                                        —Luke 2.52

Young Man, Get Up

Soon Jesus and his disciples were on their way to the town of Nain, and a big crowd was going along with them. ¹²As they came near the gate of the town, they saw people carrying out the body of a widow's only son. Many people from the town were walking along with her.

¹³When the Lord saw the woman, he felt sorry for her and said, "Don't cry!"

¹⁴Jesus went over and touched the stretcher on which the people were carrying the dead boy. They stopped, and Jesus said, "Young man, get up!" ¹⁵The boy sat up and began to speak. Jesus then gave him back to his mother.

¹⁶Everyone was frightened and praised God. They said, "A great prophet is here with us! God has come to his people."

¹⁷News about Jesus spread all over Judea and everywhere else in that part of the country.

¹⁸⁻¹⁹John's followers told John everything that was being said about Jesus. So he sent two of them to ask the Lord, "Are you the one we should be looking for? Or must we wait for someone else?"

²¹At that time Jesus was healing many people who were sick or in pain or were troubled by evil spirits, and he was giving sight to a lot of blind people. ²²Jesus said to the messengers sent by John, "Go and tell John what you have seen and heard. Blind people are now able to see, and the lame can walk. People who have leprosyª are being healed, and the deaf can now hear. The dead are raised to life, and the poor are hearing the good news. ²³God will bless everyone who doesn't reject me because of what I do."

ª7.22 *leprosy:* In biblical times the word "leprosy" was used for many different kinds of skin diseases.

Prayer Starter: Thank you, Lord, for helping those with problems.

Memory Verse: Jesus became wise, and he grew strong. God was pleased with him and so were the people.   *—Luke 2.52*

A Woman
Washes
Jesus'
Feet

A Pharisee invited Jesus to have dinner with him. So Jesus went to the Pharisee's home and got ready to eat.[a]

37When a sinful woman in that town found out that Jesus was there, she bought an expensive bottle of perfume. 38Then she came and stood behind Jesus. She cried and started washing his feet with her tears and drying them with her hair. The woman kissed his feet and poured the perfume on them.

39The Pharisee who had invited Jesus saw this and said to himself, "If this man really were a prophet, he would know what kind of woman is touching him! He would know that she is a sinner."

40Jesus said to the Pharisee, "Simon, I have something to say to you."

"Teacher, what is it?" Simon replied.

41Jesus told him, "Two people were in debt to a moneylender. One of them owed him five hundred silver coins, and the other owed him fifty. 42Since neither of them could pay him back, the moneylender said that they didn't have to pay him anything. Which one of them will like him more?"

43Simon answered, "I suppose it would be the one who had owed more and didn't have to pay it back."

"You are right," Jesus said.

44He turned toward the woman and said to Simon, "Have you noticed this woman? When I came into your home, you didn't give me any water

so I could wash my feet. But she has washed my feet with her tears and dried them with her hair. ⁴⁵You didn't greet me with a kiss, but from the time I came in, she has not stopped kissing my feet. ⁴⁶You didn't even pour olive oil on my head,ᵇ but she has poured expensive perfume on my feet. ⁴⁷So I tell you that all her sins are forgiven, and that is why she has shown great love. But anyone who has been forgiven for only a little will show only a little love."

⁴⁸Then Jesus said to the woman, "Your sins are forgiven."

⁴⁹Some other guests started saying to one another, "Who is this who dares to forgive sins?"

⁵⁰But Jesus told the woman, "Because of your faith, you are now saved.ᶜ May God give you peace!"

ᵃ7.36 *got ready to eat:* On special occasions the Jewish people often followed the Greek and Roman custom of lying down on their left side and leaning on their left elbow, while eating with their right hand. This is how the woman could come up behind Jesus and wash his feet. ᵇ7.44-46 *washed my feet . . . greet me with a kiss . . . pour olive oil on my head:* Guests in a home were usually offered water so they could wash their feet, because most people either went barefoot or wore sandals and would come in the house with very dusty feet. Guests were also greeted with a kiss on the cheek, and special ones often had sweet-smelling olive oil poured on their head. ᶜ7.50 *saved:* Or "healed." The Greek word may have either meaning.

Prayer Starter: Help me to love you more and more and more.

Memory Verse: Look at the crows! . . .   *—Luke 12.24*

The Good Samaritan

An expert in the Law of Moses stood up and asked Jesus a question to see what he would say. "Teacher," he asked, "what must I do to have eternal life?"

26Jesus answered, "What is written in the Scriptures? How do you understand them?"

27The man replied, "The Scriptures say, 'Love the Lord your God with all your heart, soul, strength, and mind.' They also say, 'Love your neighbors as much as you love yourself.'"

28Jesus said, "You have given the right answer. If you do this, you will have eternal life."

29But the man wanted to show that he knew what he was talking about. So he asked Jesus, "Who are my neighbors?"

30Jesus replied:

As a man was going down from Jerusalem to Jericho, robbers attacked him and grabbed everything he had. They beat him up and ran off, leaving him half dead. 31A priest happened to be going down the same road. But when he saw the man, he walked by on the other side. 32Later a temple helper[a] came to the same place. But when he saw the man who had been beaten up, he also went by on the other side.

33A man from Samaria then came traveling along that road. When he saw the man, he felt sorry for him 34and went over to him. He treated his wounds with olive oil and wine[b] and bandaged them. Then he put him on his own donkey and took him to an inn, where he took care of him. 35The next morning he gave the innkeeper two silver coins and said, "Please take care of the man. If you spend more than this on him, I will pay you when I return."

36Then Jesus asked, "Which one of these three people was a real neighbor to the man who was beaten up by robbers?

37The teacher answered, "The one who showed pity."

Jesus said, "Go and do the same!"

[a]10.32 *temple helper:* A man from the tribe of Levi, whose job it was to work around the temple.
[b]10.34 *olive oil and wine:* In New Testament times these were used as medicine. Sometimes olive oil is a symbol for healing by means of a miracle.

Prayer Starter: Show me someone I can help this week, Lord.

Memory Verse: Look at the crows! They don't plant or harvest . . .
—*Luke 12.24*

A Rich Fool

Aman in a crowd said to Jesus, "Teacher, tell my brother to give me my share of what our father left us when he died."

¹⁴Jesus answered, "Who gave me the right to settle arguments between you and your brother?"

¹⁵Then he said to the crowd, "Don't be greedy! Owning a lot of things won't make your life safe."

¹⁶So Jesus told them this story:

A rich man's farm produced a big crop, ¹⁷and he said to himself, "What can I do? I don't have a place large enough to store everything."

¹⁸Later, he said, "Now I know what I'll do. I'll tear down my barns and build bigger ones, where I can store all my grain and other goods. ¹⁹Then I'll say to myself, 'You have stored up enough good things to last for years to come. Live it up! Eat, drink, and enjoy yourself.'"

²⁰But God said to him, "You fool! Tonight you will die. Then who will get what you have stored up?"

²¹"This is what happens to people who store up everything for themselves, but are poor in the sight of God."

Prayer Starter: Thank you for taking care of all the birds, Lord, and for taking care of me.

Memory Verse: Look at the crows! They don't plant or harvest, and they don't have . . .   *—Luke 12.24*

Healing on the Sabbath

One Sabbath, Jesus was teaching in a Jewish meeting place, ¹¹and a woman was there who had been crippled by an evil spirit for eighteen years. She was completely bent over and could not straighten up. ¹²When Jesus saw the woman, he called her over and said, "You are now well." ¹³He placed his hands on her, and right away she stood up straight and praised God.

¹⁴The man in charge of the meeting place was angry because Jesus had healed someone on the Sabbath. So he said to the people, "Each week has six days when we can work. Come and be healed on one of those days, but not on the Sabbath."

¹⁵The Lord replied, "Are you trying to fool someone? Won't any one of you untie your ox or donkey and lead it out to drink on a Sabbath? ¹⁶This woman belongs to the family of Abraham, but Satan has kept her bound for eighteen years. Isn't it right to set her free on the Sabbath?" ¹⁷Jesus' words made his enemies ashamed. But everyone else in the crowd was happy about the wonderful things he was doing.

¹⁸Jesus said, "What is God's kingdom like? What can I compare it

with? ¹⁹It is like what happens when someone plants a mustard seed in a garden. The seed grows as big as a tree, and birds nest in its branches."

²⁰Then Jesus said, "What can I compare God's kingdom with? ²¹It is like what happens when a woman mixes yeast into three batches of flour. Finally, all the dough rises."

Prayer Starter: Lord, please help those who are sick today.

Memory Verse: Look at the crows! They don't plant or harvest, and they don't have storehouses or barns. . . .   *—Luke 12.24*

Jesus' Stories

Tax collectors[a] and sinners were all crowding around to listen to Jesus. [2]So the Pharisees and the teachers of the Law of Moses started grumbling, "This man is friendly with sinners. He even eats with them."

[3]Then Jesus told them this story:

[4]"If any of you has a hundred sheep, and one of them gets lost, what will you do? Won't you leave the ninety-nine in the field and go look for the lost sheep until you find it? [5]And when you find it, you will be so glad that you will put it on your shoulder [6]and carry it home. Then you will call in your friends and neighbors and say, "Let's celebrate! I've found my lost sheep."

[7]Jesus said, "In the same way there is more happiness in heaven because of one sinner who turns to God than over ninety-nine good people who don't need to."

[8]Jesus told the people another story:

What will a woman do if she has ten silver coins and loses one of them? Won't she light a lamp, sweep the floor, and look carefully until she finds it? [9]Then she will call in her friends and neighbors and say, "Let's celebrate! I've found the coin I lost."

[10]Jesus said, "In the same way God's angels are happy when even one person turns to him."

---

[a]15.1 *Tax collectors:* These were usually Jewish people who paid the Romans for the right to collect taxes. They were hated by other Jews who thought of them as traitors to their country and to their religion.

Prayer Starter: May more and more people turn to you, O Lord.

Memory Verse: Look at the crows! They don't plant or harvest, and they don't have storehouses or barns. But God takes care of them.

—Luke 12.24

A Son Comes Home

Jesus also told them another story:

Once a man had two sons. ¹²The younger son said to his father, "Give me my share of the property." So the father divided his property between his two sons.

¹³Not long after that, the younger son packed up everything he owned and left for a foreign country, where he wasted all his money in wild living. ¹⁴He had spent everything, when a bad famine spread through that whole land. Soon he had nothing to eat.

¹⁵He went to work for a man in that country, and the man sent him out to take care of his pigs.ᵃ ¹⁶He would have been glad to eat what the pigs were eating,ᵇ but no one gave him a thing.

¹⁷Finally, he came to his senses and said, "My father's workers have plenty to eat, and here I am, starving to death! ¹⁸I will go to my father and say to him, 'Father, I have sinned against God in heaven and against you. ¹⁹I am no longer good enough to be called your son. Treat me like one of your workers.'"

²⁰The younger son got up and started back to his father. But when he was still a long way off, his father saw him and felt sorry for him. He ran to his son and hugged and kissed him.

²¹The son said, "Father, I have sinned against God in heaven and against you. I am no longer good enough to be called your son."

²²But his father said to the servants, "Hurry, and bring the best clothes and put them on him. Give him a ring for his finger and sandalsᶜ for his feet. ²³Get the best calf and prepare it, so we can eat and celebrate. ²⁴This son of mine was dead, but has now come back to life. He was lost and has now been found." And they began to celebrate.

²⁵The older son had been out in the field. But when he came near the house, he heard the music and dancing. ²⁶So he called one of the servants over and asked, "What's going on here?"

²⁷The servant answered, "Your brother has come home safe and sound, and your father ordered us to kill the best calf." ²⁸The older brother got so angry that he would not even go into the house.

His father came out and begged him to go in. ²⁹But he said to his father, "For years I have worked for you like a slave and have always obeyed you. But you have never even given me a little goat, so that I could give a dinner for my friends. [30]This other son of yours wasted your money on prostitutes. And now that he has come home, you ordered the best calf to be killed for a feast."

[31]His father replied, "My son, you are always with me, and everything I have is yours. [32]But we should be glad and celebrate! Your brother was dead, but he is now alive. He was lost and has now been found."

[a]15.15 *pigs:* The Jewish religion taught that pigs were not fit to eat or even to touch. A Jewish man would have felt terribly insulted if he had to feed pigs, much less eat with them. [b]15.16 *what the pigs were eating:* The Greek text has "(bean) pods," which came from a tree in Palestine. These were used to feed animals. Poor people sometimes ate them too. [c]15.22 *ring . . . sandals:* These show that the young man's father fully accepted him as his son. A ring was a sign of high position in the family. Sandals showed that he was a son instead of a slave, since slaves did not usually wear sandals.

Prayer Starter: Give us love in our family for each other, Lord.

Memory Verse: He told them . . .   *—Luke 24.46*

J esus told his disciples a story about how they should keep on praying and never give up:

A Widow and a Judge

²In a town there was once a judge who didn't fear God or care about people. ³In that same town there was a widow who kept going to the judge and saying, "Make sure that I get fair treatment in court."

⁴For a while the judge refused to do anything. Finally, he said to himself, "Even though I don't fear God or care about people, ⁵I will help this widow because she keeps on bothering me. If I don't help her, she will wear me out."

⁶The Lord said:

Think about what that crooked judge said. ⁷Won't God protect his chosen ones who pray to him day and night? Won't he be concerned for them? ⁸He will surely hurry and help them. But when the Son of Man comes, will he find on this earth anyone with faith?

19Jesus was going through Jericho, ²where a man named Zacchaeus lived. He was in charge of collecting taxes ͣ and was very rich. ³⁻⁴Jesus was heading his way, and Zacchaeus wanted to see what he was like. But Zacchaeus was a short man and could not see over the crowd. So he ran ahead and climbed up into a sycamore tree.

⁵When Jesus got there, he looked up and said, "Zacchaeus, hurry down! I want to stay with you today." ⁶Zacchaeus hurried down and gladly welcomed Jesus.

[7]Everyone who saw this started grumbling, "This man Zacchaeus is a sinner! And Jesus is going home to eat with him."

[8]Later that day Zacchaeus stood up and said to the Lord, "I will give half of my property to the poor. And I will now pay back four times as much[b] to everyone I have ever cheated."

[9]Jesus said to Zacchaeus, "Today you and your family have been saved,[c] because you are a true son of Abraham.[d] [10]The Son of Man came to look for and to save people who are lost."

[a]19.2 *in charge of collecting taxes:* Tax collectors were usually Jewish people who paid the Romans for the right to collect taxes. They were hated by other Jews who thought of them as traitors to their country and to their religion. [b]19.8 *pay back four times as much:* Both Jewish and Roman law said that a person must pay back four times the amount that was taken. [c]19.9 *saved:* Zacchaeus was Jewish, but it is only now that he is rescued from sin and placed under God's care. [d]19.9 *son of Abraham:* As used in this verse, the words mean that Zacchaeus is truly one of God's special people.

Prayer Starter: Help me to keep on praying, Lord, and never give up.

Memory Verse: He told them: "The Scriptures say . . ."   —*Luke 24.46*

Jesus went out to the Mount of Olives, as he often did, and his disciples went with him.

Not What I Want

[40]When they got there, he told them, "Pray that you won't be tested."

[41]Jesus walked on a little way before he knelt down and prayed, [42]"Father, if you will, please don't make me suffer by having me drink from this cup.[a] But do what you want, and not what I want."

[43]Then an angel from heaven came to help him. [44]Jesus was in great pain and prayed so sincerely that his sweat fell to the ground like drops of blood.[b]

[45]Jesus got up from praying and went over to his disciples. They were asleep and worn out from being so sad. [46]He said to them, "Why are you asleep? Wake up and pray that you won't be tested."

[47]While Jesus was still speaking, a crowd came up. It was led by Judas, one of the twelve apostles. He went over to Jesus and greeted him with a kiss.[c]

[48]Jesus asked Judas, "Are you betraying the Son of Man with a kiss?"

[49]When Jesus' disciples saw what was about to happen, they asked, "Lord, should we attack them with a sword?" [50]One of the disciples even struck at the high priest's servant with his sword and cut off the servant's right ear.

[51]"Enough of that!" Jesus said. Then he touched the servant's ear and healed it.

[52]Jesus spoke to the chief priests, the temple police, and the leaders who had come to arrest him. He said, "Why do you come out with swords and clubs and treat me like a criminal? [53]I was with you every day in the temple, and you didn't arrest me. But this is your time, and darkness[d] is in control."

---

[a]22.42 *having me drink from this cup:* In the Scriptures "to drink from a cup" sometimes means to suffer. [b]22.43,44 *Then an angel . . . like drops of blood:* Verses 43,44 are not in some manuscripts. [c]22.47 *greeted him with a kiss:* It was the custom for people to greet each other with a kiss on the cheek. [d]22.53 *darkness:* Darkness stands for the power of the devil.

Prayer Starter: Lord, teach me to pray as Jesus did.

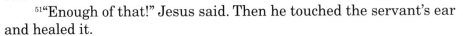

Memory Verse: He told them: "The Scriptures say that the Messiah must suffer . . ."
                                                              —*Luke 24.46*

Travelers to Emmaus

That same day two of Jesus' disciples were going to the village of Emmaus, which was about seven miles from Jerusalem. ¹⁴As they were talking and thinking about what had happened, ¹⁵Jesus came near and started walking along beside them. ¹⁶But they did not know who he was.

¹⁷Jesus asked them, "What were you talking about as you walked along?"

The two of them stood there looking sad and gloomy. ¹⁸Then the one named Cleopas asked Jesus, "Are you the only person from Jerusalem who didn't know what was happening there these last few days?"

¹⁹"What do you mean?" Jesus asked.

They answered:

Those things that happened to Jesus from Nazareth. By what he did and said he showed that he was a powerful prophet, who pleased God and all the people. ²⁰Then the chief priests and our leaders had him arrested and sentenced to die on a cross.

²⁵Then Jesus asked the two disciples, "Why can't you understand? How can you be so slow to believe all that the prophets said? ²⁶Didn't you know that the Messiah would have to suffer before he was given his glory?" ²⁷Jesus then explained everything written about himself in the Scriptures, beginning with the Law of Moses and the Books of the Prophets.ᵃ

ᵃ24.27 *the Law of Moses and the Books of the Prophets:* The Jewish Scriptures, that is, the Old Testament.

Prayer Starter: I'm so glad Jesus is alive, Lord! Hallelujah!

Memory Verse: He told them: "The Scriptures say that the Messiah must suffer, then three days later he will rise . . ."   —*Luke 24.46*

Jesus Returns to Heaven

While Jesus' disciples were talking about what had happened, Jesus appeared and greeted them. ³⁷They were frightened and terrified because they thought they were seeing a ghost.

³⁸But Jesus said, "Why are you so frightened? Why do you doubt? ³⁹Look at my hands and my feet and see who I am! Touch me and find out for yourselves. Ghosts don't have flesh and bones as you see I have."

⁴⁰After Jesus said this, he showed them his hands and his feet. ⁴¹The disciples were so glad and amazed that they could not believe it. Jesus then asked them, "Do you have something to eat?" ⁴²They gave him a piece of baked fish. ⁴³He took it and ate it as they watched.

⁴⁴Jesus said to them, "While I was still with you, I told you that everything written about me in the Law of Moses, the Books of the Prophets, and in the Psalmsᵃ had to happen."

⁴⁵Then he helped them understand the Scriptures. ⁴⁶He told them:

The Scriptures say that the Messiah must suffer, then three days later he will rise from death. ⁴⁷They also say that all people of every nation must be told in my name to turn to God, in order to be forgiven. So beginning in Jerusalem, ⁴⁸you must tell everything that has happened. ⁴⁹I will send you the one my Father has promised,ᵇ but you must stay in the city until you are given power from heaven.

⁵⁰Jesus led his disciples out to Bethany, where he raised his hands and blessed them. ⁵¹As he was doing this, he left and was taken up to heaven.ᶜ

ᵃ24.44 *Psalms:* The Jewish Scriptures were made up of three parts: (1) the Law of Moses, (2) the Books of the Prophets, and (3) the Writings, which included the Psalms. Sometimes the Scriptures were just called the Law or the Law (of Moses) and the Books of the Prophets. ᵇ24.49 *the one my Father has promised:* Jesus means the Holy Spirit. ᶜ24.51 *and was taken up to heaven:* These words are not in some manuscripts.

Prayer Starter: Dear God, help me to understand the Bible better.

Memory Verse: He told them: "The Scriptures say that the Messiah must suffer, then three days later he will rise from death." *—Luke 24.46*

A Wedding in Cana

Three days later Mary, the mother of Jesus, was at a wedding feast in the village of Cana in Galilee. [2]Jesus and his disciples had also been invited and were there.

[3]When the wine was all gone, Mary said to Jesus, "They don't have any more wine."

[4]Jesus replied, "Mother, my time hasn't yet come![a] You must not tell me what to do."

[5]Mary then said to the servants, "Do whatever Jesus tells you to do."

[6]At the feast there were six stone water jars that were used by the people for washing themselves in the way that their religion said they must. Each jar held about twenty or thirty gallons. [7]Jesus told the servants to fill them to the top with water. Then after the jars had been filled, [8]he said, "Now take some water and give it to the man in charge of the feast."

The servants did as Jesus told them, [9]and the man in charge drank some of the water that had now turned into wine. He did not know where the wine had come from, but the servants did. He called the bridegroom over [10]and said, "The best wine is always served first. Then after the guests have had plenty, the other wine is served. But you have kept the best until last!"

[11]This was Jesus' first miracle,[b] and he did it in the village of Cana in Galilee. There Jesus showed his glory, and his disciples put their faith in him. [12]After this, he went with his mother, his brothers, and his disciples to the town of Capernaum, where they stayed for a few days.

[a]2.4 *my time hasn't yet come!:* The time when the true glory of Jesus would be seen, and he would be recognized as God's Son. [b]2.11 *miracle:* The Greek text has "sign." In the Gospel of John the word "sign" is used for the miracle itself and as a way of pointing to Jesus as the Son of God.

Prayer Starter: Help me to do whatever Jesus tells me to, Lord.

Memory Verse: God loved the people of this world so much . . .

—John 3.16

Nicodemus Visits Jesus

There was a man named Nicodemus who was a Pharisee and a Jewish leader. ²One night he went to Jesus and said, "Sir, we know that God has sent you to teach us. You could not work these miracles, unless God were with you."

³Jesus replied, "I tell you for certain that you must be born from above[a] before you can see God's kingdom!"

⁴Nicodemus asked, "How can a grown man ever be born a second time?"

⁵Jesus answered:

I tell you for certain that before you can get into God's kingdom, you must be born not only by water, but by the Spirit. ⁶Humans give life to their children. Yet only God's Spirit can change you into a child of God. ⁷Don't be surprised when I say that you must be born from above. ⁸Only God's Spirit gives new life. The Spirit is like the wind that blows wherever it wants to. You can hear the wind, but you don't know where it comes from or where it is going.

⁹"How can this be?" Nicodemus asked.

¹⁰Jesus replied:

How can you be a teacher of Israel and not know these things? ¹¹I tell you for certain that we know what we are talking about because we have seen it ourselves. But none of you will accept what we say. ¹²If you don't believe when I talk to you about things on earth, how can you possibly believe if I talk to you about things in heaven?

[a]3.3 *from above:* Or "in a new way."

Prayer Starter: Thank you, God, for loving the people of this world enough to give your only Son to save them.

Memory Verse: God loved the people of this world so much that he gave his only Son . . .   *—John 3.16*

The Woman at the Well

Jesus left Judea and started for Galilee again. [4]This time he had to go through Samaria, [5]and on his way he came to the town of Sychar. It was near the field that Jacob had long ago given to his son Joseph. [6-8]The well that Jacob had dug was still there, and Jesus sat down beside it because he was tired from traveling. It was noon, and after Jesus' disciples had gone into town to buy some food, a Samaritan woman came to draw water from the well.

Jesus asked her, "Would you please give me a drink of water?"

[9]"You are a Jew," she replied, "and I am a Samaritan woman. How can you ask me for a drink of water when Jews and Samaritans won't have anything to do with each other?"[a]

[10]Jesus answered, "You don't know what God wants to give you, and you don't know who is asking you for a drink. If you did, you would ask me for the water that gives life."

[11]"Sir," the woman said, "you don't even have a bucket, and the well is deep. Where are you going to get this life-giving water? [12]Our ancestor Jacob dug this well for us, and his family and animals got water from it. Are you greater than Jacob?"

[13]Jesus answered, "Everyone who drinks this water will get thirsty again. [14]But no one who drinks the water I give will ever be thirsty again. The water I give is like a flowing fountain that gives eternal life."

[a]4.9 *won't have anything to do with each other:* Or "won't use the same cups." The Samaritans lived in the land between Judea and Galilee. They worshiped God differently from the Jews and did not get along with them.

Prayer Starter: You give me the water of life, Lord. Thank you.

Memory Verse: God loved the people of this world so much that he gave his only Son, so that everyone who has faith . . .　　　—*John 3.16*

Jesus' Brothers

Jesus decided to leave Judea and to start going through Galilee because the leaders of the people wanted to kill him. ²It was almost time for the Festival of Shelters, ³and Jesus' brothers said to him, "Why don't you go to Judea? Then your disciples can see what you are doing. ⁴No one does anything in secret, if they want others to know about them. So let the world know what you are doing!" ⁵Even Jesus' own brothers had not yet become his followers.

⁶Jesus answered, "My time hasn't yet come,ᵃ but your time is always here. ⁷The people of this world cannot hate you. They hate me, because I tell them that they do evil things. ⁸Go on to the festival. My time hasn't yet come, and I am not going." ⁹Jesus said this and stayed on in Galilee.

¹⁰After Jesus' brothers had gone to the festival, he went secretly, without telling anyone.

¹¹During the festival the leaders looked for Jesus and asked, "Where is he?" ¹²The crowds even got into an argument about him. Some were saying, "Jesus is a good man," while others were saying, "He is lying to everyone." ¹³But the people were afraid of their leaders, and none of them talked in public about him.

³⁷On the last and most important day of the festival, Jesus stood up and shouted, "If you are thirsty, come to me and drink! ³⁸Have faith in me, and you will have life-giving water flowing from deep inside you, just as the Scriptures say." ³⁹Jesus was talking about the Holy Spirit, who would be given to everyone that had faith in him.

ᵃ7.6 *My time hasn't yet come:* The time when the true glory of Jesus would be seen, and he would be recognized as God's Son.

Prayer Starter: Father, help me to share the water of life with others.

Memory Verse: God loved the people of this world so much that he gave his only Son, so that everyone who has faith in him will have eternal life . . .
—*John 3.16*

The Blind Man

As Jesus walked along, he saw a man who had been blind since birth. ²Jesus' disciples asked, "Teacher, why was this man born blind? Was it because he or his parents sinned?"

³"No, it wasn't!" Jesus answered. "But because of his blindness, you will see God work a miracle for him.

⁴As long as it is day, we must do what the one who sent me wants me to do. When night comes, no one can work. ⁵While I am in the world, I am the light for the world."

⁶After Jesus said this, he spit on the ground. He made some mud and smeared it on the man's eyes. ⁷Then he said, "Go and wash off the mud in Siloam Pool." The man went and washed in Siloam, which means "One Who Is Sent." When he had washed off the mud, he could see.

⁸The man's neighbors and the people who had seen him begging wondered if he really could be the same man. ⁹Some of them said he was the same beggar, while others said he only looked like him. But he told them, "I am that man."

¹⁰"Then how can you see?" they asked.

¹¹He answered, "Someone named Jesus made some mud and smeared it on my eyes. He told me to go and wash it off in Siloam Pool. When I did, I could see."

¹²"Where is he now?" they asked.

"I don't know," he answered.

¹³⁻¹⁴The day when Jesus made the mud and healed the man was a Sabbath. So the people took the man to the Pharisees. ¹⁵They asked him how he was able to see, and he answered, "Jesus made some mud and smeared it on my eyes. Then after I washed it off, I could see."

¹⁶Some of the Pharisees said, "This man Jesus doesn't come from God. If he did, he would not break the law of the Sabbath."

Others asked, "How could someone who is a sinner work such a miracle?"ᵃ

Since the Pharisees could not agree among themselves, ¹⁷they asked the man, "What do you say about this one who healed your eyes?"

"He is a prophet!" the man told them.

²⁴The leaders called the man back and said, "Swear by God to tell the truth! We know that Jesus is a sinner."

²⁵The man replied, "I don't know if he is a sinner or not. All I know is that I used to be blind, but now I can see!"

ᵃ9.16 *miracle:* The Greek text has "sign." In the Gospel of John the word "sign" is used for the miracle itself and as a way of pointing to Jesus as the Son of God.

Prayer Starter: I'm amazed at Jesus' power! I praise and worship him.

Memory Verse: God loved the people of this world so much that he gave his only Son, so that everyone who has faith in him will have eternal life and never really die.   *—John 3.16*

The Good Shepherd

Jesus said:

I tell you for certain that I am the gate for the sheep. ⁸Everyone who came before me was a thief or a robber, and the sheep did not listen to any of them. ⁹I am the gate. All who came in through me will be saved. Through me they will come and go and find pasture.

¹⁰A thief comes only to rob, kill and destroy. I came so that everyone would have life, and have it in its fullest. ¹¹I am the good shepherd, and the good shepherd gives up his life for his sheep. ¹²Hired workers are not like the shepherd. They don't own the sheep, and when they see a wolf coming, they run off and leave the sheep. Then the wolf attacks and scatters the flock. ¹³Hired workers run away because they don't care about the sheep.

¹⁴I am the good shepherd. I know my sheep, and they know me. ¹⁵Just as the Father knows me, I know the Father, and I give up my life for my sheep. ¹⁶I have other sheep that are not in this sheep pen. I must bring them together too, when they hear my voice. Then there will be one flock of sheep and one shepherd.

Prayer Starter: Lord, give me life to the fullest!

Memory Verse: A thief comes only to rob . . .   *—John 10.10*

Lazarus, Come Out!

Jesus then said, "I am the one who raises the dead to life! Everyone who has faith in me will live, even if they die. ²⁶And everyone who lives because of faith in me will never really die. Do you believe this?"

²⁷"Yes, Lord!" she replied. "I believe that you are Christ, the Son of God. You are the one we hoped would come into the world."

²⁸After Martha said this, she went and privately said to her sister Mary, "The Teacher is here, and he wants to see you." ²⁹As soon as Mary heard this, she got up and went out to Jesus. ³⁰He was still outside the village where Martha had gone to meet him. ³¹Many people had come to comfort Mary, and when they saw her quickly leave the house, they thought she was going out to the tomb to cry. So they followed her.

³²Mary went to where Jesus was. Then as soon as she saw him, she knelt at his feet and said, "Lord, if you had been here, my brother would not have died."

³³When Jesus saw that Mary and the people with her were crying, he was terribly upset ³⁴and asked, "Where have you put his body?"

They replied, "Lord, come and you will see."

³⁵Jesus started crying, ³⁶and the people said, "See how much he loved Lazarus."

³⁷Some of them said, "He gives sight to the blind. Why couldn't he have kept Lazarus from dying?"

³⁸Jesus was still terribly upset. So he went to the tomb, which was a cave with a stone rolled against the entrance. ³⁹Then he told the people to roll the stone away. But Martha said, "Lord, you know that Lazarus has been dead four days, and there will be a bad smell."

⁴⁰Jesus replied, "Didn't I tell you that if you had faith, you would see the glory of God?"

⁴¹After the stone had been rolled aside, Jesus looked up toward heaven and prayed, "Father, I thank you for answering my prayer. ⁴²I know that you always answer my prayers. But I said this, so that the people here would believe that you sent me."

⁴³When Jesus had finished praying, he shouted, "Lazarus, come out!" ⁴⁴The man who had been dead came out. His hands and feet were wrapped with strips of burial cloth, and a cloth covered his face.

Jesus then told the people, "Untie him and let him go."

Prayer Starter: Father, I thank you for answering my prayers.

Memory Verse: A thief comes only to rob, kill, and destroy. . . .

—John 10.10

Washing Feet

It was before Passover, and Jesus knew that the time had come for him to leave this world and to return to the Father. He had always loved his followers in this world, and he loved them to the very end.

²Even before the evening meal started, the devil had made Judas, the son of Simon Iscariot,ᵃ decide to betray Jesus.

³Jesus knew that he had come from God and would go back to God. He also knew that the Father had given him complete power. ⁴So during the meal Jesus got up, removed his outer garment, and wrapped a towel around his waist. ⁵He put some water into a large bowl. Then he began washing his disciples' feet and drying them with the towel he was wearing.

⁶But when he came to Simon Peter, that disciple asked, "Lord, are you going to wash my feet?"

⁷Jesus answered, "You don't really know what I am doing, but later you will understand."

⁸"You will never wash my feet!" Peter replied.

"If I don't wash you," Jesus told him, "you don't really belong to me."

⁹Peter said, "Lord, don't wash just my feet. Wash my hands and my head."

[10]Jesus answered, "People who have bathed and are clean all over need to wash just their feet. And you, my disciples, are clean, except for one of you." [11]Jesus knew who would betray him. That is why he said, "except for one of you."

[12]After Jesus had washed his disciples' feet and had put his outer garment back on, he sat down again.[b] Then he said:

> Do you understand what I have done? [13]You call me your teacher and Lord, and you should, because that is who I am. [14]And if your Lord and teacher has washed your feet, you should do the same for each other. [15]I have set the example, and you should do for each other exactly what I have done for you. [16]I tell you for certain that servants are not greater than their master, and messengers are not greater than the one who sent them. [17]You know these things, and God will bless you, if you do them.

[a]13.2 *Iscariot:* This may mean "a man from Kerioth" (a place in Judea). But more probably it means "a man who was a liar" or "a man who was a betrayer." [b]13.12 *sat down again:* On special occasions the Jewish people followed the Greek and Roman custom of lying down on their left side and leaning on their left elbow while eating with their right hand.

Prayer Starter: Make me a humble servant, just like the Lord Jesus.

Memory Verse: A thief comes only to rob, kill, and destroy. I came so that everyone would have life . . .   —*John 10.10*

Jesus Is Arrested

When Jesus had finished praying, he and his disciples crossed the Kidron Valley and went into a garden.[a] [2]Jesus had often met there with his disciples, and Judas knew where the place was.

[3-5]Judas had promised to betray Jesus. So he went to the garden with some Roman soldiers and temple police, who had been sent by the chief priests and the Pharisees. They carried torches, lanterns, and weapons. Jesus already knew everything that was going to happen, but he asked, "Who are you looking for?"

They answered, "We are looking for Jesus from Nazareth!"

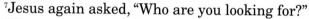

Jesus told them, "I am Jesus!"[b] [6]At once they all backed away and fell to the ground.

[7]Jesus again asked, "Who are you looking for?"

"We are looking for Jesus from Nazareth," they answered.

[8]This time Jesus replied, "I have already told you that I am Jesus. If I am the one you are looking for, let these others go. [9]Then everything will happen, just as the Scriptures say, 'I did not lose anyone you gave me.'"

[10]Simon Peter had brought along a sword. He now pulled it out and struck at the servant of the high priest. The servant's name was Malchus, and Peter cut off his right ear. [11]Jesus told Peter, "Put your sword away. I must drink from the cup[c] that the Father has given me."

[12]The Roman officer and his men, together with the temple police, arrested Jesus and tied him up.

[a]18.1 *garden:* The Greek word is usually translated "garden," but probably referred to an olive orchard. [b]18.3-5 *I am Jesus:* The Greek text has "I am." [c]18.11 *drink from the cup:* In the Scriptures a cup is sometimes used as a symbol of suffering. To "drink from the cup" is to suffer.

Prayer Starter: Help me to be patient, Lord, with people I don't like.

Memory Verse: A thief comes only to rob, kill, and destroy. I came so that everyone would have life, and have it . . . —*John 10.10*

King of the Jews

Pilate ordered the charge against Jesus to be written on a board and put above the cross. It read, "Jesus of Nazareth, King of the Jews." [20]The words were written in Hebrew, Latin, and Greek.

The place where Jesus was taken wasn't far from the city, and many of the people read the charge against him. [21]So the chief priests went to Pilate and said, "Why did you write that he is King of the Jews? You should have written, 'He claimed to be King of the Jews.'"

[22]But Pilate told them, "What is written will not be changed!"

[23]After the soldiers had nailed Jesus to the cross, they divided up his clothes into four parts, one for each of them. But his outer garment was made from a single piece of cloth, and it did not have any seams. [24]The soldiers said to each other, "Let's not rip it apart. We will gamble to see who gets it." This happened so that the Scriptures would come true, which say,

"They divided up my clothes
    and gambled for my garments."

The soldiers then did what they had decided.

²⁵Jesus' mother stood beside his cross with her sister and Mary the wife of Clopas. Mary Magdalene was standing there too.ᵃ ²⁶When Jesus saw his mother and his favorite disciple with her, he said to his mother, "This man is now your son." ²⁷Then he said to the disciple, "She is now your mother." From then on, that disciple took her into his own home.

²⁸Jesus knew that he had now finished his work. And in order to make the Scriptures come true, he said, "I am thirsty!" ²⁹A jar of cheap wine was there. Someone then soaked a sponge with the wine and held it up to Jesus' mouth on the stem of a hyssop plant. ³⁰After Jesus drank the wine, he said, "Everything is done!" He bowed his head and died.

ᵃ19.25 *Jesus' mother stood beside his cross with her sister and Mary the wife of Clopas. Mary Magdalene was standing there too:* The Greek text may also be understood to include only three women ("Jesus' mother stood beside the cross with her sister, Mary the mother of Clopas. Mary Magdalene was standing there too.") or merely two women ("Jesus' mother was standing there with her sister Mary of Clopas, that is Mary Magdalene."). "Of Clopas" may mean "daughter of" or "mother of."

Prayer Starter: Thank you for the cross of Jesus, and for the empty tomb.

Memory Verse: A thief comes only to rob, kill, and destroy. I came so that everyone would have life, and have it in its fullest.   —*John 10.10*

The Empty Tomb

Joseph from Arimathea was one of Jesus' disciples. He had kept it secret though, because he was afraid of the Jewish leaders. But now he asked Pilate to let him have Jesus' body. Pilate gave him permission, and Joseph took it down from the cross.

³⁹Nicodemus also came with about seventy-five pounds of spices made from myrrh and aloes. This was the same Nicodemus who had visited Jesus one night. ⁴⁰The two men

wrapped the body in a linen cloth, together with the spices, which was how the Jewish people buried their dead. ⁴¹In the place where Jesus had been nailed to a cross, there was a garden with a tomb that had never been used. ⁴²The tomb was nearby, and since it was the time to prepare for the Sabbath, they were in a hurry to put Jesus' body there.

20 On Sunday morning while it was still dark, Mary Magdalene went to the tomb and saw that the stone had been rolled away from the entrance. ²She ran to Simon Peter and to Jesus' favorite disciple and said, "They have taken the Lord from the tomb! We don't know where they have put him."

³Peter and the other disciple started for the tomb. ⁴They ran side by

side, until the other disciple ran faster than Peter and got there first. ⁵He bent over and saw the strips of linen cloth lying inside the tomb, but he did not go in.

⁶When Simon Peter got there, he went into the tomb and saw the strips of cloth. ⁷He also saw the piece of cloth that had been used to cover Jesus' face. It was rolled up and in a place by itself. ⁸The disciple who got there first then went into the tomb, and when he saw it, he believed. ⁹At that time Peter and the other disciple did not know that the Scriptures said Jesus would rise to life. ¹⁰So the two of them went back to the other disciples.

Prayer Starter: Remind me each day, Lord, that Jesus is alive.

Memory Verse: But the Holy Spirit will come upon you . . . —*Acts 1.8*

Jesus Appears to Mary

Mary Magdalene stood crying outside the tomb. She was still weeping, when she stooped down [12]and saw two angels inside. They were dressed in white and were sitting where Jesus' body had been. One was at the head and the other was at the foot. [13]The angels asked Mary, "Why are you crying?"

She answered, "They have taken away my Lord's body! I don't know where they have put him."

[14]As soon as Mary said this, she turned around and saw Jesus standing there. But she did not know who he was. [15]Jesus asked her, "Why are you crying? Who are you looking for?"

She thought he was the gardener and said, "Sir, if you have taken his body away, please tell me, so I can go and get him."

[16]Then Jesus said to her, "Mary!"

She turned and said to him. "Rabboni." The Aramaic word "Rabboni" means "Teacher."

[17]Jesus told her, "Don't hold on to me! I have not yet gone to the Father. But tell my disciples that I am going to the one who is my Father and my God, as well as your Father and your God." [18]Mary Magdalene then went and told the disciples that she had seen the Lord. She also told them what he had said to her.

Prayer Starter: Help me to tell others the good news that Jesus rose from the dead.

Memory Verse: But the Holy Spirit will come upon you and give you power. . . .
—Acts 1.8

Jesus and Thomas

The disciples were afraid of the Jewish leaders, and on the evening of that same Sunday they locked themselves in a room. Suddenly, Jesus appeared in the middle of the group. He greeted them ²⁰and showed them his hands and his side. When the disciples saw the Lord, they became very happy.

²¹After Jesus had greeted them again, he said, "I am sending you, just as the Father has sent me." ²²Then he breathed on them and said, "Receive the Holy Spirit. ²³If you forgive anyone's sins, they will be forgiven. But if you don't forgive their sins, they will not be forgiven."

²⁴Although Thomas the Twin was one of the twelve disciples, he wasn't with the others when Jesus appeared to them. ²⁵So they told him, "We have seen the Lord!"

But Thomas said, "First, I must see the nail scars in his hands and touch them with my finger. I must put my hand where the spear went into his side. I won't believe unless I do this!"

²⁶A week later the disciples were together again. This time, Thomas was with them. Jesus came in while the doors were still locked and stood in the middle of the group. He greeted his disciples ²⁷and said to Thomas, "Put your finger here and look at my hands! Put your hand into my side. Stop doubting and have faith!"

²⁸Thomas replied, "You are my Lord and my God!"

Prayer Starter: Thank you, heavenly Father, for Jesus who is my Lord and my God.

Memory Verse: But the Holy Spirit will come upon you and give you power. Then you will tell everyone about me in Jerusalem . . .

—*Acts 1.8*

Two Men Dressed in White

For forty days after Jesus had suffered and died, he proved in many ways that he had been raised from death. He appeared to his apostles and spoke to them about God's kingdom. ⁴While he was still with them, he said:

Don't leave Jerusalem yet. Wait here for the Father to give you the Holy Spirit, just as I told you he has promised to do. ⁵John baptized with water, but in a few days you will be baptized with the Holy Spirit.

⁶While the apostles were still with Jesus, they asked him, "Lord, are you now going to give Israel its own king again."[a]

⁷Jesus said to them, "You don't need to know the time of those events that only the Father controls. ⁸But the Holy Spirit will come upon you and give you power. Then you will tell everyone about me in Jerusalem, in all Judea, in Samaria, and everywhere in the world." ⁹After Jesus had said this and while they were watching, he was taken up into a cloud. They could not see him, ¹⁰but as he went up, they kept looking up into the sky.

Suddenly two men dressed in white clothes were standing there beside them. ¹¹They said, "Why are you men from Galilee standing here and looking up into the sky? Jesus has been taken to heaven. But he will come back in the same way that you have seen him go."

[a]*1.6 are you now going to give Israel its own king again?:* Or "Are you now going to rule Israel as its king?"

Prayer Starter: Please hurry and come back to earth, Lord. We love you.

Memory Verse: But the Holy Spirit will come upon you and give you power. Then you will tell everyone about me in Jerusalem, in all Judea, in Samaria . . .
　　　　　　　　　　　　　　　　　　　　　　　　—Acts 1.8

The Disciples Meet

After the apostles returned to the city, they went upstairs to the room where they had been staying.

¹⁴The apostles often met together and prayed with a single purpose in mind.ᵃ The women and Mary the mother of Jesus would meet with them, and so would his brothers. ¹⁵One day there were about one hundred twenty of the Lord's followers meeting together, and Peter stood up to speak to them. ¹⁶⁻¹⁷He said:

My friends, long ago by the power of the Holy Spirit, David said something about Judas, and what he said has now happened. Judas was one of us and had worked with us, but he brought the mob to arrest Jesus.

²¹⁻²²So we need someone else to help us tell others that Jesus has been raised from death. He must also be one of the men who was with us from the very beginning. He must have been with us from the time the Lord Jesus was baptized by John until the day he was taken to heaven.

²³Two men were suggested: One of them was Joseph Barsabbas, known as Justus, and the other was Matthias. ²⁴Then they all prayed, "Lord, you know what everyone is like! Show us the one you have chosen ²⁵to be an apostle and to serve in place of Judas, who got what he deserved." ²⁶They drew names, and Matthias was chosen to join the group of the eleven apostles.

ᵃ1.14 *met together and prayed with a single purpose in mind:* Or "met together in a special place for prayer."

Prayer Starter: Show me your choices for me, each day, O Lord.

Memory Verse: But the Holy Spirit will come upon you and give you power. Then you will tell everyone about me in Jerusalem, in all Judea, in Samaria, and everywhere in the world.   —*Acts 1.8*

The Day
of Pentecost

On the day of Pentecost[a] all the Lord's followers were together in one place. ²Suddenly there was a noise from heaven like the sound of a mighty wind! It filled the house where they were meeting. ³Then they saw what looked like fiery tongues moving in all directions, and a tongue came and settled on each person there. ⁴The Holy Spirit took control of everyone, and they began speaking whatever languages the Spirit let them speak.

⁵Many religious Jews from every country in the world were living in Jerusalem. ⁶And when they heard this noise, a crowd gathered. But they were surprised, because they were hearing everything in their own languages. ⁷They were excited and amazed, and said:

Don't all these who are speaking come from Galilee? ⁸Then why do we hear them speaking our very own languages? ⁹Some of us are from Parthia, Media, and Elam. Others are from Mesopotamia, Judea, Cappadocia, Pontus, Asia, ¹⁰Phrygia, Pamphylia, Egypt, parts of Libya near Cyrene, Rome, ¹¹Crete, and Arabia. Some of us were born Jews, and others of us have chosen to be Jews. Yet we all hear them using our own languages to tell the wonderful things God has done.

[a]2.1 *Pentecost:* A Jewish festival that came fifty days after Passover and celebrated the wheat harvest. Jews later celebrated Pentecost as the time when they were given the Law of Moses.

Prayer Starter: Thank you for giving me a tongue for speaking. Help me to use it to share Christ with others.

Memory Verse: Only Jesus has the power . . .   —*Acts 4.12*

Peter Heals a Lame Man

The time of prayer[a] was about three o'clock in the afternoon, and Peter and John were going into the temple. ²A man who had been born lame was being carried to the temple door. Each day he was placed beside this door, known as the Beautiful Gate. He sat there and begged from the people who were going in.

³The man saw Peter and John entering the temple, and he asked them for money. ⁴But they looked straight at him and said, "Look up at us!"

⁵The man stared at them and thought he was going to get something. ⁶But Peter said, "I don't have any silver or gold! But I will give you what I do have. In the name of Jesus Christ from Nazareth, get up and start walking." ⁷Peter then took him by the right hand and helped him up.

At once the man's feet and ankles became strong, ⁸and he jumped up and started walking. He went with Peter and John into the temple, walking and jumping and praising God. ⁹Everyone saw him walking around and praising God. ¹⁰They knew that he was the beggar who had been lying beside the Beautiful Gate, and they were completely surprised. They could not imagine what had happened to the man.

[a]3.1 *The time of prayer:* Many of the Jewish people prayed in their homes at regular times each day, and on special occasions they prayed in the temple.

Prayer Starter: Thank you for my feet and legs. Thank you for giving me energy each day.

Memory Verse: Only Jesus has the power to save! . . .   —*Acts 4.12*

Peter and John Arrested

The apostles were still talking to the people, when some priests, the captain of the temple guard, and some Sadducees arrived. ²These men were angry because the apostles were teaching the people that the dead would be raised from death, just as Jesus had been raised from death. ³It was already late in the afternoon, and they arrested Peter and John and put them in jail for the night. ⁴But a lot of people who had heard the message believed it. So by now there were about five thousand followers of the Lord.

⁵The next morning the leaders, the elders, and the teachers of the Law of Moses met in Jerusalem. ⁶The high priest Annas was there, as well as Caiaphas, John, Alexander, and other members of the high priest's family. ⁷They brought in Peter and John and made them stand in the middle while they questioned them. They asked, "By what power and in whose name have you done this?"

⁸Peter was filled with the Holy Spirit and told the nation's leaders and the elders:

⁹You are questioning us today about a kind deed in which a crippled man was healed. ¹⁰But there is something we must tell you and

everyone else in Israel. This man is standing here completely well because of the power of Jesus Christ from Nazareth. You put Jesus to death on a cross, but God raised him to life. ¹¹He is the stone that you builders thought was worthless, and now he is the most important stone of all.

¹²Only Jesus has the power to save! His name is the only one in all the world that can save anyone.

¹³The officials were amazed to see how brave Peter and John were, and they knew that these two apostles were only ordinary men and not well educated. The officials were certain that these men had been with Jesus. ¹⁴But they could not deny what had happened. The man who had been healed was standing there with the apostles.

¹⁵The officials commanded them to leave the council room. Then the officials said to each other, ¹⁶"What can we do with these men? Everyone in Jerusalem knows about this miracle, and we cannot say it didn't happen. ¹⁷But to keep this thing from spreading, we will warn them never again to speak to anyone about the name of Jesus." ¹⁸So they called the two apostles back in and told them that they must never, for any reason, teach anything about the name of Jesus.

¹⁹Peter and John answered, "Do you think God wants us to obey you or to obey him? ²⁰We cannot keep quiet about what we have seen and heard."

²¹⁻²²The officials could not find any reason to punish Peter and John. So they threatened them and let them go. The man who was healed by this miracle was more than forty years old, and everyone was praising God for what had happened.

Prayer Starter: Lord, your name is the only one in all the earth that can save anyone.

Memory Verse: Only Jesus has the power to save! His name is the only one . . .
—*Acts 4.12*

Ananias and Sapphira

Joseph was one of the followers who had sold a piece of property and brought the money to the apostles. He was a Levite from Cyprus, and the apostles called him Barnabas, which means, "one who encourages others."

5 Ananias and his wife Sapphira also sold a piece of property. ²But they agreed to cheat and keep some of the money for themselves.

So when Ananias took the rest of the money to the apostles, ³Peter said, "Why has Satan made you keep back some of the money from the sale of the property? Why have you lied to the Holy Spirit? ⁴The property was yours before you sold it, and even after you sold it, the money was still yours. What made you do such a thing? You didn't lie to people. You lied to God!"

⁵As soon as Ananias heard this, he dropped dead, and everyone who heard about it was frightened. ⁶Some young men came in and wrapped up his body. Then they took it out and buried it.

⁷Three hours later Sapphira came in, but she did not know what had happened to her husband. ⁸Peter asked her, "Tell me, did you sell the property for this amount?"

"Yes," she answered, "that's the amount."

⁹Then Peter said, "Why did the two of you agree to test the Lord's Spirit? The men who buried Ananias are by the door, and they will carry you out!" ¹⁰At once she fell at Peter's feet and died.

When the young men came back in, they found Sapphira lying there dead. So they carried her out and buried her beside her husband. ¹¹The church members were afraid, and so was everyone else who heard what had happened.

Prayer Starter: Help me always be honest, Lord. Keep me from cheating and lying.

Memory Verse: Only Jesus has the power to save! His name is the only one in all the world . . .
—Acts 4.12

| Many Miracles |

The apostles worked many miracles and wonders among the people. All of the Lord's followers often met in the part of the temple known as Solomon's Porch.[a] [13]No one outside their group dared join them, even though everyone liked them very much.

[14]Many men and women started having faith in the Lord. [15]Then sick people were brought out to the road and placed on cots and mats. It was hoped that Peter would walk by, and

his shadow would fall on them and heal them. [16]A lot of people living in the towns near Jerusalem brought those who were sick or troubled by evil spirits, and they were all healed.

[17]The high priest and all the other Sadducees who were with him became jealous. [18]They arrested the apostles and put them in the city jail. [19]But that night an angel from the Lord opened the doors of the jail and led the apostles out. The angel said, [20]"Go to the temple and tell the people everything about this new life." [21]So they went into the temple before sunrise and started teaching.

The high priest and his men called together their council, which included all of Israel's leaders. Then they ordered the apostles to be brought to them from the jail. [22]The temple police who were sent to the jail did not find the apostles. They returned and said, [23]"We found the jail locked tight and the guards standing at the doors. But when we opened the doors and went in we didn't find anyone there." [24]The captain of the temple police and the chief priests listened to their report, but they did not know what to think about it.

[25]Just then someone came in and said, "Right now those men you put in jail are in the temple, teaching the people!" [26]The captain went with some of the temple police and brought the apostles back. But they did not use force. They were afraid that the people might start throwing stones at them.

[a]5.12 *Solomon's Porch:* A public place with tall columns along the east side of the temple.

Prayer Starter: Thank you, Lord, for the angels who watch over us.

Memory Verse: Only Jesus has the power to save! His name is the only one in all the world that can save anyone. —*Acts 4.12*

Apostles Beaten

When the apostles were brought before the council, the high priest said to them, [28]"We told you plainly not to teach in the name of Jesus. But look what you have done! You have been teaching all over Jerusalem, and you are trying to blame us for his death."

[29]Peter and the apostles replied:

We don't obey people. We obey God. [30]You killed Jesus by nailing him to a cross. But the God our ancestors worshiped raised him to life [31]and made him our Leader and Savior. Then God gave him a place at his right side,[a] so that the people of Israel would turn back to him and be forgiven. [32]We are here to tell you about all this, and so is the Holy Spirit, who is God's gift to everyone who obeys God.

[33]When the council members heard this, they became so angry that they wanted to kill the apostles. [34]But one of the members was the Pharisee Gamaliel, a highly respected teacher. He ordered the apostles to be taken out of the room for a little while. [35]Then he said to the council:

Be careful what you do with these men. [36]Not long ago Theudas claimed to be someone inportant, and about four hundred men joined him. But he was killed. All his followers were scattered, and that was the end of that.

[37]Later, when the people of our nation were being counted, Judas from Galilee showed up. A lot of people followed him, but he was killed, and all his followers were scattered.

[38]So I advise you to stay away from these men. Leave them alone. If what they are planning is something of their own doing, it will fail. [39]But if God is behind it, you cannot stop it anyway, unless you want to fight against God.

The council members agreed with what he said, [40]and they called the apostles back in. They had them beaten with a whip and warned them not to speak in the name of Jesus. Then they let them go.

[41]The apostles left the council and were happy, because God had considered them worthy to suffer for the sake of Jesus. [42]Every day they spent time in the temple and in one home after another. They never stopped teaching and telling the good news that Jesus is the Messiah.

[a]5.31 *right side:* The place of honor and power.

Prayer Starter: Lord, give me the courage to be your follower, even when it's hard.

Memory Verse: The Lord's followers . . .   *—Acts 8.4*

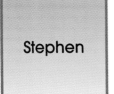

Stephen

The twelve apostles called the whole group of followers together and said, "We should not give up preaching God's message in order to serve at tables.[a] [3]My friends, choose seven men who are respected and wise and filled with God's Spirit. We will put them in charge of these things. [4]We can spend our time praying and serving God by preaching."

[5]This suggestion pleased everyone, and they began by choosing Stephen. He had great faith and was filled with the Holy Spirit. Then they chose Philip, Prochorus, Nicanor, Timon, Parmenas, and also Nicolaus, who worshiped with the Jewish people[b] in Antioch.

[8]God gave Stephen the power to work great miracles and wonders among the people. [9]But some men from Cyrene and Alexandria were members of a group who called themselves "Free Men."[c] They started arguing with Stephen. Some others from Cilicia and Asia also argued with him. [10]But they were no match for Stephen, who spoke with the great wisdom that the Spirit gave him. [11]So they talked some men into saying, "We heard Stephen say terrible things against Moses and God!"

[12]They turned the people and their leaders and the teachers of the Law of Moses against Stephen. Then they all grabbed Stephen and dragged him in front of the council.

[13]Some men agreed to tell lies about Stephen, and they said, "This man keeps on saying terrible things about this holy temple and the Law of Moses. [14]We have heard him claim that Jesus from Nazareth will destroy this place and change the customs that Moses gave us." [15]Then all the council members stared at Stephen. They saw that his face looked like the face of an angel.

[a]6.2 *to serve at tables:* This may mean either that they were in charge of handing out food to the widows or that they were in charge of the money, since the Greek word "table" may also mean "bank." [b]6.5 *worshiped with the Jewish people:* This translates the Greek word "proselyte" that means a Gentile who had accepted the Jewish religion. [c]6.9 *Free Men:* A group of Jewish men who had once been slaves, but had been freed.

Prayer Starter: Lord, give me faith and wisdom like Stephen's.

Memory Verse: The Lord's followers who had been scattered . . .
                                                —*Acts 8.4*

**Stephen
Stoned to
Death**

When the council members heard Stephen's speech, they were angry and furious. [55]But Stephen was filled with the Holy Spirit. He looked toward heaven, where he saw our glorious God and Jesus standing at his right side.[a] [56]Then Stephen said, "I see heaven open and the Son of Man standing at the right side of God!"

[57]The council members shouted and covered their ears. At once they all attacked Stephen [58]and dragged him out of the city. Then they started throwing stones at him. The men who had brought charges against him put their coats at the feet of a young man named Saul.[b]

[59]As Stephen was being stoned to death, he called out, "Lord Jesus, please welcome me!" [60]He knelt down and shouted, "Lord, don't blame them for what they have done." Then he died.

8 Saul approved the stoning of Stephen. Some faithful followers of the Lord buried Stephen and mourned very much for him.

At that time the church in Jerusalem suffered terribly. All of the Lord's followers, except the apostles, were scattered everywhere in Judea and Samaria. [3]Saul started making a lot of trouble for the church. He went from house to house, arresting men and women and putting them in jail.

⁴The Lord's followers who had been scattered went from place to place, telling the good news. ⁵Philip went to the city of Samaria and told the people about Christ. ⁶They crowded around Philip because they were eager to hear what he was saying and to see him work miracles. ⁷Many people with evil spirits were healed, and the spirits went out of them with a shout. A lot of crippled and lame people were also healed. ⁸Everyone in that city was very glad because of what was happening.

ª7.55 *standing at his right side:* The "right side" is the place of honor and power. "Standing" may mean that Jesus is welcoming Stephen. ᵇ7.58 *Saul:* Better known as Paul, who became a famous follower of Jesus.

Prayer Starter: Lord, as I go from place to place, may I tell the good news.

Memory Verse: The Lord's followers who had been scattered went from place to place . . .   *—Acts 8.4*

Simon

For some time a man named Simon had lived in the city of Samaria and had amazed the people. He practiced witchcraft and claimed to be somebody great. [10]Everyone, rich and poor, crowded around him. They said, "This man is the power of God called 'The Great Power.'"

[11]For a long time, Simon had used witchcraft to amaze the people, and they kept crowding around him. [12]But when they believed what Philip was saying about God's kingdom and about the name of Jesus Christ, they were all baptized. [13]Even Simon believed and was baptized. He stayed close to Philip, because he marveled at all the miracles and wonders.

[14]The apostles in Jerusalem heard that some people in Samaria had accepted God's message, and they sent Peter and John. [15]When the two apostles arrived, they prayed that the people would be given the Holy Spirit. [16]Before this, the Holy Spirit had not been given to anyone in Samaria, though some of them had been baptized in the name of the Lord Jesus. [17]Peter and John then placed their hands on everyone who had faith in the Lord, and they were given the Holy Spirit.

[18]Simon noticed that the Spirit was given only when the apostles placed their hands on the people. So he brought money [19]and said to Peter and John, "Let me have this power too! Then anyone I place my hands on will also be given the Holy Spirit."

[20]Peter said to him, "You and your money will both end up in hell if you think you can buy God's gift! [21]You don't have any part in this, and God sees that your heart isn't right. [22]Get rid of these evil thoughts and ask God to forgive you.

Prayer Starter: Lord, keep me from loving money too much.

Memory Verse: The Lord's followers who had been scattered went from place to place, telling . . .
—Acts 8.4

Philip and the Ethiopian

The Lord's angel said to Philip, "Go south[a] along the desert road that leads from Jerusalem to Gaza."[b] ²⁷So Philip left.

An important Ethiopian official happened to be going along that road in his chariot. He was the chief treasurer for Candace, the Queen of Ethiopia. The official had gone to Jerusalem to worship ²⁸and was now on his way home. He was sitting in his chariot, reading the book of the prophet Isaiah.

²⁹The Spirit told Philip to catch up with the chariot. ³⁰Philip ran up close and heard the man reading aloud from the book of Isaiah. Philip asked him, "Do you understand what you are reading?"

³¹The official answered, "How can I understand unless someone helps me?" He then invited Philip to come up and sit beside him.

³²The man was reading the passage that said,

"He was led like a sheep on its way to be killed.
He was silent as a lamb whose wool is being cut off,
     and he did not say a word.
³³ He was treated like a nobody
     and did not receive a fair trial.
How can he have children,
     if his life is snatched away?"

³⁴The official said to Philip, "Tell me, was the prophet talking about himself or about someone else?" ³⁵So Philip began at this place in the Scriptures and explained the good news about Jesus.

[a]8.26 *Go south:* Or "About noon go." [b]8.26 *the desert road that leads from Jerusalem to Gaza:* Or "the road that leads from Jerusalem to Gaza in the desert."

Prayer Starter: Lord, bless all your preachers, teachers, and evangelists who are explaining the good news about Jesus.

Memory Verse: The Lord's followers who had been scattered went from place to place, telling the good news.   —*Acts 8.4*

**Saul Meets
Jesus**

Saul kept on threatening to kill the Lord's followers. He even went to the high priest ²and asked for letters to their leaders in Damascus. He did this because he wanted to arrest and take to Jerusalem any man or woman who had accepted the Lord's Way.ᵃ ³When Saul had almost reached Damascus, a bright light from heaven suddenly flashed around him. ⁴He fell to the ground and heard a voice that said, "Saul! Saul! Why are you so cruel to me?"

⁵"Who are you?" Saul asked.

"I am Jesus," the Lord answered. "I am the one you are so cruel to. ⁶Now get up and go into the city, where you will be told what to do."

⁷The men with Saul stood there speechless. They had heard the voice, but they had not seen anyone. ⁸Saul got up from the ground, and when he opened his eyes, he could not see a thing. Someone then led him by the hand to Damascus, ⁹and for three days he was blind and did not eat or drink.

¹⁰A follower named Ananias lived in Damascus, and the Lord spoke to him in a vision. Ananias answered, "Lord, here I am."

¹¹The Lord said to him, "Get up and go to the house of Judas on Straight Street. When you get there, you will find a man named Saul from the city of Tarsus. Saul is praying, ¹²and he has seen a vision. He saw a man named Ananias coming to him and putting his hands on him, so that he could see again."

¹³Ananias replied: "Lord, a lot of people have told me about the terrible things this man has done to your followers in Jerusalem. ¹⁴Now the chief priests have given him the power to come here and arrest anyone who worships in your name."

¹⁵The Lord said to Ananias, "Go! I have chosen him to tell foreigners, kings, and the people of Israel about me. ¹⁶I will show him how much he must suffer for worshiping in my name."

¹⁷Ananias left and went into the house where Saul was staying. Ananias placed his hands on him and said, "Saul, the Lord Jesus has sent me. He is the same one who appeared to you along the road. He wants you to be able to see and to be filled with the Holy Spirit."

¹⁸Suddenly something like fish scales fell from Saul's eyes, and he could see. He got up and was baptized.

ᵃ9.2 *accepted the Lord's Way:* In the book of Acts, this means to become a follower of the Lord Jesus.

Prayer Starter: May my friends who don't know Christ come to love and trust him, just as Saul did.

Memory Verse: God is pleased . . .   *—Acts 10.35*

Saul Escapes Damascus

For several days Saul stayed with the Lord's followers in Damascus. [20]Soon he went to the Jewish meeting places and started telling people that Jesus is the Son of God. [21]Everyone who heard Saul was amazed and said, "Isn't this the man who caused so much trouble for those people in Jerusalem who worship in the name of Jesus? Didn't he come here to arrest them and take them to the chief priests?"

[22]Saul preached with such power that he completely confused the Jewish people in Damascus, as he tried to show them that Jesus is the Messiah.

[23]Later some of them made plans to kill Saul, [24]but he found out about it. He learned that they were guarding the gates of the city day and night in order to kill him. [25]Then one night his followers let him down over the city wall in a large basket.

[26]When Saul arrived in Jerusalem, he tried to join the followers. But they were all afraid of him, because they did not believe he was a true follower. [27]Then Barnabas helped him by taking him to the apostles. He explained how Saul had seen the Lord and how the Lord had spoken to him. Barnabas also said that when Saul was in Damascus, he had spoken bravely in the name of Jesus.

[28]Saul moved about freely with the followers in Jerusalem and told everyone about the Lord. [29]He was always arguing with the Jews who spoke Greek, and so they tried to kill him. [30]But the followers found out about this and took Saul to Caesarea. From there they sent him to the city of Tarsus.

[31]The church in Judea, Galilee, and Samaria now had a time of peace and kept on worshiping the Lord. The church became stronger, as the Holy Spirit encouraged it and helped it grow.

Prayer Starter: Help me to speak bravely in the name of the Lord.

Memory Verse: God is pleased with everyone who worships him . . .
—*Acts 10.35*

Dorcas

While Peter was traveling from place to place, he visited the Lord's followers who lived in the town of Lydda. [33]There he met a man named Aeneas, who for eight years had been sick in bed and could not move. [34]Peter said to Aeneas, "Jesus Christ has healed you! Get up and make your bed."[a] Right away he stood up.

[35]Many people in the towns of Lydda and Sharon saw Aeneas and became followers of the Lord.

[36]In Joppa there was a follower named Tabitha. Her Greek name was Dorcas, which means "deer." She was always doing good things for people and had given much to the poor. [37]But she got sick and died, and her body was washed and placed in an upstairs room. [38]Joppa wasn't far from Lydda, and the followers heard that Peter was there. They sent two men to say to him, "Please come with us as quickly as you can!" [39]Right away, Peter went with them.

The men took Peter upstairs into the room. Many widows were there crying. They showed him the coats and clothes that Dorcas had made while she was still alive.

⁴⁰After Peter had sent everyone out of the room, he knelt down and prayed. Then he turned to the body of Dorcas and said, "Tabitha, get up!" The woman opened her eyes, and when she saw Peter, she sat up. ⁴¹He took her by the hand and helped her to her feet.

Peter called in the widows and the other followers and showed them that Dorcas had been raised from death. ⁴²Everyone in Joppa heard what had happened, and many of them put their faith in the Lord. ⁴³Peter stayed on for a while in Joppa in the house of a man named Simon, who made leather.

ᵃ9.34 *and make up your bed:* Or "and fix something to eat."

Prayer Starter: I love to read your Bible each day, Lord. Thank you for stories like this one.

Memory Verse: God is pleased with everyone who worships him and does right . . .
—Acts 10.35

Peter's Chains Fall Off

At that time King Herod[a] caused terrible suffering for some members of the church. [2]He ordered soldiers to cut off the head of James, the brother of John. [3]When Herod saw that this pleased the Jewish people, he had Peter arrested during the Festival of Thin Bread. [4]He put Peter in jail and ordered four squads of soldiers to guard him. Herod planned to put him on trial in public after the festival.

[5]While Peter was being kept in jail, the church never stopped praying to God for him.

[6]The night before Peter was to be put on trial, he was asleep and bound by two chains. A soldier was guarding him on each side, and two other soldiers were guarding the entrance to the jail. [7]Suddenly an angel from the Lord appeared, and light flashed around in the cell. The angel poked Peter in the side and woke him up. Then he said, "Quick! Get up!"

The chains fell off his hands, [8]and the angel said, "Get dressed and put on your sandals." Peter did what he was told. Then the angel said, "Now put on your coat and follow me." [9]Peter left with the angel, but he thought everything was only a dream. [10]They went past the two groups of soldiers, and when they came to the iron gate to the city, it opened by itself. They went out and were going along the street, when all at once the angel disappeared.

[11]Peter now realized what had happened, and he said, "I am certain that the Lord sent his angel to rescue me from Herod and from everything the Jewish leaders planned to do to me." [12]Then Peter went to the house of Mary the mother of John whose other name was Mark. Many of the Lord's followers had come together there and were praying.

[13]Peter knocked on the gate, and a servant named Rhoda came to answer. [14]When she heard Peter's voice, she was too excited to open the gate. She ran back into the house and said that Peter was standing there.

[15]"You are crazy!" everyone told her. But she kept saying that it was Peter. Then they said, "It must be his angel."[b] [16]But Peter kept on knocking, until finally they opened the gate. They saw him and were completely amazed.

[17]Peter motioned for them to keep quiet. Then he told how the Lord had led him out of jail. He also said, "Tell James[c] and the others what has happened." After that, he left and went somewhere else.

[18]The next morning the soldiers who had been on guard were terribly worried and wondered what had happened to Peter. [19]Herod ordered his

own soldiers to search for him, but they could not find him. Then he questioned the guards and had them put to death. After this, Herod left Judea to stay in Caesarea for a while.

^a12.1 *Herod:* Herod Agrippa I, the grandson of Herod the Great. ^b12.15 *his angel:* Probably meaning "his guardian angel." ^c12.17 *James:* The brother of the Lord.

Prayer Starter: Send your angels to watch over us, Lord, just as they cared for Peter.

Memory Verse: God is pleased with everyone who worships him and does right, no matter what nation . . .   —*Acts 10.35*

Elymas, Son of the Devil

The church at Antioch had several prophets and teachers. They were Barnabas, Simeon, also called Niger, Lucius from Cyrene, Manaen, who was Herod's[a] close friend, and Saul. [2]While they were worshiping the Lord and going without eating,[b] the Holy Spirit told them, "Appoint Barnabas and Saul to do the work for which I have chosen them." [3]Everyone prayed and went without eating for a while longer. Next, they placed their hands on Barnabas and Saul to show that they had been appointed to do this work. Then everyone sent them on their way.

[4]After Barnabas and Saul had been sent by the Holy Spirit, they went to Seleucia. From there they sailed to the island of Cyprus. [5]They arrived at Salamis and began to preach God's message in the Jewish meeting places. They also had John[c] as a helper.

[6]Barnabas and Saul went all the way to the city of Paphos on the other end of the island, where they met a Jewish man named Bar-Jesus. He practiced witchcraft and was a false prophet. [7]He also worked for Sergius Paulus, who was very smart and was the governor of the island. Sergius Paulus wanted to hear God's message, and he sent for Barnabas and Saul. [8]But Bar-Jesus, whose other name was Elymas, was against them. He even tried to keep the governor from having faith in the Lord.

[9]Then Saul, better known as Paul, was filled with the Holy Spirit. He looked straight at Elymas [10]and said, "You son of the devil! You are a liar, a crook, and an enemy of everything that is right. When will you stop speaking against the true ways of the Lord? [11]The Lord is going to punish you by making you completely blind for a while."

Suddenly the man's eyes were covered by a dark mist, and he went around trying to get someone to lead him by the hand. [12]When the governor saw what had happened, he was amazed at this teaching about the Lord. So he put his faith in the Lord.

[a]13.1 *Herod's:* Herod Antipas, the son of Herod the Great. [b]13.2 *going without eating:* The Jews often went without eating as a way of showing how much they loved God. This is also called "fasting." [c]13.5 *John:* Whose other name was Mark.

Prayer Starter: Thank you for my eyes, ears, nose, and mouth.

Memory Verse: God is pleased with everyone who worships him and does right, no matter what nation they come from. —*Acts 10.35*

Paul and Barnabas Preach

When David was alive, he obeyed God. Then after he died, he was buried in the family grave, and his body decayed. [37]But God raised Jesus from death, and his body did not decay.

[38]My friends, the message is that Jesus can forgive your sins! The Law of Moses could not set you free from all your sins. [39]But everyone who has faith in Jesus is set free. [40]Make sure that what the prophets have said doesn't happen to you. They said,

[41] "Look, you people who make fun of God!
    Be amazed and disappear.
I will do something today that you won't believe,
    even if someone tells you about it!"

[42]As Paul and Barnabas were leaving the meeting, the people begged them to say more about these same things on the next Sabbath. [43]After the service, many Jews and a lot of Gentiles who worshiped God went with them. Paul and Barnabas begged them all to remain faithful to God, who had been so kind to them.

[44]The next Sabbath almost everyone in town came to hear the message about the Lord.[a] [45]When the Jewish people saw the crowds, they were very jealous. They insulted Paul and spoke against everything he said.

[46]But Paul and Barnabas bravely said:

We had to tell God's message to you before we told it to anyone else. But you rejected the message! This proves that you don't deserve eternal life. Now we are going to the Gentiles. [47]The Lord has given us this command,

"I have placed you here as a light for the Gentiles.
You are to take the saving power of God
    to people everywhere on earth."

[48]This message made the Gentiles glad, and they praised what they had heard about the Lord.[b] Everyone who had been chosen for eternal life then put their faith in the Lord.

[49]The message about the Lord spread all over the region.

[a]13.44 *the Lord:* Some manuscripts have "God." [b]13.48 *the Lord:* Some manuscripts have "God."

Prayer Starter: I want to trust you, Lord, when things seem to be going badly.

Memory Verse: Stop all your dirty talk. . . .   —*Ephesians 4.29*

Paul's Stoning

In Lystra there was a man who had been born with crippled feet and had never been able to walk. ⁹The man was listening to Paul speak, when Paul saw that he had faith in Jesus and could be healed. So he looked straight at the man ¹⁰and shouted, "Stand up!" The man jumped up and started walking around.

¹¹When the crowd saw what Paul had done, they yelled out in the language of Lycaonia, "The gods have turned into humans and have come down to us!" ¹²The people then gave Barnabas the name Zeus, and they gave Paul the name Hermes,ᵃ because he did the talking.

¹³The temple of Zeus was near the entrance to the city. Its priest and the crowds wanted to offer a sacrifice to Barnabas and Paul. So the priest brought some bulls and flowers to the city gates. ¹⁴When the two apostles found out about this, they tore their clothes in horror and ran to the crowd, shouting:

¹⁵Why are you doing this? We are humans just like you. Please give up all this foolishness. Turn to the living God, who made the sky, the earth, the sea, and everything in them. ¹⁶In times past, God let each nation go its own way. ¹⁷But he showed that he was there by the good things he did. God sends rain from heaven and makes your crops grow. He gives food to you and makes your hearts glad.

¹⁸Even after Paul and Barnabas had said all this, they could hardly keep the people from offering a sacrifice to them.

¹⁹Some Jewish leaders from Antioch and Iconium came and turned the crowds against Paul. They hit him with stones and dragged him out of the city, thinking he was dead. ²⁰But when the Lord's followers gathered around Paul, he stood up and went back into the city. The next day he and Barnabas went to Derbe.

ᵃ14.12 *Hermes:* The Greeks thought of Hermes as the messenger of the other gods, especially of Zeus, their chief god.

Prayer Starter: Thank you for giving us food and making our hearts glad.

Memory Verse: Stop all your dirty talk. Say the right thing . . .
—*Ephesians 4.29*

The Jerusalem Meeting

Some people came from Judea and started teaching the Lord's followers that they could not be saved, unless they were circumcised as Moses had taught. ²This caused trouble, and Paul and Barnabas argued with them about this teaching. So it was decided to send Paul and Barnabas and a few others to Jerusalem to discuss this problem with the apostles and the church leaders.

³The men who were sent by the church went through Phoenicia and Samaria, telling how the Gentiles had turned to God. This news made the Lord's followers very happy. ⁴When the men arrived in Jerusalem, they were welcomed by the church, including the apostles and the leaders. They told them everything God had helped them do. ⁵But some Phar-

isees had become followers of the Lord. They stood up and said, "Gentiles who have faith in the Lord must be circumcised and told to obey the Law of Moses."

⁶The apostles and church leaders met to discuss this problem about Gentiles. ⁷They had talked it over for a long time, when Peter got up and said:

My friends, you know that God decided long ago to let me be the one from your group to preach the good news to the Gentiles. God did this so that they would hear and obey him. ⁸He knows what is in everyone's heart. And he showed that he had chosen the Gentiles, when he gave them the Holy Spirit, just as he had given his Spirit to us. ⁹God treated them in the same way that he treated us. They put their faith in him, and he made their hearts pure.

¹⁰Now why are you trying to make God angry by placing a heavy burden on these followers? This burden was too heavy for us or our ancestors. ¹¹But our Lord Jesus was kind to us, and we are saved by faith in him, just as the Gentiles are.

¹²Everyone kept quiet and listened as Barnabas and Paul told how God had given them the power to work a lot of miracles and wonders for the Gentiles.

Prayer Starter: Thank you for your church, dear Lord.

Memory Verse: Stop all your dirty talk. Say the right thing at the right time . . . *—Ephesians 4.29*

The Apostles' Letter

The apostles, the leaders, and all the church members decided to send some men to Antioch along with Paul and Barnabas. They chose Silas and Judas Barsabbas,[a] who were two leaders of the Lord's followers. [23]They wrote a letter that said:

We apostles and leaders send friendly greetings to all of you Gentiles who are followers of the Lord in Antioch, Syria, and Cilicia.

[24]We have heard that some people from here have terribly upset you by what they said. But we did not send them! [25]So we met together and decided to choose some men and to send them to you along with our good friends Barnabas and Paul. [26]These men have risked their lives for our Lord Jesus Christ. [27]We are also sending Judas and Silas, who will tell you in person the same things that we are writing.

[28]The Holy Spirit has shown us that we should not place any extra burden on you. [29]But you should not eat anything offered to idols. You should not eat any meat that still has the blood in it or any meat of any animal that has been strangled. You must also not commit any terrible sexual sins. If you follow these instructions, you will do well.

We send our best wishes.

[30]The four men left Jerusalem and went to Antioch. Then they called the church members together and gave them the letter. [31]When the letter was read, everyone was pleased and greatly encouraged.

[a]15.22 *Judas Barsabbas:* He may have been a brother of Joseph Barsabbas, but the name "Barsabbas" was often used by the Jewish people.

Prayer Starter: Bless those who have gone to other nations, taking the message of Jesus.

Memory Verse: Stop all your dirty talk. Say the right thing at the right time and help others . . .
—*Ephesians 4.29*

Paul's Travels

Paul and Silas went back to Derbe and Lystra, where there was a follower named Timothy. His mother was also a follower. She was Jewish, and his father was Greek. ²The Lord's followers in Lystra and Iconium said good things about Timothy, ³and Paul wanted him to go with them. But Paul first had him circumcised, because all the Jewish people around there knew that Timothy's father was Greek.ᵃ

⁴As Paul and the others went from city to city, they told the followers what the apostles and leaders in Jerusalem had decided, and they urged them to follow these instructions. ⁵The churches became stronger in their faith, and each day more people put their faith in the Lord.

⁶Paul and his friends went through Phrygia and Galatia, but the Holy Spirit would not let them preach in Asia. ⁷After they arrived in Mysia, they tried to go into Bithynia, but the Spirit of Jesus would not let them. ⁸So they went on throughᵇ Mysia until they came to Troas.

⁹During the night, Paul had a vision of someone from Macedonia who was standing there begging him, "Come over to Macedonia and help us!" ¹⁰After Paul had seen the vision, we began looking for a way to go to Macedonia. We were sure that God had called us to preach the good news there.

ᵃ16.3 *had him circumcised . . . Timothy's father was Greek:* Timothy would not have been acceptable to the Jews unless he had been circumcised, and Greeks did not circumcise their sons. ᵇ16.8 *went on through:* Or "passed by."

Prayer Starter: Lead me day by day, dear Lord, just as you led the apostle Paul.

Memory Verse: Stop all your dirty talk. Say the right thing at the right time and help others by what you say. —*Ephesians 4.29*

Followers in Philippi

We sailed straight from Troas to Samothrace, and the next day we arrived in Neapolis. [12]From there we went to Philippi, which is a Roman colony in the first district of Macedonia.[a]

We spent several days in Philippi. [13]Then on the Sabbath we went outside the city gate to a place by the river, where we thought there would be a Jewish meeting place for prayer. We sat down and talked with the women who came. [14]One of them was Lydia, who was from the city of Thyatira and sold expensive purple cloth. She was a worshiper of the Lord God, and he made her willing to accept what Paul was saying. [15]Then after she and her family were baptized, she kept on begging us, "If you think I really do have faith in the Lord, come stay in my home." Finally, we accepted her invitation.

[a]16.12 *in the first district of Macedonia:* Some manuscripts have "and the leading city of Macedonia."

Prayer Starter: Teach me to pray each day, to talk to you friend-to-friend.

Memory Verse: They replied . . .   *—Acts 16.31a*

What Must I Do?

The crowd joined in the attack on Paul and Silas. Then the officials tore the clothes off the two men and ordered them to be beaten with a whip. ²³After they had been badly beaten, they were put in jail, and the jailer was told to guard them carefully. ²⁴The jailer did as he was told. He put them deep inside the jail and chained their feet to heavy blocks of wood.

²⁵About midnight Paul and Silas were praying and singing praises to God, while the other prisoners listened. ²⁶Suddenly a strong earthquake shook the jail to its foundations. The doors opened, and the chains fell from all the prisoners.

²⁷When the jailer woke up and saw that the doors were open, he thought that the prisoners had escaped. He pulled out his sword and was about to kill himself. ²⁸But Paul shouted, "Don't harm yourself! No one has escaped."

²⁹The jailer asked for a torch and went into the jail. He was shaking all over as he knelt down in front of Paul and Silas. ³⁰After he had led them out of the jail, he asked, "What must I do to be saved?"

³¹They replied, "Have faith in the Lord Jesus and you will be saved! This is also true for everyone who lives in your home."

³²Then Paul and Silas told him and everyone else in his house about the Lord. ³³While it was still night, the jailer took them to a place where he could wash their cuts and bruises. Then he and everyone in his home were baptized. ³⁴They were very glad that they had put their faith in God. After this, the jailer took Paul and Silas to his home and gave them something to eat.

Prayer Starter: Be with those in the jails and prisons, Lord, and give them the hope of the Lord Jesus.

Memory Verse: They replied, "Have faith . . ."   —*Acts 16.31a*

Paul's Sermon in Athens

While Paul was waiting in Athens, he was upset to see all the idols in the city. [17]He went to the Jewish meeting place to speak to the Jews and to anyone who worshiped with them. Day after day he also spoke to everyone he met in the market. [18]Some of them were Epicureans[a] and some were Stoics,[b] and they started arguing with him.

People were asking, "What is this know-it-all trying to say?"

Some even said, "Paul must be preaching about foreign gods! That's what he means when he talks about Jesus and about people rising from death."[c]

[19]They brought Paul before a council called the Areopagus, and said, "Tell us what your new teaching is all about. [20]We have heard you say some strange things, and we want to know what you mean."

[21]More than anything else the people of Athens and the foreigners living there loved to hear and to talk about anything new. [22]So Paul stood up in front of the council and said:

People of Athens, I see that you are very religious. [23]As I was going through your city and looking at the things you worship, I found an altar with the words, "To an Unknown God." You worship this God, but you don't really know him. So I want to tell you about him. [24]This God made the world and everything in it. He is Lord of heaven and earth, and he doesn't live in temples built by human hands. [25]He doesn't need help from anyone. He gives life, breath, and everything else to all people. [26]From one person God made all nations who live on earth, and he decided when and where every nation would be.

[a]17.18 *Epicureans:* People who followed the teaching of a man named Epicurus, who taught that happiness should be the main goal in life. [b]17.18 *Stoics:* Followers of a man named Zeno, who taught that people should learn self-control and be guided by their consciences. [c]17.18 *people rising from death:* Or "a goddess named 'Rising from Death.'"

Prayer Starter: Show me those I can invite to church and tell about you.

Memory Verse: They replied, "Have faith in the Lord Jesus . . ."

—Acts 16.31a

Making Tents

Paul left Athens and went to Corinth, ²where he met Aquila, a Jewish man from Pontus. Not long before this, Aquila had come from Italy with his wife Priscilla, because Emperor Claudius had ordered the Jewish people to leave Rome.ᵃ Paul went to see Aquila and Priscilla ³and found out that they were tent makers. Paul was a tent maker too. So he stayed with them, and they worked together.

⁴Every Sabbath, Paul went to the Jewish meeting place. He spoke to Jews and Gentilesᵇ and tried to win them over. ⁵But after Silas and Timothy came from Macedonia, he spent all his time preaching to the Jews about Jesus the Messiah. ⁶Finally, they turned against him and insulted him. So he shook the dust from his clothesᶜ and told them, "Whatever happens to you will be your own fault! I am not to blame. From now on I am going to preach to the Gentiles."

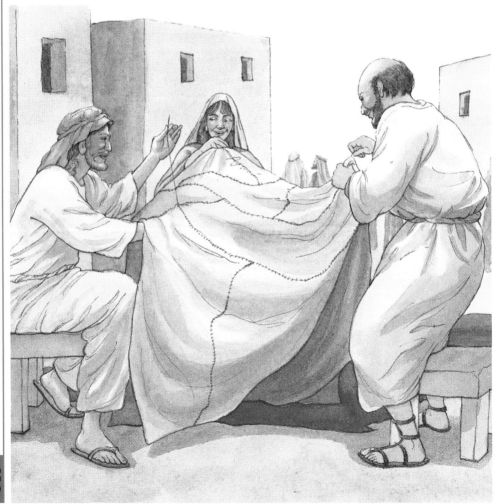

⁷Paul then moved into the house of a man named Titius Justus, who worshiped God and lived next door to the meeting place. ⁸Crispus was the leader of the meeting place. He and everyone in his family put their faith in the Lord. Many others in Corinth also heard the message, and all the people who had faith in the Lord were baptized.

ᵃ18.2 *Emperor Claudius had ordered the Jewish people to leave Rome:* Probably A.D. 49, though it may have been A.D. 41. ᵇ18.4 *Gentiles:* Here the word is "Greeks." ᶜ18.6 *shook the dust from his clothes:* This means the same as shaking dust from the feet.

Prayer Starter: Give me good friends, Lord, who will help me be stronger.

Memory Verse: They replied, "Have faith in the Lord Jesus and you . . ."
—*Acts 16.31a*

I Am
with You

One night, Paul had a vision, and in it the Lord said, "Don't be afraid to keep on preaching. Don't stop! [10]I am with you, and you won't be harmed. Many people in this city belong to me." [11]Paul stayed on in Corinth for a year and a half, teaching God's message to the people.

[12]While Gallio was governor of Achaia, some of the Jewish leaders got together and grabbed Paul. They brought him into court [13]and said, "This man is trying to make our people worship God in a way that is against our Law!"

[14]Even before Paul could speak, Gallio said, "If you were charging this man with a crime or some other wrong, I would have to listen to you. [15]But since this concerns only words, names, and your own law, you will have to take care of it. I refuse to judge such matters." [16]Then he sent them out of the court. [17]The crowd grabbed Sosthenes, the Jewish leader, and beat him up in front of the court. But none of this mattered to Gallio.

[18]After Paul had stayed for a while with the Lord's followers in Corinth, he told them good-by and sailed on to Syria with Aquila and Priscilla. But before he left, he had his head shaved[a] at Cenchreae because he had made a promise to God.

[a]18.18 *he had his head shaved:* Paul had promised to be a "Nazirite" for a while. This meant that for the time of the promise, he could not cut his hair or drink wine. When the time was over, he would have to cut his hair and offer a sacrifice to God.

Prayer Starter: Give strength to Christians around the world who are being mistreated because of their faith in you.

Memory Verse: They replied, "Have faith in the Lord Jesus and you will be saved!"   —*Acts 16.31a*

Priscilla, Aquila, and Apollos

The three of them arrived in Ephesus, where Paul left Priscilla and Aquila. He then went into the Jewish meeting place to talk with the people there. ²⁰They asked him to stay longer, but he refused. ²¹He told them good-by and said, "If God lets me, I will come back."

²²Paul sailed to Caesarea, where he greeted the church. Then he went on to Antioch. ²³After staying there for a while, he left and visited several places in Galatia and Phyrgia. He helped the followers there to become stronger in their faith.

²⁴A Jewish man named Apollos came to Ephesus. Apollos had been born in the city of Alexandria. He was a very good speaker and knew a lot about the Scriptures. ²⁵He also knew much about the Lord's Way,ᵃ and he spoke about it with great excitement. What he taught about Jesus was right, but all he knew was John's message about baptism.

²⁶Apollos started speaking bravely in the Jewish meeting place. But when Priscilla and Aquila heard him, they took him to their home and helped him understand God's Way even better.

²⁷Apollos decided to travel through Achaia. So the Lord's followers wrote letters, encouraging the followers there to welcome him. After Apollos arrived in Achaia, he was a great help to  everyone who had put their faith in the Lord Jesus because of God's kindness. ²⁸He got into fierce arguments with the Jewish people, and in public he used the Scriptures to prove that Jesus is the Messiah.

19 While Apollos was in Corinth, Paul traveled across the hill country to Ephesus, where he met some of the Lord's followers. ²He asked them, "When you put your faith in Jesus, were you given the Holy Spirit?"

"No!" they answered. "We have never even heard of the Holy Spirit."

³"Then why were you baptized?" Paul asked.

They answered, "Because of what John taught."ᵇ

⁴Paul replied, "John baptized people so that they would turn to God. But he also told them that someone else was coming, and that they should put their faith in him. Jesus is the one that John was talking about." ⁵After the people heard Paul say this, they were baptized in the name of the Lord Jesus.

ᵃ18.25 *the Lord's Way:* In the book of Acts, this means to become a follower of the Lord Jesus.
ᵇ19.3 *Then why were you baptized? . . . Because of what John taught:* Or "In whose name were you baptized? . . . We were baptized in John's name."

Prayer Starter: You are so kind, dear Lord. Give me a kind heart, too.

Memory Verse: Remember . . .   *—Acts 20.35b*

Riot at Ephesus

After all of this had happened, Paul decided[a] to visit Macedonia and Achaia on his way to Jerusalem. Paul had said, "From there I will go on to Rome." [22]So he sent his two helpers, Timothy and Erastus, to Macedonia. But he stayed on in Asia for a while.

[23]At that time there was serious trouble because of the Lord's Way.[b] [24]A silversmith named Demetrius had a business that made silver models of the temple of the goddess Artemis. Those who worked for him earned a lot of money. [25]Demetrius brought together everyone who was in the same business and said:

Friends, you know that we make a good living at this. [26]But you have surely seen and heard how this man Paul is upsetting a lot of people, not only in Ephesus, but almost everywhere in Asia. He claims that the gods we humans make are not really gods at all. [27]Everyone will start saying terrible things about our business. They will stop respecting the temple of the goddess Artemis, who is worshiped in Asia and all over the world. Our great goddess will be forgotten!

[28]When the workers heard this, they got angry and started shouting, "Great is Artemis, the goddess of the Ephesians!" [29]Soon the whole city was in a riot, and some men grabbed Gaius and Aristarchus, who had come from Macedonia with Paul. Then everyone in the crowd rushed to the place where the town meetings were held.

[30]Paul wanted to go out and speak to the people, but the Lord's followers would not let him. [31]A few of the local officials were friendly to Paul, and they sent someone to warn him not to go.

[a]19.21 *Paul decided:* Or "Paul was led by the Holy Spirit." [b]19.23 *the Lord's Way:* In the book of Acts, this means to become a follower of the Lord Jesus.

Prayer Starter: Comfort and encourage me today, heavenly Father.

Memory Verse: Remember that our Lord Jesus said . . . —*Acts 20.35b*

Sleeping in Church

When the riot was over, Paul sent for the followers and encouraged them. He then told them good-by and left for Macedonia. [2]As he traveled from place to place, he encouraged the followers with many messages. Finally, he went to Greece[a] [3]and stayed there for three months.

Paul was about to sail to Syria. But some of the Jewish leaders plotted against him, so he decided to return by way of Macedonia. [4]With him were Sopater, son of Pyrrhus from Berea, and

Aristarchus and Secundus from Thessalonica. Gaius from Derbe was also with him, and so were Timothy and the two Asians, Tychicus and Trophimus. [5]They went on ahead to Troas and waited for us there. [6]After the Festival of Thin Bread, we sailed from Philippi. Five days later we met them in Troas and stayed there for a week.

[7]On the first day of the week[b] we met to break bread together.[c] Paul spoke to the people until midnight because he was leaving the next morning. [8]In the upstairs room where we were meeting, there were a lot of lamps. [9]A young man by the name of Eutychus was sitting on a window sill. While Paul was speaking, the young man got very sleepy. Finally, he went to sleep and fell three floors all the way down to the ground. When they picked him up, he was dead.

[10]Paul went down and bent over Eutychus. He took him in his arms and said, "Don't worry! He's alive." [11]After Paul had gone back upstairs, he broke bread, and ate with us. He then spoke until dawn and left. [12]Then the followers took the young man home alive and were very happy.

[13]Paul decided to travel by land to Assos. The rest of us went on

ahead by ship, and we were to take him aboard there. ¹⁴When he met us in Assos, he came aboard, and we sailed on to Mitylene. ¹⁵The next day we came to a place near Chios, and the following day we reached Samos. The day after that we sailed to Miletus. ¹⁶Paul had decided to sail on past Ephesus, because he did not want to spend too much time in Asia. He was in a hurry and wanted to be in Jerusalem in time for Pentecost.ᵈ

ᵃ20.2 *Greece:* Probably Corinth. ᵇ20.7 *On the first day of the week:* Since the Jewish day began at sunset, the meeting would have begun in the evening. ᶜ20.7 *break bread together:* They ate together and celebrated the Lord's Supper. ᵈ20.16 *in time for Pentecost:* The Jewish people liked to be in Jerusalem for this festival.

Prayer Starter: God, bless me when I'm at church. May I worship you and learn about you there.

Memory Verse: Remember that our Lord Jesus said, "More blessings . . ."

—*Acts 20.35b*

Church Leaders from Ephesus

From Miletus, Paul sent a message for the church leaders at Ephesus to come and meet with him. ¹⁸When they got there, he said:

You know everything I did during the time I was with you when I first came to Asia. ¹⁹Some of the Jews plotted against me and caused me a lot of sorrow and trouble. But I served the Lord and was humble. ²⁰When I preached in public or taught in your homes, I didn't hold back from telling anything that would help you. ²¹I told Jews and Gentiles to turn to God and have faith in our Lord Jesus.

²²I don't know what will happen to me in Jerusalem, but I must obey God's Spirit and go there. ²³In every city I visit, I am told by the Holy Spirit that I will be put in jail and will be in trouble in Jerusalem. ²⁴But I don't care what happens to me, as long as I finish the work that the Lord Jesus gave me to do. And that work is to tell the good news about God's great kindness.

²⁵I have gone from place to place, preaching to you about God's kingdom, but now I know that none of you will ever see me again. ²⁶I tell you today that I am no longer responsible for any of you! ²⁷I have told you everything God wants you to know. ²⁸Look after yourselves and everyone the Holy Spirit has placed in your care. Be like shepherds to God's church. It is the flock that he bought with the blood of his own Son.ᵃ

²⁹I know that after I am gone, others will come like fierce wolves to attack you. ³⁰Some of your own people will tell lies to win over the Lord's followers. ³¹Be on your guard! Remember how day and night for three years I kept warning you with tears in my eyes.

³²I now place you in God's care. Remember the message about his great kindness! This message can help you and give you what belongs to you as God's people. ³³I have never wanted anyone's money or clothes. ³⁴You know how I have worked with my own hands to make a living for myself and my friends. ³⁵By everything I did, I showed how you should work to help everyone who is weak. Remember that our Lord Jesus said, "More blessings come from giving than from receiving."

³⁶After Paul had finished speaking, he knelt down with all of them and prayed. ³⁷Everyone cried and hugged and kissed him. ³⁸They were especially sad because Paul had told them, "You will never see me again."

Then they went with him to the ship.

ᵃ20.28 *the blood of his own Son:* Or "his own blood."

Prayer Starter: Help me remember that more blessings come from giving than receiving.

Memory Verse: Remember that our Lord Jesus said, "More blessings come from giving . . ."
                                                              —*Acts 20.35b*

Philip's Daughters

After saying good-by, we sailed straight to Cos. The next day we reached Rhodes and from there sailed on to Patara. ²We found a ship going to Phoenicia, so we got on board and sailed off.

³We came within sight of Cyprus and then sailed south of it on to the port of Tyre in Syria, where the ship was going to unload its cargo. ⁴We looked up the Lord's followers and stayed with them for a week. The Holy Spirit had told them to warn Paul not to go on to Jerusalem. ⁵But when the week was over, we started on our way again. All the men, together with their wives and children, walked with us from the town to the seashore. We knelt on the beach and prayed. ⁶Then after saying good-by to each other, we got into the ship, and they went back home.

⁷We sailed from Tyre to Ptolemais, where we greeted the followers and stayed with them for a day. ⁸The next day we went to Caesarea and stayed with Philip, the preacher. He was one of the seven men who helped the apostles, ⁹and he had four unmarried[a] daughters who prophesied.

¹⁰We had been in Caesarea for several days, when the prophet Agabus came to us from Judea. ¹¹He took Paul's belt, and with it he tied up his own hands and feet. Then he told us, "The Holy Spirit says that some of the Jewish leaders in Jerusalem will tie up the man who owns this belt. They will also hand him over to the Gentiles." ¹²After Agabus said this, we and the followers living there begged Paul not to go to Jerusalem.

¹³But Paul answered, "Why are you crying and breaking my heart? I am not only willing to be put in jail for the Lord Jesus. I am even willing to die for him in Jerusalem!"

¹⁴Since we could not get Paul to change his mind, we gave up and prayed, "Lord, please make us willing to do what you want."

[a]21.9 *unmarried:* Or "virgin."

Prayer Starter: Cause more and more people to place their faith in Jesus Christ.

Memory Verse: Remember that our Lord Jesus said, "More blessings come from giving than from receiving."   *—Acts 20.35b*

Paul Speaks to a Mob

The commander told him he could speak, so Paul stood on the steps and motioned to the people. When they were quiet, he spoke to them in Aramaic:

22 "My friends and leaders of our nation, listen as I explain what happened!" [2]When the crowd heard Paul speak to them in Aramaic, they became even quieter. Then Paul said:

[3]I am a Jew, born and raised in the city of Tarsus in Cilicia. I was a student of Gamaliel and was taught to follow every single law of our ancestors. In fact, I was just as eager to obey God as any of you are today.

[4]I made trouble for everyone who followed the Lord's Way,[a] and I even had some of them killed. I had others arrested and put in jail. I didn't care if they were men or women. [5]The high priest and all the council members can tell you that this is true. They even gave me letters to the Jewish leaders in Damascus, so that I could arrest people there and bring them to Jerusalem to be punished.

[6]One day about noon I was getting close to Damascus, when a bright light from heaven suddenly flashed around me. [7]I fell to the ground and heard a voice asking, "Saul, Saul, why are you so cruel to me?"

[8]"Who are you?" I answered.

The Lord replied, "I am Jesus from Nazareth!"

[a]22.4 *followed the Lord's Way:* In the book of Acts, this means to become a follower of the Lord Jesus.

Prayer Starter: Please protect the men and women in the armed forces who are helping protect our country.

Memory Verse: Cheer up! . . .   *—Acts 27.25*

The Plot Against Paul

The next morning more than forty Jewish men got together and vowed that they would not eat or drink anything until they had killed Paul. ¹⁴Then some of them went to the chief priests and the nation's leaders and said, "We have promised God that we would not eat a thing until we have killed Paul. ¹⁵You and everyone in the council must go to the commander and pretend that you want to find out more about the charges against Paul. Ask for him to brought before your court. Meanwhile, we will be waiting to kill him before he gets there."

¹⁶When Paul's nephew heard about the plot, he went to the fortress and told Paul about it. ¹⁷So Paul said to one of the army officers, "Take this young man to the commander. He has something to tell him."

¹⁸The officer took him to the commander and said, "The prisoner named Paul asked me to bring this young man to you, because he has something to tell you."

¹⁹The commander took the young man aside and asked him in private, "What do you want to tell me?"

²⁰He answered, "Some men are planning to ask you to bring Paul down to the Jewish council tomorrow. They will claim that they want to find out more about him. ²¹But please don't do what they say. More than forty men are going to attack Paul. They have made a vow not to eat or drink anything until they have killed him. Even now they are waiting to hear what you decide."

²²The commander sent the young man away after saying to him, "Don't let anyone know that you told me this."

Prayer Starter: Protect me from the evil one.

Memory Verse: Cheer up! I am sure . . .   *—Acts 27.25*

Agrippa and Bernice

The next day Agrippa and Bernice made a big show as they came into the meeting room. High ranking army officers and leading citizens of the town were also here. Festus then ordered Paul to be brought in ²⁴and said:

King Agrippa and other guests, look at this man! Every Jew from Jerusalem and Caesarea has come to me, demanding for him to be put to death. ²⁵I have not found him guilty of any crime deserving death. But because he has asked to be judged by the Emperor, I have decided to send him to Rome.

26 Agrippa told Paul, "You may now speak for yourself." Paul stretched out his hand and said:

²King Agrippa, I am glad for this chance to defend myself before you today on all these charges that my own people have brought against me. ³You know a lot about our religious customs and the beliefs that divide us. So I ask you to listen patiently to me.

Prayer Starter: May the leaders of this world bow down and worship you.

Memory Verse: Cheer up! I am sure that God will do . . . —*Acts 27.25*

Storm on the Mediterranean

When a gentle wind from the south started blowing, the men thought it was a good time to do what they had planned. So they pulled up the anchor, and we sailed along the coast of Crete. [14]But soon a strong wind called "The Northeaster" blew against us from the island. [15]The wind struck the ship, and we could not sail against it. So we let the wind carry the ship.

[16]We went along the island of Cauda on the side that was protected from the wind. We had a hard time holding the lifeboat in place, [17]but finally we got it where it belonged. Then the sailors wrapped ropes around the ship to hold it together. They lowered the sail and let the ship drift along, because they were afraid it might hit the sandbanks in the gulf of Syrtis.

[18]The storm was so fierce that the next day they threw some of the ship's cargo overboard. [19]Then on the third day, with their bare hands they threw overboard some of the ship's gear. [20]For several days we could not see either the sun or the stars. A strong wind kept blowing, and we finally gave up all hope of being saved.

[21]Since none of us had eaten anything for a long time, Paul stood up and told the men:

You should have listened to me! If you had stayed on in Crete, you would not have had this damage and loss. [22]But now I beg you to cheer up, because you will be safe. Only the ship will be lost.

[23]I belong to God, and I worship him. Last night he sent an angel [24]to tell me, "Paul, don't be afraid! You will stand trial before the Emperor. And because of you, God will save the lives of everyone on the ship." [25]Cheer up! I am sure that God will do exactly what he promised. [26]But we will first be shipwrecked on some island!

[29]The sailors were afraid that we might hit some rocks, and they let down four anchors from the back of the ship. Then they prayed for daylight.

Prayer Starter: Help me to cheer up, Lord, for I believe you will do all you have promised.

Memory Verse: Cheer up! I am sure that God will do exactly . . .
—Acts 27.25

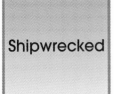

Shipwrecked

The sailors wanted to escape from the ship. So they lowered the lifeboat into the water, pretending that they were letting down an anchor from the front of the ship. ³¹But Paul said to Captain Julius and the soldiers, "If the sailors don't stay on the ship, you won't have any chance to save your lives." ³²The soldiers then cut the ropes that held the lifeboat and let it fall into the sea.

³³Just before daylight Paul begged the people to eat something. He told them, "For fourteen days you have been so worried that you haven't eaten a thing. ³⁴I beg you to eat something. Your lives depend on it. Do this and not one of you will be hurt."

³⁵After Paul had said this, he took a piece of bread and gave thanks to God. Then in front of everyone, he broke the bread and ate some. ³⁶They all felt encouraged, and each of them ate something. ³⁷There were 276 people on the ship, ³⁸and after everyone had eaten, they threw the cargo of wheat into the sea to make the ship lighter.

³⁹Morning came, and the ship's crew saw a coast that they did not recognize. But they did see a cove with a beach. So they decided to try to run the ship aground on the beach. ⁴⁰They cut the anchors loose and let them sink into the sea. At the same time they untied the ropes that were holding the rudders. Next, they raised the sail at the front of the ship and let the wind carry the ship toward the beach. ⁴¹But it ran aground on

a sandbank. The front of the ship stuck firmly in the sand, and the rear was being smashed by the force of the waves.

⁴²The soldiers decided to kill the prisoners to keep them from swimming away and escaping. ⁴³But Captain Julius wanted to save Paul's life, and he did not let the soldiers do what they had planned. Instead, he ordered everyone who could swim to dive into the water and head for shore. ⁴⁴Then he told the others to hold on to planks of wood or parts of the ship. At last, everyone safely reached shore.

28When we came ashore, we learned that the island was called Malta.

Prayer Starter: Thank you for food, for all you give us to eat.

Memory Verse: Cheer up! I am sure that God will do exactly what he promised.
—Acts 27.25

Paul Bitten by a Snake

The local people were very friendly, and they welcomed us by building a fire, because it was rainy and cold.

³After Paul had gathered some wood and had put it on the fire, the heat caused a snake to crawl out, and it bit him on the hand. ⁴When the local people saw the snake hanging from Paul's hand, they said to each other, "This man must be a murderer! He didn't drown in the sea, but the goddess of justice will kill him anyway."

⁵Paul shook the snake off into the fire and wasn't harmed. ⁶The people kept thinking that Paul would either swell up or suddenly drop dead. They watched him for a long time, and when nothing happened to him, they changed their minds and said, "This man is a god."

¹¹Three months later we sailed in a ship that had been docked at Malta for the winter. The ship was from Alexandria in Egypt and was known as "The Twin Gods."^a ¹²We arrrived in Syracuse and stayed for three days. ¹³From there we sailed to Rhegium. The next day a south wind began to blow, and two days later we arrived in Puteoli. ¹⁴There we found some of the Lord's followers, who begged us to stay with them. A week later we left for the city of Rome.

---

^a28.11 *known as "The Twin Gods":* Or "carried on its bow a wooden carving of the Twin Gods." These gods were Castor and Pollux, two of the favorite gods among sailors.

Prayer Starter: Thank you for fish and birds, even for reptiles and insects.

Memory Verse: I am proud of the good news! . . . *—Romans 1.16*

**Paul
in Rome**

Some of the followers in Rome heard about us and came to meet us at the market of Appius and at the Three Inns. When Paul saw them, he thanked God and was encouraged.

¹⁶We arrived in Rome, and Paul was allowed to live in a house by himself with a soldier to guard him.

¹⁷Three days after we got there, Paul called together some of the Jewish leaders and said:

My friends, I have never done anything to hurt our people, and I have never gone against the customs of our ancestors. But in Jerusalem I was handed over as a prisoner to the Romans. ¹⁸They looked into the charges against me and wanted to release me. They found that I had not done anything deserving death. ¹⁹The Jewish leaders disagreed, so I asked to be tried by the Emperor.

But I don't have anything to say against my own nation. ²⁰I am bound by these chains because of what we people of Israel hope for. That's why I have called you here to talk about this hope of ours. ²¹The leaders replied, "No one from Judea has written us a letter about you. And not one of them has come here to report on you or to say anything against you. ²²But we would like to hear what you have to say. We understand that people everywhere are against this new group."

²³They agreed on a time to meet with Paul, and many of them came to his house. From early morning until late in the afternoon, Paul talked to them about God's kingdom. He used the Law of Moses and the Books of the Prophets[a] to try to win them over to Jesus.

³⁰For two years Paul stayed in a rented house and welcomed everyone who came to see him. ³¹He bravely preached about God's kingdom and taught about the Lord Jesus Christ, and no one tried to stop him.

[a]28.23 *Law of Moses and the Books of the Prophets:* The Jewish Bible, that is, the Old Testament.

Prayer Starter: Help me be an encouraging friend.

Memory Verse: I am proud of the good news! It is God's powerful way . . .
—*Romans 1.16*

From Paul, a servant of Christ Jesus.

God chose me to be an apostle, and he appointed me to preach the good news ²that he promised long ago by what his prophets said in the holy Scriptures. ³⁻⁴This good news is about his Son, our Lord Jesus Christ! As a human, he was from the family of David. But the Holy Spirit[a] proved that Jesus is the powerful Son of God,[b] because he was raised from death.

⁵Jesus was kind to me and chose me to be an apostle,[c] so that people of all nations would obey and have faith. ⁶You are some of those people chosen by Jesus Christ.

⁷This letter is to all of you in Rome. God loves you and has chosen you to be his very own people.

I pray that God our father and our Lord Jesus Christ will be kind to you and will bless you with peace!

⁸First, I thank God in the name of Jesus Christ for all of you. I do this because people everywhere in the world are talking about your faith. ⁹God has seen how I never stop praying for you, while I serve him with all my heart and tell the good news about his Son.

¹⁰In all my prayers, I ask God to make it possible for me to visit you. ¹¹I want to see you and share with you the same blessings that God's Spirit has given me. Then you will grow stronger in your faith. ¹²What I am saying is that we can encourage each other by the faith that is ours.

¹³My friends, I want you to know that I have often planned to come

for a visit. But something has always kept me from doing it. I want to win followers to Christ in Rome, as I have done in many other places. [14-15]It doesn't matter if people are civilized and educated, or if they are uncivilized and uneducated. I must tell the good news to everyone. That's why I am eager to visit all of you in Rome.

[16]I am proud of the good news! It is God's powerful way of saving all people who have faith, whether they are Jews or Gentiles. [17]The good news tells how God accepts everyone who has faith, but only those who have faith.[d] It is just as the Scriptures say, "The people God accepts because of their faith will live."[e]

[a]1.3,4 *the Holy Spirit:* Or "his own spirit of holiness." [b]1.3,4 *proved that Jesus is the powerful Son of God:* Or "proved in a powerful way that Jesus is the Son of God." [c]1.5 *Jesus was kind to me and chose me to be an apostle:* Or "Jesus was kind to us and chose us to be his apostles." [d]1.17 *but only those who have faith:* Or "and faith is all that matters." [e]1.17 *The people God accepts because of their faith will live:* Or "The people God accepts will live because of their faith."

Prayer Starter: Make me proud of the good news about Jesus, dear God.

Memory Verse: I am proud of the good news! It is God's powerful way of saving all people . . .   *—Romans 1.16*

371

This Is My Body

Your worship services do you more harm than good. I am certainly not going to praise you for this. ¹⁸I am told that you can't get along with each other when you worship, and I am sure that some of what I have heard is true. ¹⁹You are bound to argue with each other, but it is easy to see which of you have God's approval.

²⁰When you meet together, you don't really celebrate the Lord's Supper. ²¹You even start eating before everyone gets to the meeting, and some of you go hungry, while others get drunk. ²²Don't you have homes where you can eat and drink? Do you hate God's church? Do you want to embarrass people who don't have anything? What can I say to you? I certainly cannot praise you.

²³I have already told you what the Lord Jesus did on the night he was betrayed. And it came from the Lord himself.

He took some bread in his hands. ²⁴Then after he had given thanks, he broke it and said, "This is my body, which is given for you. Eat this and remember me."

²⁵After the meal, Jesus took a cup of wine in his hands and said, "This is my blood, and with it God makes his new agreement with you. Drink this and remember me."

²⁶The Lord meant that when you eat this bread and drink from this cup, you tell about his death until he comes.

²⁷But if you eat the bread and drink the wine in a way that isn't worthy of the Lord, you sin against his body and blood. ²⁸That's why you must examine the way you eat and drink.

Prayer Starter: Help me be well behaved in church and school, Lord. Help me to respect my teachers.

Memory Verse: I am proud of the good news! It is God's powerful way of saving all people who have faith . . .   *—Romans 1.16*

Paul Corrects Peter

James, Peter,[a] and John realized that God had given me the message about his undeserved kindness. And these men are supposed to be the backbone of the church. They even gave Barnabas and me a friendly handshake. This was to show that we would work with Gentiles and that they would work with Jews. [10]They only asked us to remember the poor, and that was something I had always been eager to do.

[11]When Peter came to Antioch, I told him face-to-face that he was wrong. [12]He used to eat with Gentile followers of the Lord, until James sent some Jewish followers. Peter was afraid of the Jews and soon stopped eating with Gentiles. [13]He and the others hid their true feelings so well that even Barnabas was fooled. [14]But when I saw that they were not really obeying the truth that is in the good news, I corrected Peter in front of everyone and said:

Peter, you are a Jew, but you live like a Gentile. So how can you force Gentiles to live like Jews?

¹⁵We are Jews by birth and are not sinners like Gentiles. ¹⁶But we know that God accepts only those who have faith in Jesus Christ. No one can please God by simply obeying the Law. So we put our faith in Christ Jesus, and God accepted us because of our faith.

¹⁷When we Jews started looking for a way to please God, we discovered that we are sinners too. Does this mean that Christ is the one who makes us sinners? No, it doesn't! ¹⁸But if I tear down something and then build it again, I prove that I was wrong at first. ¹⁹It was the Law itself that killed me and freed me from its power, so that I could live for God.

I have been nailed to the cross with Christ. ²⁰I have died, but Christ lives in me. And I now live by faith in the Son of God, who loved me and gave his life for me.

ᵃ2.9 *Peter:* The Greek text has "Cephas," which is an Aramaic name meaning "rock."

Prayer Starter: Give me wisdom, Lord, to know when to tell others that they are wrong.

Memory Verse: I am proud of the good news! It is God's powerful way of saving all people who have faith, whether they are Jews or Gentiles.   —*Romans 1.16*

**Christ Brings
Spiritual
Blessings**

From Paul, chosen by God to be an apostle of Christ Jesus.

To God's people who live in Ephesus and[a] are faithful followers of Christ Jesus.

[2]I pray that God our Father and our Lord Jesus Christ will be kind to you and will bless you with peace!

[3]Praise the God and Father of our Lord Jesus Christ for the spiritual blessings that Christ has brought us from heaven! [4]Before the world was created, God had Christ choose us to live with him and to be his holy and innocent and loving people. [5]God was kind[b] and decided that Christ would choose us to be God's own adopted children. [6]God was very kind to us because of the Son he dearly loves, and so we should praise God.

⁷⁻⁸Christ sacrificed his life's blood to set us free, which means that our sins are now forgiven. Christ did this because God was so kind to us. God has great wisdom and understanding, ⁹and by what Christ has done, God has shown us his own mysterious ways. ¹⁰Then when the time is right, God will do all that he has planned, and Christ will bring together everything in heaven and on earth.

¹¹God always does what he plans, and that's why he had Christ choose us. ¹²He did this so that we Jews would bring honor to him and be the first ones to have hope because of him. ¹³Christ also brought you the truth, which is the good news about how you can be saved. You put your faith in Christ and were given the promised Holy Spirit to show that you belong to God. ¹⁴The Spirit also makes us sure that we will be given what God has stored up for his people. Then we will be set free, and God will be honored and praised.

¹⁵I have heard about your faith in the Lord Jesus and your love for all of God's people. ¹⁶So I never stop being grateful for you, as I mention you in my prayers. ¹⁷I ask the glorious Father and God of our Lord Jesus Christ to give you his Spirit. The Spirit will make you wise and let you understand what it means to know God. ¹⁸My prayer is that light will flood your hearts and that you will understand the hope that was given to you when God chose you. Then you will discover the glorious blessings that will be yours together with all of God's people.

ᵃ1.1 *live in Ephesus and:* Some manuscripts do not have these words. ᵇ1.4,5 *holy and innocent and loving people.* ⁵*God was kind:* Or "holy and innocent people. God was loving ⁵and kind."

Prayer Starter: I praise you, Father, for the spiritual blessings Christ brought from heaven.

Memory Verse: Don't worry . . .   —*Philippians 4.6*

The Armor that God Gives

Finally, let the mighty strength of the Lord make you strong. ¹¹Put on all the armor that God gives, so you can defend yourself against the devil's tricks. ¹²We are not fighting against humans. We are fighting against forces and authorities and against rulers of darkness and powers in the spiritual world. ¹³So put on all the armor that God gives. Then when that evil day* comes, you will be able to defend yourself. And when the battle is over, you will still be standing firm.

[14]Be ready! Let the truth be like a belt around your waist, and let God's justice protect you like armor. [15]Your desire to tell the good news about peace should be like shoes on your feet. [16]Let your faith be like a shield, and you will be able to stop all the flaming arrows of the evil one. [17]Let God's saving power be like a helmet, and for a sword use God's message that comes from the Spirit.

[18]Never stop praying, especially for others. Always pray by the power of the Spirit. Stay alert and keep praying for God's people. [19]Pray that I will be given the message to speak and that I may fearlessly explain the mystery about the good news. [20]I was sent to do this work, and that's the reason I am in jail. So pray that I will be brave and will speak as I should.

[21-22]I want you to know how I am getting along and what I am doing. That's why I am sending Tychicus to you. He is a dear friend, as well as a faithful servant of the Lord. He will tell you how I am doing, and he will cheer you up.

[23]I pray that God the Father and the Lord Jesus Christ will give peace, love, and faith to every follower! [24]May God be kind to everyone who keeps on loving our Lord Jesus Christ.

[a]6.13 *that evil day:* Either the present or "the day of death" or "the day of judgment."

Prayer Starter: Help me to stay alert, Lord, and to keep praying for your people.

Memory Verse: Don't worry about anything . . .   *—Philippians 4.6*

Timothy and
Epaphroditus

My dear friends, you always obeyed when I was with you. Now that I am away, you should obey even more. So work with fear and trembling to discover what it really means to be saved. ¹³God is working in you to make you willing and able to obey him.

¹⁴Do everything without grumbling or arguing. ¹⁵Then you will be the pure and innocent children of God. You live among people who are crooked and evil, but you must not do anything that they can say is wrong. Try to shine as lights among the people of this world, ¹⁶as you hold firmly to^a the message that gives life. Then on the day when Christ returns, I can take pride in you. I can also know that my work and efforts were not useless.

¹⁷Your faith in the Lord and your service are like a sacrifice offered to him. And my own blood may have to be poured out with the sacrifice.ᵇ If this happens, I will be glad and rejoice with you. ¹⁸In the same way, you should be glad and rejoice with me.

¹⁹I want to be encouraged by news about you. So I hope the Lord Jesus will soon let me send Timothy to you. ²⁰I don't have anyone else who cares about you as much as he does. ²¹The others think only about what interests them and not about what concerns Christ Jesus. ²²But you know what kind of person Timothy is. He has worked with me like a son in spreading the good news. ²³I hope to send him to you, as soon as I find out what is going to happen to me. ²⁴And I feel sure that the Lord will also let me come soon.

²⁵I think I ought to send my dear friend Epaphroditus back to you. He is a follower and a worker and a soldier of the Lord, just as I am. You sent him to look after me, ²⁶but now he is eager to see you. He is worried, because you heard he was sick. ²⁷In fact, he was very sick and almost died. But God was kind to him, and also to me, and he kept me from being burdened down with sorrow.

²⁸Now I am more eager than ever to send Epaphroditus back again. You will be glad to see him, and I won't have to worry any longer. ²⁹Be sure to give him a cheerful welcome, just as people who serve the Lord deserve. ³⁰He almost died working for Christ, and he risked his own life to do for me what you could not.

ᵃ2.16 *hold firmly to:* Or "offer them." ᵇ2.17 *my own blood may have to be poured out with the sacrifice:* Offerings of water or wine were sometimes poured out when animals were sacrificed on the altar.

Prayer Starter: Please help those who are sick, Lord, and keep us well.

Memory Verse: Don't worry about anything, but pray about every-thing. . . .
                                                            —Philippians 4.6

I Keep on Running

All I want is Christ ⁹and to know that I belong to him. I could not make myself acceptable to God by obeying the Law of Moses. God accepted me simply because of my faith in Christ. ¹⁰All I want is to know Christ and the power that raised him to life. I want to suffer and die as he did, ¹¹so that somehow I also may be raised to life.

¹²I have not yet reached my goal, and I am not perfect. But Christ has taken hold of me. So I keep on running and struggling to take hold of the prize. ¹³My friends, I don't feel that I have already arrived. But I forget what is behind, and I struggle for what is ahead. ¹⁴I run toward the goal, so that I can win the prize of being called to heaven. This is the prize that God offers because of what Christ Jesus has done. ¹⁵All of us who are mature should think in this same way. And if any of you think differently, God will make it clear to you. ¹⁶But we must keep going in the direction that we are now headed.

¹⁷My friends, I want you to follow my example and learn from others who closely follow the example we set for you.

Prayer Starter: Lord, I can hardly wait for the Lord Jesus Christ who is coming again from heaven.

Memory Verse: Don't worry about anything, but pray about everything. With thankful hearts . . .
—*Philippians 4.6*

I Beg You

Dear friends, I love you and long to see you. Please keep on being faithful to the Lord. You are my pride and joy.

²Euodia and Syntyche, you belong to the Lord, so I beg you to stop arguing with each other. ³And, my true partner,[a] I ask you to help them. These women have worked together with me and with Clement and with the others in spreading the good news. Their names are now written in the book of life.[b]

⁴Always be glad because of the Lord! I will say it again: Be glad. ⁵Always be gentle with others. The Lord will soon be here. ⁶Don't worry about anything, but pray about everything. With thankful hearts offer up your prayers and requests to God. ⁷Then, because you belong to Christ Jesus, God will bless you with peace that no one can completely understand. And this peace will control the way you think and feel.

⁸Finally, my friends, keep your minds on whatever is true, pure, right, holy, friendly, and proper. Don't ever stop thinking about what is truly worthwhile and worthy of praise. ⁹You know the teachings I gave you, and you know what you heard me say and saw me do. So follow my example. And God, who gives peace, will be with you.

[a]4.3 *partner:* Or "Syzygus," a person's name.
[b]4.3 *the book of life:* A book in which the names of God's people are written.

Prayer Starter: Help me not to worry about anything, but to pray about everything.

Memory Verse: Don't worry about anything, but pray about everything. With thankful hearts offer up your prayers and requests to God.

—*Philippians 4.6*

**The Lord
Will Return**

My friends, we want you to understand how it will be for those followers who have already died. Then you won't grieve over them and be like people who don't have any hope. [14]We believe that Jesus died and was raised to life. We also believe that when God brings Jesus back again, he will bring with him all who had faith in Jesus before they died. [15]Our Lord Jesus told us that when he comes, we won't go up to meet him ahead of his followers who have already died.

[16]With a loud command and with the shout of the chief angel and a blast of God's trumpet, the Lord will return from heaven. Then those who

had faith in Christ before they died will be raised to life. [17]Next, all of us who are still alive will be taken up into the clouds together with them to meet the Lord in the sky. From that time on we will all be with the Lord forever. [18]Encourage each other with these words.

5 I don't need to write you about the time or date when all this will happen. [2]You surely know that the Lord's return[a] will be as a thief coming at night.

[a]5.2 *the Lord's return:* The Greek text has "the day of the Lord."

Prayer Starter: Thank you, Lord, for all your promises about the future.

Teach These Things

If you teach these things to other followers, you will be a good servant of Christ Jesus. You will show that you have grown up on the teachings about our faith and on the good instructions you have obeyed. ⁷Don't have anything to do with worthless, senseless stories. Work hard to be truly religious. ⁸⁻⁹As the saying goes,

"Exercise is good for your body,
but religion helps you in every way.
   It promises life now and forever."

These words are worthwhile and should not be forgotten. ¹⁰We have put our hope in the living God, who is the Savior of everyone, but especially of those who have faith. That's why we work and struggle so hard.ᵃ

¹¹Teach these things and tell everyone to do what you say. ¹²Don't let anyone make fun of you, just because you are young. Set an example for other followers by what you say and do, as well as by your love, faith, and purity.

¹³Until I arrive, be sure to keep on reading the Scriptures in worship, and don't stop preaching and teaching. ¹⁴Use the gift you were given when the prophets spoke and the group of church leaders[b] blessed you by placing their hands on you. ¹⁵Remember these things and think about them, so everyone can see how well you are doing. ¹⁶Be careful about the way you live and about what you teach. Keep on doing this, and you will save not only yourself, but the people who hear you.

5 Don't correct an older man. Encourage him, as you would your own father. Treat younger men as you would your own brother, ²and treat older women as you would your own mother. Show the same respect to younger women that you would to your sister.

[a]4.10 *struggle so hard:* Some manuscripts have "are treated so badly." [b]4.14 *group of church leaders:* Or "group of elders" or "group of presbyters" or "group of priests."

Prayer Starter: Forgive me, Father, for the times I haven't treated other people nicely.

Memory Verse: You surely know that the Lord's return . . .
— 1 Thessalonians 5.2

**Eunice
and Lois**

From Paul, an apostle of Christ Jesus.
God himself chose me to be an apostle, and he gave me the promised life that Jesus Christ makes possible.

²Timothy, you are like a dear child to me. I pray that God our Father and our Lord Christ Jesus will be kind and merciful to you and will bless you with peace!

³Night and day I mention you in my prayers. I am always grateful for you, as I pray to the God my ancestors and I have served with a clear conscience. ⁴I remember how you cried, and I want to see you, because that will make me truly happy. ⁵I also remember the genuine faith of your mother Eunice. Your grandmother Lois had the same sort of faith, and I am sure that you have it as well. ⁶So I ask you to make full use of the gift that God gave you when I placed my hands on you.ᵃ Use it well. ⁷God's Spiritᵇ doesn't make cowards out of us. The Spirit gives us power, love, and self-control.

⁸Don't be ashamed to speak for our Lord. And don't be ashamed of

me, just because I am in jail for serving him. Use the power that comes from God and join with me in suffering for telling the good news.

⁹ God saved us and chose us to be his holy people.
     We did nothing to deserve this,
         but God planned it because he is so kind.
     Even before time began
         God planned for Christ Jesus to show kindness to us.

¹⁰ Now Christ Jesus has come to show us the kindness of God.
     Christ our Savior defeated death
         and brought us the good news.
     It shines like a light and offers life that never ends.

¹¹My work is to be a preacher, an apostle, and a teacher.ᶜ ¹²That's why I am suffering now. But I am not ashamed! I know the one I have faith in, and I am sure that he can guard until the last day what he has trusted me with.ᵈ ¹³Now follow the example of the correct teaching I gave you, and let the faith and love of Christ Jesus be your model. ¹⁴You have been trusted with a wonderful treasure. Guard it with the help of the Holy Spirit, who lives within you.

ᵃ1.6 *when I placed my hands on you:* Church leaders placed their hands on people who were being appointed to preach or teach (see 1 Timothy 4.14). ᵇ1.7 *God's Spirit:* Or "God." ᶜ1.11 *teacher:* Some manuscripts add "of the Gentiles." ᵈ1.12 *what he has trusted me with:* Or "what I have trusted him with."

Prayer Starter: Thank you, God, for all the people who love me.

Memory Verse: You surely know that the Lord's return will be as a thief . . .
                     —1 Thessalonians 5.2

Philemon

Philemon, each time I mention you in my prayers, I thank God. ⁵I hear about your faith in our Lord Jesus and about your love for all of God's people. ⁶As you share your faith with others, I pray that they may come to know all the blessings Christ has given us. ⁷My friend, your love has made me happy and has greatly encouraged me. It has also cheered the hearts of God's people.

⁸Christ gives me the courage to tell you what to do. ⁹But I would rather ask you to do it simply because of love. Yes, as someoneᵃ in jail for Christ, ¹⁰I beg you to help Onesimus!ᵇ He is like a son to me because I led him to Christ here in jail. ¹¹Before this, he was useless to you, but now he is useful both to you and to me.

¹²Sending Onesimus back to you makes me very sad. ¹³I would like to keep him here with me, where he could take your place in helping me while I am here in prison for preaching the good news. ¹⁴But I won't do anything unless you agree to it first. I want your act of kindness to come from your heart, and not be something you feel forced to do.

¹⁵Perhaps Onesimus was taken from you for a little while so that you could have him back for good, ¹⁶but not as a slave. Onesimus is much more than a slave. To me he is a dear friend, but to you he is even more, both as a person and as a follower of the Lord.

¹⁷If you consider me a friend because of Christ, then welcome Onesimus as you would welcome me. ¹⁸If he has cheated you or owes you anything, charge it to my account. ¹⁹With my own hand I write: I, PAUL, WILL PAY YOU BACK. But don't forget that you owe me your life.

ᵃ9 *someone:* Greek "a messenger" or "an old man." ᵇ10 *Onesimus:* In Greek this name means "useful."

Prayer Starter: Lord, use my love to make others happy.

Faith

Enoch had faith and did not die. He pleased God, and God took him up to heaven. That's why his body was never found. ⁶But without faith no one can please God. We must believe that God is real and that he rewards everyone who searches for him.

⁷Because Noah had faith, he was warned about something that had not yet happened. He obeyed and built a boat that saved him and his family. In this way the people of the world were judged, and Noah was given the blessings that come to everyone who pleases God.

⁸Abraham had faith and obeyed God. He was told to go to the land that God had said would be his, and he left for a country he had never seen. ⁹Because Abraham had faith, he lived as a stranger in the promised land. He lived there in a tent, and so did Isaac and Jacob, who were later given the same promise. ¹⁰Abraham did this, because he was waiting for the eternal city that God had planned and built.

¹³Every one of those people died. But they still had faith, even though they had not received what they had been promised. They were glad just to see these things from far away, and they agreed that they were only strangers and foreigners on this earth. ¹⁴When people talk this way, it is clear that they are looking for a place to call their own. ¹⁵If they had been talking about the land where they had once lived, they could have gone back at any time. ¹⁶But they were looking forward to a better home in  heaven. That's why God wasn't ashamed for them to call him their God. He even built a city for them.

Prayer Starter: Increase my faith, Lord. Help me believe that you are real and that you reward those who seek you.

Memory Verse: You surely know that the Lord's return will be as a thief coming at night. *—1 Thessalonians 5.2*

Religion that Pleases God

Obey God's message! Don't fool yourselves by just listening to it. ²³If you hear the message and don't obey it, you are like people who stare at themselves in a mirror ²⁴and forget what they look like as soon as they leave. ²⁵But you must never stop looking at the perfect law that sets you free. God will bless you in everything you do, if you listen and obey, and don't just hear and forget.

²⁶If you think you are being religious, but can't control your tongue, you are fooling yourself, and everything you do is useless. ²⁷Religion that pleases God the Father must be pure and spotless. You must help needy orphans and widows and not let this world make you evil.

2 My friends, if you have faith in our glorious Lord Jesus Christ, you won't treat some people better than others. ²Suppose a rich person wearing fancy clothes and a gold ring comes to one of your meetings. And suppose a poor person dressed in worn-out clothes also comes. ³You must not give the best seat to the one in fancy clothes and tell the one who is poor to stand at the side or sit on the floor. ⁴That is the same as saying that some people are better than others, and you would be acting like a crooked judge.

⁵My dear friends, pay attention. God has given a lot of faith to the poor people in this world. He has also promised them a share in his kingdom that he will give to everyone who loves him. ⁶You mistreat the poor. But isn't it the rich who boss you around and drag you off to court? ⁷Aren't they the ones who make fun of your Lord?

⁸You will do all right, if you obey the most important law[a] in the Scriptures. It is the law that commands us to love others as much as we love ourselves. ⁹But if you treat some people better than others, you have done wrong, and the Scriptures teach that you have sinned.

¹⁰If you obey every law except one, you are still guilty of breaking them all. ¹¹The same God who told us to be faithful in marriage also told us not to murder. So even if you are faithful in marriage, but murder someone, you still have broken God's Law.

¹²Speak and act like people who will be judged by the law that sets us free. ¹³Do this, because on the day of judgment there will be no pity for those who have not had pity on others. But even in judgment, God is merciful![b]

¹⁴My friends, what good is it to say you have faith, when you don't do anything to show that you really do have faith? Can that kind of faith save you? ¹⁵If you know someone who doesn't have any clothes or food, ¹⁶you shouldn't just say, "I hope all goes well for you. I hope you will be warm and have plenty to eat." What good is it to say this, unless you do something to help? ¹⁷Faith that doesn't lead us to do good deeds is all alone and dead!

---

[a]2.8 *most important law:* The Greek text has "royal law," meaning the one given by the king (that is, God). [b]2.13 *But even in judgment, God is merciful!:* Or "So be merciful, and you will be shown mercy on the day of judgment."

Prayer Starter: Give me love and concern for those who don't have as much as I have.

Memory Verse: But if we confess our sins . . .   *— 1 John 1.9*

You Should Pray

My friends, be patient until the Lord returns. Think of farmers who wait patiently for the spring and summer rains to make their valuable crops grow. ⁸Be patient like those farmers and don't give up. The Lord will soon be here! ⁹Don't grumble about each other or you will be judged, and the judge is right outside the door.

¹⁰My friends, follow the example of the prophets who spoke for the Lord. They were patient, even when they had to suffer. ¹¹In fact, we praise the ones who endured the most. You remember how patient Job was and how the Lord finally helped him. The Lord did this because he is so merciful and kind.

¹²My friends, above all else, don't take an oath. You must not swear by heaven or by earth or by anything else. "Yes" or "No" is all you need to say. If you say anything more, you will be condemned.

¹³If you are having trouble, you should pray. And if you are feeling good, you should sing praises. ¹⁴If you are sick, ask the church leadersᵃ to

come and pray for you. Ask them to put olive oil[b] on you in the name of the Lord. [15]If you have faith when you pray for sick people, they will get well. The Lord will heal them, and if they have sinned, he will forgive them.

[16]If you have sinned, you should tell each other what you have done. Then you can pray for one another and be healed. The prayer of an innocent person is powerful, and it can help a lot. [17]Elijah was just as human as we are, and for three and a half years his prayers kept the rain from falling. [18]But when he did pray for rain, it fell from the skies and made the crops grow.

[19]My friends, if any followers have wandered away from the truth, you should try to lead them back. [20]If you turn sinners from the wrong way, you will save them from death, and many of their sins will be forgiven.

[a]5.14 *church leaders:* Or "elders" or "presbyters" or "priests." [b]5.14 *olive oil:* The Jewish people used olive oil for healing.

Prayer Starter: Teach me to sing praises to you, Lord, especially when I am feeling good.

Memory Verse: But if we confess our sins to God . . .   *—1 John 1.9*

A Message for Church Leaders

Church leaders,[a] I am writing to encourage you. I too am a leader, as well as a witness to Christ's suffering, and I will share in his glory when it is shown to us.

[2]Just as shepherds watch over their sheep, you must watch over everyone God has placed in your care. Do it willingly in order to please God, and not simply because you think you must. Let it be something you want to do, instead of something you do merely to make money. [3]Don't be bossy to those people who are in your care, but set an example for them. [4]Then when Christ the Chief Shepherd returns, you will be given a crown that will never lose its glory.

[5]All of you young people should obey your elders. In fact, everyone should be humble toward everyone else. The Scriptures say,

"God opposes proud people,
but he helps everyone who is humble."

[6]Be humble in the presence of God's mighty power, and he will honor you when the time comes. [7]God cares for you, so turn all your worries over to him.

[8]Be on your guard and stay awake. Your enemy, the devil, is like a roaring lion, sneaking around to find someone to attack. [9]But you must resist the devil and stay strong in your faith. You know that all over the world the Lord's followers are suffering just as you are. [10]But God shows undeserved kindness to everyone. That's why he had Christ Jesus choose you to share in his eternal glory. You will suffer for a while, but God will make you complete, steady, strong, and firm. [11]God will be in control forever! Amen.

[a]5.1 *Church leaders:* Or "Elders" or "Presbyters" or "Priests."

Prayer Starter: Bless and encourage the pastor of my church, O Lord.

Memory Verse: But if we confess our sins to God, he can always be trusted . . .
—1 John 1.9

God Is Light

The Word that gives life was from the beginning, and this is the one our message is about.

Our ears have heard, our own eyes have seen, and our hands touched this Word.

²The one who gives life appeared! We saw it happen, and we are witnesses to what we have seen. Now we are telling you about this eternal life that was with the Father and appeared to us. ³We are telling you what we have seen and heard, so that you may share in this life with us. And we share in it with the Father and with his Son Jesus Christ. ⁴We are writing to tell you these things, because this makes us* truly happy.

⁵Jesus told us that God is light and doesn't have any darkness in him. Now we are telling you.

⁶If we say that we share in life with God and keep on living in the dark, we are lying and are not living by the truth. ⁷But if we live in the light, as God does, we share in life with each other. And the blood of his Son Jesus washes all our sins away. ⁸If we say that we have not sinned,

we are fooling ourselves, and the truth isn't in our hearts. ⁹But if we confess our sins to God, he can always be trusted to forgive us and take our sins away.

¹⁰If we say that we have not sinned, we make God a liar, and his message isn't in our hearts.ᵇ

ᵃ1.4 *us:* Some manuscripts have "you." ᵇ1.10 *and his message isn't in our hearts:* Or "because we have not accepted his message."

Prayer Starter: Show me when I sin, Father, so that I can ask for your forgiveness.

Memory Verse: But if we confess our sins to God, he can always be trusted to forgive us . . . —*1 John 1.9*

On Patmos Island

I am John, a follower together with all of you. We suffer because Jesus is our king, but he gives us the strength to endure. I was sent to Patmos Island,[a] because I had preached God's message and had told about Jesus. [10]On the Lord's day the Spirit took control of me, and behind me I heard a loud voice that sounded like a trumpet. [11]The voice said, "Write in a book what you see. Then send it to the seven churches in Ephesus, Smyrna, Pergamum, Thyatira, Sardis, Philadelphia, and Laodicea."[b]

[12]When I turned to see who was speaking to me, I saw seven gold lampstands. [13]There with the lampstands was someone who seemed to be the Son of Man.[c] He was wearing a robe that reached down to his feet, and a gold cloth was wrapped around his chest. [14]His head and his hair were white as wool or snow, and his eyes looked like flames of fire. [15]His feet were glowing like bronze being heated in a furnace, and his voice sounded like the roar of a waterfall. [16]He held seven stars in his right hand, and a sharp double-edged sword was coming from his mouth. His face was shining as bright as the sun at noon.

[17]When I saw him, I fell at his feet like a dead person. But he put his right hand on me and said:

> Don't be afraid! I am the first, the last, [18]and the living one. I died, but now I am alive forevermore, and I have the keys to death and the world of the dead.[d]

[a]1.9 *Patmos Island:* A small island where prisoners were sometimes kept by the Romans. [b]1.11 *Ephesus . . . Laodicea:* Ephesus was in the center with the six other cities forming a half-circle around it. [c]1.13 *Son of Man:* That is, Jesus. [d]1.18 *keys to death and the world of the dead:* That is, power over death and the world of the dead.

Prayer Starter: Help me realize how glorious Jesus Christ really is.

Memory Verse: But if we confess our sins to God, he can always be trusted to forgive us and take our sins away.   *—1 John 1.9*

I'm Knocking at Your Door

T his is what you must write to the angel of the church in Laodicea:

I am the one called Amen![a] I am the faithful and true witness and the source[b] of God's creation. Listen to what I say.

[15]I know everything you have done, and you are not cold or hot. I wish you were either one or the other. [16]But since you are lukewarm and neither cold nor hot, I will spit you out of my mouth. [17]You claim to be rich and successful and to have everything you need. But you don't know how bad off you are. You are pitiful, poor, blind, and naked.

[18]Buy your gold from me. It has been refined in a fire, and it will make you rich. Buy white clothes from me. Wear them and you can cover up your shameful nakedness. Buy medicine for your eyes, so that you will be able to see.

[19]I correct and punish everyone I love. So make up your minds to turn away from your sins. [20]Listen! I am standing and knocking at your door. If you hear my voice and open the door, I will come in and we will eat together. [21]Everyone who wins the victory will sit with me on my throne, just as I won the victory and sat with my Father on his throne.

[22]If you have ears, listen to what the Spirit says to the churches.

[a]3.14 *Amen:* Meaning "Trustworthy." [b]3.14 *source:* Or "beginning."

Prayer Starter: Keep me from being lukewarm about you, dear God.

Memory Verse: The one who has spoken these things . . .

—Revelation 22.20

The Lamb

In the right hand of the one sitting on the throne I saw a scroll[a] that had writing on the inside and on the outside. And it was sealed in seven places. [2]I saw a mighty angel ask with a loud voice, "Who is worthy to open the scroll and break its seals?" [3]No one in heaven or on earth or under the earth was able to open the scroll or see inside it.

[4]I cried hard because no one was found worthy to open the scroll or see inside it. [5]Then one of the elders said to me, "Stop crying and look! The one who is called both the 'Lion from the Tribe of Judah'[b] and 'King David's Great Descendant'[c] has won the victory. He will open the book and its seven seals."

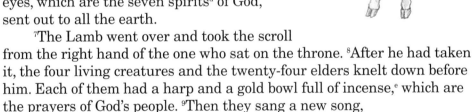

[6]Then I looked and saw a Lamb standing in the center of the throne that was surrounded by the four living creatures and the elders. The Lamb looked as if it had once been killed. It had seven horns and seven eyes, which are the seven spirits[d] of God, sent out to all the earth.

[7]The Lamb went over and took the scroll from the right hand of the one who sat on the throne. [8]After he had taken it, the four living creatures and the twenty-four elders knelt down before him. Each of them had a harp and a gold bowl full of incense,[e] which are the prayers of God's people. [9]Then they sang a new song,

"You are worthy to receive the scroll and open its seals,
    because you were killed.
And with your own blood you bought for God
    people from every tribe, language, nation, and race.

[a]5.1 *scroll:* A roll of paper or special leather used for writing on. Sometimes a scroll would be sealed on the outside with one or more pieces of wax. [b]5.5 *'Lion from the Tribe of Judah':* In Genesis 49.9 the tribe of Judah is called a young lion, and King David was from Judah. [c]5.5 *'King David's Great Descendant':* The Greek text has "the root of David" which is a title for the Messiah based on Isaiah 11.1,10. [d]5.6 *the seven spirits:* Some manuscripts have "the spirits." [e]5.8 *incense:* A material that produces a sweet smell when burned. Sometimes it is a symbol for the prayers of God's people.

Prayer Starter: You, Lord, are worthy of all my love and worship.

Memory Verse: The one who has spoken these things says . . .
—*Revelation 22.20*

Worship in Heaven

After this, I saw a large crowd with more people than could be counted. They were from every race, tribe, nation, and language, and they stood before the throne and before the Lamb. They wore white robes and held palm branches in their hands, [10]as they shouted,

"Our God, who sits upon the throne,
has the power to save his people,
    and so does the Lamb."

[11]The angels who stood around the throne knelt in front of it with their faces to the ground. The elders and the four living creatures knelt there with them. Then they all worshiped God [12]and said,

"Amen! Praise, glory, wisdom, thanks, honor, power,
    and strength belong to our God forever and ever! Amen!"

[13]One of the elders asked me, "Do you know who these people are that are dressed in white robes? Do you know where they come from?" [14]"Sir," I answered, "you must know."
Then he told me:

"These are the ones
    who have gone through the great suffering.
They have washed their robes in the blood of the Lamb
    and have made them white.

Prayer Starter: Amen! Praise, glory, wisdom, thanks, and strength belong to our God forever and ever! Amen!

Memory Verse: The one who has spoken these things says, "I am coming soon!" . . .
—Revelation 22.20

**King
of Kings**

I looked and saw that heaven was open, and a white horse was there. Its rider was called Faithful and True, and he is always fair when he judges or goes to war. ¹²He had eyes like flames of fire, and he was wearing a lot of crowns. His name was written on him, but he was the only one who knew what the name meant.

¹³The rider wore a robe that was covered with[a] blood, and he was known as "The Word of God." ¹⁴He was followed by armies from heaven that rode on horses and were dressed in pure white linen. ¹⁵From his mouth a sharp sword went out to attack the nations. He will rule them with an iron rod and will show the fierce anger of God All-Powerful by trampling the grapes in the pit where wine is made. ¹⁶On the part of the robe that covered his thigh was written, "KING OF KINGS AND LORD OF LORDS."

¹⁷I then saw an angel standing on the sun, and he shouted to all the birds flying in the sky, "Come and join in God's great feast! ¹⁸You can eat the flesh of kings, rulers, leaders, horses, riders, free people, slaves, important people, and everyone else."

¹⁹I also saw the beast and all kings of the earth come together. They fought against the rider on the white horse and against his army. ²⁰But the beast was captured and so was the false prophet.

[a]19.13 *covered with:* Some manuscripts have "sprinkled with."

Prayer Starter: You, O Lord God, are King of kings and Lord of lords.

Memory Verse: The one who has spoken these things says, "I am coming soon!" So, Lord Jesus . . .   *—Revelation 22.20*

Please Come Soon

I saw a new heaven and a new earth. The first heaven and the first earth had disappeared, and so had the sea. ²Then I saw New Jerusalem, that holy city, coming down from God in heaven. It was like a bride dressed in her wedding gown and ready to meet her husband.

³I heard a loud voice shout from the throne:

God's home is now with his people. He will live with them, and they will be his own. Yes, God will make his home among his people. ⁴He will wipe all tears from their eyes, and there will be no more death, suffering, crying, or pain. These things of the past are gone forever.

¹⁰Then with the help of the Spirit, he took me to the top of a very high mountain. There he showed me the holy city of Jerusalem coming down from God in heaven.

¹¹The glory of God made the city bright. It was dazzling and crystal clear like a precious jasper stone.

22 Then I was told:

I am coming soon! And when I come, I will reward everyone for what they have done. ¹³I am Alpha and Omega,ᵃ the first and the last, the beginning and the end.

¹⁶I am Jesus! And I am the one who sent my angel to tell all of you these things for the churches. I am David's Great Descendant,ᵇ and I am also the bright morning star.ᶜ

¹⁷The Spirit and the bride say, "Come!" Everyone who hears thisᵈ should say, "Come!"

If you are thirsty, come! If you want life-giving water, come and take it. It's free!

²⁰The one who has spoken these things says, "I am coming soon!" So, Lord Jesus, please come soon!"

²¹I pray that the Lord Jesus will be kind to all of you.

ᵃ22.13 *Alpha and Omega:* The first and last letters of the Greek alphabet, which sometimes mean "first" and "last." ᵇ22.16 *David's Great Descendant:* The Greek text has "the root of David" which is a title for the Messiah based on Isaiah 11.1,10. ᶜ22.16 *the bright morning star:* Probably thought of as the brightest star. ᵈ22.17 *who hears this:* The reading of the book of Revelation in a service of worship.

Prayer Starter: Lord Jesus, please come soon!

Memory Verse: The one who has spoken these things says, "I am coming soon!" So, Lord Jesus, please come soon!   *—Revelation 22.20*

Subject List